The Story of the Stone
A Translator's Notebooks
David Hawkes

《紅樓夢》
英译笔记

〔英〕霍克思 著

David Hawkes 霍克思

图书在版编目（CIP）数据

《红楼梦》英译笔记 = The Story of the Stone: A Translator's Notebooks / (英) 霍克思著. —北京：商务印书馆，2023
ISBN 978-7-100-21598-5

Ⅰ. ①红…　Ⅱ. ①霍…　Ⅲ. ①《红楼梦》—英语—文学翻译—研究　Ⅳ. ① H315.9 ② I207.411

中国版本图书馆 CIP 数据核字（2022）第 152371 号

权利保留，侵权必究。

David Hawkes
The Story of The Stone: A Translator's Notebooks
© 2023 by John Minford
The copyright of the Chinese edition is granted by The Proprietor.
ALL RIGHTS RESERVED.

《红楼梦》英译笔记
〔英〕霍克思　著

商务印书馆出版
（北京王府井大街36号　邮政编码100710）
商务印书馆发行
北京雅昌艺术印刷有限公司印刷
ISBN 978-7-100-21598-5

2023年6月第1版	开本 889×1194　1/16
2023年6月北京第1次印刷	印张 27¾

定价：498.00元

霍克思

在牛津贝德福德街 59 号的书房,
他在那里完成了《红楼梦》的翻译。

霍克思和杨宪益

CONTENTS
目录

viii	**FOREWORD**	John Minford

001	**PART I**
	November 1970—February 1973

093	**PART II**
	February 1973—August 1975

185	**PART III**
	August 1975—

257	**PART IV**

422	后　记	范圣宇

FOREWORD
John Minford

It often comes as something of a surprise to working translators what and how much is being said about them by their theoretician colleagues. Translators themselves tend to get on with the job. For the most part they have little to say on the subject of their own "methods" of work, and what they do say tends to be either disappointingly fragmentary (inconclusive notes and desultory, self-deprecating jottings—"There's not much to be said, really. I just did it like that."); or else self-adulatory ("How I achieved the impossible and translated XYZ.... and incidentally, how much better my version is than So-and-so's....").

The true raw materials (journals, manuscripts etc.) for a sober empirical study of the craft and history of translation are tantalisingly few. There are virtually no archives. This humble tribe has left few records of its own achievements. In the past a self-effacing attitude on the part of the translator was in general considered right and proper in the wider literary community. Indeed, the translator's name was frequently not even printed on the title page of a book. By and large the job was considered to have been best done when the translator succeeded in being totally transparent, to the extent of vaporising into thin air and leaving no trace whatsoever.

And yet translation history is in itself a fascinating branch of literary history. It offers extraordinary insights into moments of inter-cultural contact, snapshots of crucial passages between cultures. The history of the translation of Chinese literature into English is no exception. Here are just a couple of potential headings for a future study of this subject.

Manuscripts nearly lost

James Legge's first draft of the *Book of Changes* was dropped into the Red Sea, and had to be virtually rewritten. Herbert Giles' manuscript of the *Liaozhai Stories* by Pu Songling (his *Strange Stories from a Chinese Studio*) was sent to London from the British Consulate in Canton, using the services of the colonial French firm Messageries Maritimes. For several months, it was lost somewhere in that distinguished company's Marseilles offices.

Collaborations

Fascinating examples include the formidable James Legge and the distinguished Shanghai littérateur Wang Tao; Judith Gautier, the poet's daughter, and her young Chinese friend in Paris; Richard Wilhelm and the veteran Chinese scholar Lao Naixuan; Witter Bynner and the "collaborator" Kiang Kang-hu; Gladys Yang and Yang Xianyi; Gerald Bullett and Tsui Chi; Florence Ayscough and Amy Lowell.

The whole field of translation history has been hugely neglected. And yet, the practising translator may benefit more from the lessons of history, from the informal insights and tips that form part of the tradition, from anecdotes and other evidence of how good translators have operated in the past, than from the reams of paper devoted to translation theory.

David Hawkes is one of the most distinguished contemporary translators from the Chinese. In everything that he has put his hand to, he has combined rigorous scholarship with literary grace. He devoted many years to translating the great eighteenth-century novel *The Story of the Stone* (*Hongloumeng*, also translated by Gladys Yang and Yang Xianyi as *A Dream of Red Mansions*). It was my good fortune to have been his student when he was still Professor of Chinese at Oxford, and later to have been his apprentice during this great undertaking, from its beginning in the early 1970s. But Hawkes himself had started reading the novel many years earlier than this, during his student days in Oxford and Peking after the Second World War, as he told Chan Oi-sum in an informal interview conducted in Oxford in December 1998:

> I'd heard about *Hongloumeng*, from students in Oxford; I think ... a friend, maybe Qiu Ke'an, showed me a copy of this great novel, so I'd heard about it. I think I tried to read the first chapter, and it was very difficult. Actually the beginning of *Hongloumeng*, if you're not familiar with either *baihua* or modern *wenyan*, is quite difficult, because it's written in a very strange style, to start with. That first chapter. I don't think I got more than— I struggled through about a page, I think! (laughs) But anyway, people talked a lot about *Hongloumeng*, Chinese students, and I thought well, I'll try and read it. So what I did, through a Chinese friend of the Empsons [William Empson, then a Visiting Professor at Beida, and his wife Hetta], a lady the Empsons knew, they found an unemployed man—I don't know what he was, I think he'd been a government clerk in Hebei, he wasn't from Peking, he came from outside, somewhere in Hebei. He hadn't got a job, he was living off his wife; they were very very poor. He was a sort of *lao xiansheng*, a very old-fashioned man. He always wore a *changpao* all through the year. Everyone used to wear a *changpao* in the winter, you wore a *mianpao*, everyone did, just to keep warm; but you never did in the summer. Unless you were a shop-keeper or something like that. But he was very old-fashioned. He used to come round, every day I think. I spent quite a lot of money on having lessons. What he did—he didn't speak a word of English, and I don't think he'd taught language before either; but with the help of some Chinese friend, I bought a copy of *Hongloumeng*, and we used to sit side by side, and we'd read it—he'd read it. He'd read it out loud—and then start explaining it. And I didn't understand what he said,

but I could see what he was talking about. So it was a sort of direct method gone mad, if you like! I wouldn't suggest it as an ideal way of learning, but it's the way I chose. I thought of it as a way of learning.... But gradually I found it did work, actually. I didn't understand a lot of what he said first of all, he was just talking away all the time; he didn't speak real *Beijing hua*, he probably spoke with rather a funny sort of accent. I expect I never learnt proper Pekinese. Anyway, none of the teachers at Beida, well very few, spoke anything like even *Putonghua*; they were practically all Southerners. I went to some classes by Yu Pingbo, and I could hardly understand a word he said! He was from Zhejiang, I think.[1]

He did his first translation of a few selections from the novel a little later during his stay in Peking:

> I should say I actually started, I did a bit, I translated a few bits of it, just little selections, while I was still in Peking; because I once was invited along with Luo Changpei and one or two other people, to a sort of society, of mostly foreigners, somewhere in the Embassy area. I can't remember now what it was called, or what it was, but I know that two of the people there were Mr and Mrs Manning.

Over twenty years later, having held the Chair of Chinese at Oxford from 1958 (his Inaugural Lecture delivered in 1961 contains a translated extract from the novel), he finally took the plunge. As he put it in the interview, "I thought, this novel really deserves to be done properly, someone ought to do the whole thing." He embarked on his complete version of the first eighty chapters of the novel, signing a contract with Penguin Books in 1970. In order to devote himself full time to the project, he resigned from the Oxford Chair of Chinese. In the 1998 interview he explains this decision of his with characteristic humility:

> When I started translating this, I enjoyed it so much, that I thought well— I never saw myself as a very good Professor; and I thought, this is really my métier, I really ought to be a translator and not a Professor. So I decided to give the Professorship up....

He kept a number of informal notebooks or working journals during the course of the subsequent years. The first entry is dated Tuesday 10 November 1970, the last Friday 1 June 1979. These notebooks, together with a loose-leaf folder containing the drafts of some of the verse translations in the novel, have been acquired (thanks to the far-sighted initiative of Joseph Lau and C. C. Liu) by Lingnan University and are now being published in a facsimile edition. This will be an invaluable source for anyone wanting to understand the working of a creative translator's mind.

There are many references in the notebooks to books. But there are also numerous references to the various friends whom Hawkes consulted during the years he spent on this project, people like Dorothy Liu, Joseph Needham, Denis Twitchett, Tony Hyder, Cheng Teh-k'un to mention only a few. In the 1998 interview he talks about this:

> You asked me in one of your questions, what help did I have? Well, I received whatever help I could get, anywhere I could get it! It wasn't so much, "What does this mean? What does that mean?" I don't mean to say that I always know what everything means. I certainly don't. I got a lot of things wrong, made a lot of mistakes. But I don't think that was really what I was tending to ask people about much, with some exceptions. It was more often about, well—I think clothing was something that bothered me a lot. Also things like arrangements. When you're translating that novel— it's slightly claustrophobic in a way, very enclosed. It's very much in a house and in a garden, and you're always very conscious of where you are and where you're going, that sort of thing, and where everything is. Of course, people have had lots of fun trying to redesign the *Daguanyuan*. Sometimes what Cao Xueqin writes doesn't make sense; not deliberately, but I think sometimes he says west instead of east, because it was east, but he's forgotten.... So you get in a bit of a tangle. That's the sort of thing I might well have asked about—I can't remember now. It's such a long time ago, I can't remember who I asked what. I was always asking people, "Have you any idea what this is all about?" But I don't think it was very much asking what words meant.

In both the notebooks and the 1998 interview, we can see that from the very outset Hawkes wanted this to be much more than a scholarly translation. Although he read the scholarship intensively (the *hongxue*), and mastered the extraordinarily complex textual history of the novel, he did so to serve his own creative ends as a translator. The notebooks abound with references to the various manuscript transcriptions and texts of *The Stone*. On this subject, Hawkes makes the following comment in the 1998 interview:

> I've read the manuscripts very carefully, Zhiyanzhai and so on, and tried to make use of them intelligently, but I haven't edited it.... If you did study my translation with the texts all along. you'd probably find that it follows one popular edition much more closely and gets more eclectic as it

goes along, as I was learning more about it and becoming more aware of the problems involved....

It's all very fine to be scholarly, and academic.... I was simply eclectic. I just went for whatever made a good story.... It's very unscholarly, it's not the sort thing that a "serious" scholar would do....

I felt by the end of it [the International Conference on *The Stone*, held in Madison, Wisconsin] that I'd really had enough of *hongxue* to last me for two lives. It's very interesting. But a lot of it isn't very relevant to translating.

The notebooks are not always easy to decipher. They were not written for publication, and are often heavily abbreviated. In due course it would be a very worthwhile project to transcribe them and write an extended commentary, unravelling the abbreviations and allusions with which they abound. It would make an extremely interesting study of the translator at work.

For the present one or two examples from the notebooks must suffice, to characterise this precious document.

From time to time Hawkes writes little asides that capture something of his wonderful liveliness, his sense of humour, his ability to enter into the lives of his characters as if they were his own friends, or as if he were a theatre director helping his actors say their lines with the right nuances. See for example the entry for 24 June 1971:

> Zhiyanzhai's insistence that it was wanton caprice—the sort of thing you can expect from worthless actors—suggests that he was not quite so knowledgeable as he makes out. Earlier his remarks about the plays are equally *malàpropos*. Probably his *sanshinianqian* interest in the stage had more to do with pinching actors' bottoms than with studying the plays they acted.

There are numerous examples of the use of pictures and diagrams to elucidate problems in translation—see for example the entry for 8 July 1971. When a translator is trying to visualise an item of clothing, or some other physical detail of the Jia household, a picture is worth a thousand words.

The notebooks document in detail Hawkes' ingenious approach to the translation of Chinese names. Once again, he talks about this in the 1998 interview:

> Now one of the problems it presents—to some extent I suppose it's a problem translating any Chinese novel presents—is Chinese names. Chinese names are just very difficult. Well, I'm sure you've noticed. English people

are always saying, "What's your name?", and can you tell me it again, I've forgotten it, and how do you spell it, that sort of thing! (laughs) They can't remember Chinese names. Particularly if they're written in some of the spellings, like Wade-Giles. They think Chinese looks like Ching-chong ching-chong ching.... They just can't remember. If you say Jia Zheng, and Jia Zhen, and Jia Jing—it all looks the same. So you've got this problem. And there are so many of them. What do you do about this? It seemed to me that particularly in this novel where there are such a vast number of characters (it's a long novel, with hundreds of characters), it seemed to me that one thing you could do would be to divide them up and treat one class of characters in one way, and one in another way, and one in another way, so that at least—it's still difficult—but you've reduced the possibilities (when you ask "Who's this?") by a third. The method I adopted—roughly speaking—was to say that this was a novel about masters and servants; *xiaojie, guniang,* and *yatou*. And quite apart from the problem of names, there's also the difficulty that in Chinese you've got many more distinctions than are possible in English, when it comes to relationships. I mean you've got your *yi'er* and *gumu*, and *bomu*, and this that and the other, and they're all Aunt in English. So I said, well let's decide to take all the master class, they stay Chinese; so Jia Zheng, Lady Wang, and so on. The maids, the inferior class, will be translated. [Aroma, Skybright etc.] I wouldn't say that it's a good thing to do in principle regardless in translation. But in this case, I'm just talking about the problems of translating *Hongloumeng*. So that people can follow the story and know what you're talking about. Or what sort of person you're talking about. It's something if they know that this person is a maid and not a mistress. Then ... I took religious people, I said well, O.K., any Buddhists and people like that, I'll give Latin names. So I called them Sapientia and so on. Actresses I gave French names to. Parfumée and so on. That's not a general principle I have about translating names. It was just something that I hit upon in this particular instance.

The notebooks provide many instances of the attitude that underlay Hawkes' work, an attitude that later found expression in the 1998 interview:

I don't know whether I've got any principles. I suppose I have got some sort of vague principles. But so much of what I did, in so far as I had any rules, they were rules I made for translating that specific novel, because of its problems, the problems it presented.

You see, I'd thought of it in a very different sort of way [from, for example, the translation of *The Songs of the South*]. I'd thought that what

I'd like to do was a translation where I didn't have to think about academic considerations, scholarly considerations. I'd just think about how to present this book—this was Penguins, after all—in such a way that I did the whole of it but at the same time it was enjoyable for the English reader, if possible. They could get some of the pleasure out of it that I had got myself.

This in the end was his motto. He was working to share with others his own intense pleasure as a reader of great literature. As he commented in the 1998 interview, "I think that's one of the fascinating things about *Hongloumeng*, that it's a flawed book, technically—isn't it? But it's one of the best novels in the world. It's both at the same time." It seems fitting to end with the (much quoted) concluding words of the Introduction to the first volume of the translation:

> For although this is ... an "unfinished" novel, it was written (and rewritten) by a great artist with his very lifeblood. I have therefore assumed that whatever I find in it is there for a purpose and must be dealt with somehow or other. I cannot pretend always to have done so successfully, but if I can convey to the reader even a fraction of the pleasure this Chinese novel has given me, I shall not have lived in vain.

---

[1] This and all subsequent extracts are taken from a lengthy interview conducted with David Hawkes by Chan Oi-sum in December 1998, in Oxford. The complete interview (which provides a useful accompaniment to the notebooks) can be consulted as an appendix to Ms Chan's M. Phil. Thesis, "*The Story of the Stone*'s Journey to the West", Hong Kong Polytechnic University, 1999. Anyone wanting to read further should consult the three introductions by Hawkes to the first three volumes of the Penguin Classics translation, and the two articles, "*The Story of the Stone*: A Symbolist Novel", and "The Translator, the Mirror and the Dream", reprinted in his collected essays, *Classical, Modern and Humane: Essays in Chinese Literature* (Hong Kong: The Chinese University Press, 1989).

PART I

November 1970

—

February 1973

紅樓夢

November 1970 —
February 1973

Tuesday 10th November 1970

Letter from Price (9 Nov.), mostly re publication plan. More or less confirms impression that no paperback will appear until the whole transl. is in hardback.

Chap. 9 p.114 人民 ed.
宝玉：撕挤代死？我是必要回去的！
秦钟：有金荣在这裏，我是要回去的了。
宝玉：这是为代死？...

CCWang obviously right in taking 回去 in sense of "tell" (teacher what you've done).
But the 2ⁿᵈ one can't have that sense; which is impossibly awkward. (CCW leaves the second one out.)
In fact 脂砚 (庚辰)²¹⁷ and 高鈔本 ⁹/⁵ both have
有金荣在这裏，我是不在这裏念书的
which is obviously the right text. V. hard to see why it got changed. I foresee 高鈔 etc.

  Note. Can the printed text really represent Kao's own 'correction'? It seems hard to believe that he could have been so obtuse. Perhaps there was a 'Printer's reader' who corrected the whole thing & introduced such inanities.

Chap 10

Thursday 12ᵗʰ November 1970

Rough typescript finished yesterday. Corrected copy last night & recorrected this morning. Chap. 10 typed, commenced Thursday mid-morning.

Friday 13ᵗʰ

given to Friday morning. Rough typescript (cc) of Chap. 9 received from Mrs. Halsey & fair TS of Chap. 7 collected.

Drugs on p. 124 identified in ref. section of OI Library.

Sat. 14ᵗʰ November 1970

10 钱 = 1 两   60 grains = 1 dram
10 分 = 1 钱   8 drams = 1 oz.
100 分 = 1 两

∴ 1 两   ≃   1 oz.
   1 钱   ≃   1 dram
   5 分   ≃   ½ dram
   2 分   ≃   ¼ dram

Rig Tsy about medical terms.

Mem. Tell Mrs. Halsey to insert 'than' on p.5/ch.9
also 'other' on p. 12. (he)
Pao-yu / (he)
p. 14. 'that's who he is' (!)

Tuesday 17ᵗʰ NN.

Above cons. made on copy w. Halsey & Chap. seven returned for typing corrs.

chap. 10

Wednesday 18 November 1970

Mem. Give Halsey corr. on p.1 of Chap Nine.
    Also p. 2   and p. 13.
        p. 7 ↑ But   p. 11.
Not much done today. (up to 且说 p. 122.)
Mem. What are "建蓮子"?

(引用建蓮子七粒去心)

? 当归 植物圖鑑 give Ligusticum acutilobum
  薛亨字典 give Aralia edulis
      w. 植 calls '土当归'

植 says 「婦科用」of Lig. and "sarsaparilla —
    但食用」子 土当归
Read for Aralia sinensis.

II Sources used for medical & botanical transit
   Chap. 10 (mostly supplies of AH)

1. T. A. Wise, Review of the History of Medicine (2 vols)
                                    London 1867
    (Esp. v1. 2, p. 560 sq)

2. "La prise du pouls en médicine sino-vietnamienne"
                        France-Asie (?)

3. Bernard E. Read Chinese Medicinal Plants July 1936
4. Needham. Clerks & Craftsmen in China & the West
                                    Cambridge 1970
        263 — end.

Monday 23 Nov. 1970
MS. of Chap. 10 finished by lunch time.

Friday 27 Nov 1970
TS of Chap 10 given to Mrs. Haley
 (Certain corr. made since then).

Saturday 28 Nov 1970
By evening completed (of the second day's work)
the 校正 of Chap. 27 under the mistaken
impression that it was in Vol. 1. — It doesn't, of
course (26, 27, 27, NOT 27, 28, 28, as
given on the very proofs.)

Sunday 29 Nov. 1970

Monday 30 Nov. 1970
Give full corr. to Mrs. H.: p. 5 (be)
 Chap. 10 pp. 9, 10, 11,
Tuesday 1 Dec. 1970   received 8 & 9 back fr
                                        Haley.
Thursday 3rd Dec. 1970
 校正 隨想錄, returned to SOAS Library — Vol
 1 (1–2) re-borrowed (until 3 Jan).
 Give Dorothy rough TS of 10.

Monday 7 Dec. 1970
Corrected rough TS with Haley. (大亚枕,
which DL says is not 'bolster' but 'arm-rest')

Thurs. 10 Dec. 1970
Half-way thro' Ch. 11. Textual diff. is 要端一
encounter w. 凤姐笑ハ荟芳园

心中暗喜，因想道，再不想今日此奇遇，
那情景越发难堪了。

庚辰 hw:
再不想到今日的这个奇遇，那神情光景
越发不堪难看了

高抄 G. h.
再不想到今日的这个奇遇，神情光景越发
不堪的难看

Sunday 13 Dec. 1970
Rough TS of Chap. 11 completed + corrected
5 early morning.

Friday 18 Dec. 1970
Receive corr. of 9, 10 from Haley.
Send 6–10 to Price (registered) with covering letter.

22 December 1970

* Chaps. 5–10 (Copy 3) Surface mail to John Minford.

Chaps. 2–10 (Copy 2) to Dorothy Liu.

30 Dec.

Dear. Correct Chia Jong's bedroom.
May? (Gardens & Opera?)

2 Jan. 1971 (or thereabouts)

Letter from Price acknowledging receipt of 6–10

Tuesday 5 Jan. 1971

Complete rough TS of Chap. 12.

Friday Jan. 15. 1971

Rough TS of 12 given to Hawkes.

Thurs. Feb. 4 1971

Cor. fair TS of 11 returned to Hawkes & rough TS of 13.
Note. About a week before this, discussed rough TS of 13 with Dorothy in London, after evening loan of Byles.

Dear
7/16 'Chief Steward Lai Erh' must be altered to 'Lai Sheng' to bring it in line w. 10/7 and 14/1

来旺 Lai Wang must be treated as
旺兒 + household (like 興兒, 隆兒, 昭兒,
見, 壽兒, 拴兒, 嘉兒) to avoid confusion with
Lai Sheng (来旺家的, 賴汗家的) in
chap. 14.   As plans:
旺兒: Brightie
昭兒: Shiner
拴兒: Fixer
興兒: Merry
隆兒: ~~Clocky~~ Rich
嘉兒: Hoppy
壽兒: Oldie
　This means an alternative is Chap.

(拜) 水懺 → 水懺隨聞錄 →
　　慈悲道場水懺隨聞錄　　續乙 2/2-3

　　法界聖凡水陸大齋法輪寶懺
　　　　　　　　　　　　續乙 2/4-3/1

　　慈悲道場懺法　45/922-967 (1909)

　　千手千眼大悲心懺行法　續乙 2/1
　　　　　　(1/27A)

$$\underset{11-1}{子} \quad \underset{1-3}{丑}$$

Friday 12 Feb 1971

Halley returns counted 11 & 12. (12 needs no count).

Times: 卯 辰

寅 卯 辰 巳 午
3-5 5-7 7-9 9-11 11-1

寅正 means 4 a.m.
寅初 " 3 a.m.
寅正二刻 = 4.30 a.m. etc.

未 申 酉 戌 亥
1-3 3-5 5-7 7-9 9-11

初更 二更 三更 四更 五更
7-9   9-11 11-1 1-3   3-5

Wednesday 17 Feb 1971

p.154 The times are ridiculous. If she eats at 10 and doesn't see 領牌的 until 11.30, why on 三十五日 does she hear (p.157) 領牌交牌人 往來不絕 as well as roll-call (6.30) and it being all over? Why does the maid who comes in just after she has finished eating (p.157) say 「方才想起來, 再遲一步, 也飲不成了」? Why does she say to Pao-yü (p.157) 「他們來領的時候, 你還做夢呢」?

The texts are as follows:

人民：　只在午初二刻；戌初燒……
俞本：　只在午初刻。戌初燒……
王本：　same as 人民
庚辰：　只在午初刻到戌初燒……（刻→到）
甲戌：　只在午初刻戌初燒……
高抄：　只在午初戌初燒……

The primary weakness in the text is between 初 and 戌. 在 is significantly odd. Pretty strong the text ought to read 只在午初前；戌初…

Also. Perhaps 'Breakfast' and 'Dinner' is better for the meals than 'Dinner' and 'Supper'. This will need rather careful going over.

18 Feb.　　Or 'Lunch' and 'Dinner'?

19 Feb

Mrs. Halsey returns T.S. 4 XIII

Chap. 11　p.127　Let's 秦氏's illness beginning 上月……二十日 a few days b/f 中秋節. So her illness began on 八月二十日 and 'now' is 九月

p.133　这年正是十一月三十日冬至……明日大初一 i.e. beginning of 十二月 they decide she's dying.

p.137　现是腊月天气（十二月）

p.142　谁知至年冬底林如海因为身作重疾…… so 貴璉 + 代玉 leave for Yangchou in 十二月.

p.158　林姑老爷是九月初三……没的 二爷……大约赶年底回来

Clearly this is quite ridiculous. This is on, in eff
第五十五日 i.e. 35th day of mourning.
秦氏 can't have died before and after 十二月十日
That makes the date of p.158 about 正月十五日.
One can only make sense by emending 九月 to 正月, 繡?
翠? in 上月 and 年底 should be 原底 春底
keep 31 month off. 正月底
+ several days of 鐵檻寺
+ 秦鐘's cold
+ ("一日") 賈妃's birthday
+ 智能's escape ; 邦業 '三五日便唔中袁動了'
p.174 本該出月到家
It looks as though he had been expecting to arrive in
三月 but in fact arrived earlier towards end 二月.
林如海 must have died on 正月初三. but The
question is, what wd. 曉光 have said?

Wed. 24 Feb 1971
_____

Better call 北靜王 水 instead of 世
(following 1755 rather than 人民) because there are
too many "Shih's" already

Wed Mar 3 1971
_____
corr. T.S. of chap 13 back. chap 14
with Mrs. Haley.

Menu: 7/12 lunch 7/15 dinner

Menu. 祭棚: this para should read
The first of these booths was the Princess of
Tung-p'ing's, the second the Princess of Nan-ari's,
the third the Prince of Ching-ning's, & the 4th the Prince of
Pei-ching's.

念珠經 (金剛頂瑜伽念珠經)
17.727-8 (No.789)

菶荟: all MSS have 菁荟
(い. 脊令, 鶺鴒) ?!

師父 = 尼姑. 7/6. Many alterations.
7/10 Lin-an

11 Mar 1971

15/170 命婚媾: 甲戌, 庚辰 etc. Look after
this 命. 句 高 揚, Lose it. But it seems likely the
高揚 is right & the word 句. 命 was in any case fong wt.
人 offers it, but afraid for her it seems must if indeed the
阿凰 would walk inwardly unto you.
No. the 體 心 腹 了頭 already known, it myself
have been over copying to order you clearly went to
旺兄. Surely 命 is right.

Chap. 3
① 車鍪 玉 紫金冠
② 二 桶 速 珠金 抹額
③ 二 色 金 白蝶穿花大红一向和袖
④ 五彩總扎攏 坎肩 袷袍 宮縧
⑤ 五色緞剪綫（另/回 — 七寶象王.

Chap. 15.
① 東珠銀冠
② 紋龍本海珠額
③ 四蝶 闹 家袖
④ 撘裢銀帶
⑤ 剪綫 (or 15 juni)

Wednesday
31 Mar. 1971
Got back corrected
Ts of Chaps. 14, 15
from Mrs. Halsey

(Halsey paid for
typing 11 – 15)

Thursday 1 April 1971
Chaps. 11–15 sent to
Price (registered post)
Letter to Price.
Letter to JM deposits
modify

End of Chap. 16

(人民) 那都判越夺着急，忙喝起来
毕竟秦钟死说如何，且听下回分解

(俞) 都判道："放屁，俗语说的好：天下官
管天下民．．．．．．．．and a long passage in which
Ch'in Ch'g admonish Pao-yü all. 立志功名 on his deathbed

(抄稿) 判官闻听连喝不了于是欲奉槛
这般放回苏醒过来，睁眼见宝玉在傍
竟枯痰堵咽喉不能出语．．．．．．
he dies in silence.

(庚辰) is having the same as (俞).
(己) (甲戌) is also the same.

Osvald Sirén   Gardens of China
              New York 1949   CW2; Sir.

Andrew Boyd   Chinese Architecture
                              Lund 1962
Gin Djih Su   Chinese Architecture Past &
                              Contemp. HK 1964

10 May 1971
Chap 17, p.199 ~~红玉鼓~~ 二十三道箍
    Textual variants. Soong showed be
「二十四道箍」

18 May 1971
Ruph TS given to Mrs. Haley

30 May 1971
Chap. 18 p.202 作家v人民 both have
香巾 —— So have 李引, 王G, etc
俞, 高抄C, ~~颗~~ 脂砚 all have
香(珠). (俞, typically, has no mention in appendix,
though in has a trivial variant 拂座)
香巾 not in my dict. etc. 香珠 is presumably 15
cented beads.

ib. 苑内悶见
    MSS have 院. Obviously right. They aren't in
the garden yet.

2 June 1971
荇 (18/202) 二著条 fringed water lily,
floating heart. (nymphoides peltatum)

ib. 清流一带. What happened to the
    floating lanterns?

Sunday
20 June 1971

Chap. 18/206-7
MSS (高+脂) gin 五绝「万象争辉」to 探春 and 五七律「文采风流」to 李纨.
Printed ~~verins~~ eds (except 八十) gin 五绝句 to 李纨 + 五律 to 探春.
In the introductory sentence, of chap, 五律七绝 and 「李纨又勉强作成一律」, but now all 15 not now 探春 (自忖己难与薛林争衡, 只好随众塞责) unaltered, so that it becomes quite meaningless.

In chap. 37, when the 诗社 is being formed, 李纨 says ~~你们都~~「我和二姑娘 (迎春) 四姑娘 (惜春) 都不会作诗, 须得让出我们三个人去……」
but she doesn't exclude the possibility of their sometimes producing a poem (p.444「若遇见容易些的题目韵脚, 我们也随便做一首. ~~做~~」)
In fact, I don't think she ever does write any.
The present arrangement must be due to Kao's editing. I think it is an improvement — 15 MS version does seem like an inconsistency (+ even if it isn't, it's hard not to make T'an-ch'un's 绝 look

much less literate than 李渔's 律) —
& follow it in my version. But it calls for
alternates in the preceding centuries, which I have
therefore had to rewrite accordingly.

~~The second type it says~~

Probably K M's version is 'right';
but the translator needs a single speaker here.
In the last resort it of try (a very crude one)
of showing the Tai-chi, Pao-ch'ai & T'an-ch'un
one has at versifying than So-Wan, Ying-ch'un &
Hsi-ch'un is to let them write longer poems!

24 June 1971

脂硯 shows up pretty badly in his double-column
notes near the end of this chap., where he fires off
against the iniquities of players. 齡官's objection that
游園 & 惊夢 "非本角之戏" was a simple statement
of fact — she wasn't a 正旦. 脂硯's unwillingness
that it was broken caprice — the sort of thing you can
expect from worthless actors — suggests that he was not
quite so knowledgeable as he makes out. Earlier his
remarks about the plays are equally malapropos.
Probably his 三 + 年 前 interest in the stage had more
to do with pinching actors' bottoms than with studying the
plays they acted.

Thurs

24 June 1971

Can't very well call the actresses 'Mademoiselle'. All players (mas. n fem.) were '— Kuan'. Perhaps 'Player X'.

蒋玉函 (#38/332) male, player of 旦 roles, has stage name 琪官.

Finally decided to use French nouns. (Charmante, Parfumée, etc.) Prefixes seem too cumbrous, & they mustn't be confused with maids.

Sunday 27 June 1971

Fair MS copy completed. Rough typing begun (ch.18).
p. 205 燈光之中 諸般 玩耍.
Surpers B refers to "shows" of some kind (chiang, etc).
The 優伶, 百戲 of p. 210 must refer to more than the 12 actresses. (cf. 百戲)

Monday 28 June 1971

(Mem) In chap. 18 賈蘭 is made to sound very wee 3 or 4; I think the age he's given at first mention earlier is too great. Alter?

18/202 The time here goes all wrong again. About fourteen hours are unaccounted for.

It's barely daylight in 15.55ʰ when K. start waiting outside. Then fly for inches & do a few flaps. The "suddenly" the swallows come & she annis. And it's completely when she gets there.

30 June 1971

Letter from TK Cheng gives pkey bibliography:

Hawley, W.M. Chinese folk designs Hollywood 1949. (图 152 cos typ)

Kocha A. Chinese flower symbolism. Tokyo 1954 (p.21, p.20)

王端, 中國圖案集, 上海 1953 (pl.106)

—— 溪集 —— 1954 (pl.164)

Bod. 林漢傑 民间藍印花布圖案, 北京 1956
Chin.d.1020   (pl.17)

故宮博物院, 清代織繡圖花圖案
                            北京 1959
                    (pl. 61, 62, 65)

Friday 1 July 1971

212 撒骰子赶围棋作戏
216 又有赶围棋的,又有撒骰抹牌的
232 正遇见宝钗香菱莺儿三个赶围
　　棋作耍、贾环又要玩、宝钗...
　　让他上来坐在一处玩。一注
　　十个钱...谁知后来接连输了
　　几盘... (following passage has details of games)
Seems to mean racing 围棋 pieces by dice, the
winner collecting 钱 bets.

p.212「丁郎认父」and「黄伯央大摆
陰魂阵」unidentifiable. Looks like a
flea opening.

Friday 2 July 1971

18/212　The 第一个 凤姐 ... 第二个
　　宝玉 .... section reads like a series of
non-sequiturs. 凤姐 showed long cause before
「又收园中...」　　第一个...二块」
given it seems as if she did it. The 第一个
got misplaced from a way into it in that
follows, perhaps.

p.212 正在房内玩的没兴头
高抄本 has 顽的兴头
庚辰本 has 顽的没兴头

(212) 弟兄子侄...
「满街之人...」is much more fun to translate. 庚辰 has this text with the note「必有之言」
Interestingly enough, 高抄 has「满街...」crowded out and「弟兄...」substituted!

213 庚辰 has
Jues
「窗前闻得房内有呻吟之韵」
and nothing between「所训之子」and「宝玉禁不住大叫了...」

戚入民 has「听见屋里一片喘息之声」
「正在得趣,故此呻吟」诸本無
此八字, etc.

高抄:
has 房内有呻吟之韵 crowded out and
屋裡一片喘息声 substituted
and 正在得趣故此 呻吟
added ~~whichever~~ as a later addition insertion.

呻吟 are moans of ecstasy, + 喘息 ɔ

plantings. They can't both be right, 坤吟之韵 looks like 瞥's text. The other 150 one two emendations made at different times 与瞀. Probably he wanted to make it more harmonious when he put 吟 it 瞀吟 — forgot to cross out it at bot. (Which cd. be 瞀吟之韵 e.g.). 坤吟 seems more like it 美人.

_____

Schuyler Cammann   China's Dragon Robes   NY 1952
100 sq. Punning symbols or rebuses

Chavannes "L'expression des voeux dans l'art populaire chinoise" JA 9 série vol. 18 (1901)

Seikin Nozaki : Kisshō zuan Kaidai   Tientsin 1928

红蝠至天 = 鸿福致天
磬 = 庆
戟磬如意 = 吉庆如意
戟磬和瓶 = 吉庆和平
冠带般猴 = 官代侯流 (?)
鲇鲇与蝠 = 年年万福
笔锭如意 = 必定如意
瓶笙三戟 = 平升三级
卐鲇如意 = 万年...
卐鲇连蝠 = 万年连福

Costumes for 1st Forbidden City

必定如意

筆錠如意

(Hackmack, Chinese Carpets
and Rugs Plate XIII Fig. 27   Tientsin 1924)

鮎 'ugly, spotted catfish — al. sheat-fish a
eels (Parasilurus asotus L.)

Alan Priest: Costumes from the Forbidden City
New York Metropolitan   1945 16p. 54 plates
Museum of Art. (Not in Bod. (They have other
                              pub. by him))

Helen E. Fernald   Chinese Court Costumes
        Toronto 1946   51p. illus. 37 (i.e. 41)
                                    plates

V & A.   Brief Guide to Chinese embroideries
                                    1921
         Brief guide to the Chinese woven fabrics
                                    1921
Vuillemier, B. The art of silk
         weaving in China, symbolism of Chinese imperial
         ritual robes. London 1939 (Bod. 21998 d.34)

Alan Priest   Chinese textiles ...
               (1931) 1934

Paine, Wit. Pane Old Chinese embroideries 1929

Simmons, Pauline Chinese patterned silks NY NY 1948

Parish-Watson & Co.

Berthold Laufer: The gold treasure of the Empress Ch'ien-lung of China. Chicago, A Century of Progress 1934.

金銀

Perzyński, Friedrich. Chinesische Goldgegenstände und Textilien aus dem Besitze von Friedrich Perzyński, (formerly of William Cohn)

---

8 July 1971
Elmer Cotton Sports Shop, Turl St. Oxford.
Game of 圍棋, is named:

GO

or

WEI-CHI

and proprietor feels 'Go' to be 'standard' name.

吉慶有餘 from 林漢傑 17. N.b. nothing special for 吉

萬福流芳

(林 18)

#28 壽臺流芳 don't understand this one.   蓮 in different ways 2 ends (運到頭了)

#33 福壽三多   #67   平安吉慶

12 July 1971

Ch. 19/216「也有擲骰抹牌的」
R. S. Culin:
Chinese Games with Dice and Dominoes (1895)

TS of Ch. 17 returned to Mrs. Halsey for correcting.

13 July 1971
Chia Chen showed asleep to Cousin Chen, to avoid surprise at Chia Cheng. Showed asleep Chia Lien to Cousin Lien too, but fear surprise at Lin Tai-yü

丁郎尋父　The Ac. Sin. material has 5 such
titles and 2 丁郎仲狀元　a follows:—

丁郎尋父　(弹词) 19　(北方小曲) 311
　　　　　(大鼓) 94　(杂耍) 402
　　　　　(子弟書) 108　(夯歌) 502
丁郎仲狀元　(北平词曲) 24　(夯歌) 502

94 is in 4 parts (本) 1. 逛燈 2. 打夯
3. 改書　4. 奉本
This is a 嚴嵩 story. 杜景隆 is wrongly
exiled though it indicates 丁 Yea) meant 年 to whole
taken along to his wife. She is pregnant at the end, & 丁 is his son.
It is exceedingly crude, disjointed story.

「象位明公莫轻信
　此乃就是劝善文」

The 夯歌 (502) appears to be used for used 4 times.
尋父 = 大鼓 1 and 2, 仲狀元 = 大鼓 3 and 4.

A part of 4 is that Yea Sung & his wicked son
forced to write an bypass style the streets of Peking (intended
by the gods when 丁 has studied), various beatings being mentioned
by name.

陰魂陣　94 (大鼓) and 109 (快書)

94 is the middle between 黄百翔 and 孙膑 (al. 孙
百灵, 孙三郎). After 于樂毅伐齐. A v.

short extract — it doesn't even include the battle itself, only its preliminaries — + it is v. hard to tell exactly what it is my about. ("文明大鼓書詞)

Design names for 故宮博物院藏清代
織繡團花圖案 文物 Peking 1959

福壽同圖　　　　並蒂蓮
喜相逢 (2 butterflies)　蓮雲万幅
八仙慶壽　　　　蓮幅如意
鳳穿牡丹　　　　蓮生貴子
滿地嬌　　　　　芝芝蘭芳
四季如意　　　　如意壽 (plants + clouds)
四季百花　　　　五福捧壽
四季花卉　　　　百幅九壽
三秋　　　　　　金壽吉祥
富貴如意　　　　五福英慶
玉堂富貴 (peonies in mushroom-cloud surround?, asters?, crab and peony)
蓮棠富貴　　　　八仙慶壽 (symbols of 八仙)
灵仙富貴　　　　合富貴如意
灵仙祝壽
吉慶有餘
丰登大吉 (lantern)
丰登慶有餘
丹鳳朝陽 (phoenix + peony)
洪福齊天 (bats in clouds)
麟生九子 (one of in. middle + 8 round)

Culin Chinese Games with Dice & Dominoes
Smithsonian Report U.S. Nat. Museum 1898
RSL Soc. 1998 2 1.1)
p. 491 seq.

[22 July 1971]

Ch. 19/222
「再不許謗僧毀道的了」
庚辰 has
「再不了毀僧謗道、調脂弄粉、還有
要緊的一件．再不許吃人嘴上的胭脂了
則了你的化第三件．~~and the~~
~~再~~ ~~許~~ ~~吃~~ 吃人…胭脂
is evidently a more extreme instance of the kind 了化,
which means that 毀僧謗道 and 調脂弄粉
must be practically synonymous. It is wholly impossible
that 毀僧謗道 may mean anything to do with
monks. It must be an idiomatic expression the
meaning of which is ~~to~~ now lost.
(Viiing 賈 did n't understand it best.
The received or an him as far (nil-emended).)

[24 July 1971]
19/223「這時候誰帶什麼香呢？」Pings
marginis. 庚辰 text and 脂硯齋 elucidate.

「冬寒十月讌帶什麼書呢？」
　圖（夾批）「口頭語，猶在寒冷
　　　　　　　　　之時」

Sunday 25 July 1971
MS of Chap. 19 completed, 3 p.m.

30 July 1971
Dwitz returns Chaps 2-10 (Copy 2)

31 July 1971
Give Dwitz Chaps. 11-17 (Copy 2)

10 Aug 1971
Eve of holiday. Deposit 16-19
[16④, 17①, 18 top copy roph TS,
19 unique copy roph TS] in red box
in OI for safety.

28 Aug. 1971
Best TS of 18 finished.
Answer letter from Mrs. Hawkins re Bussell
translation.

11 Sept. 1971
11-20 Copy 3 to John Minford.

Friday 17 Sept. 1971

Inquiry to Price abt. receipt of 16-20
(Registered post 1 Sept. 1971. Letter announcing
despatch dated 31 ~~Sept~~ Aug.)

Monday 20 Sept. 1971

Price acknowledges 16-20.
Dorothy returns 11-17 with suggested corrections
Gin Dorrit 18-20

15 October 1971

Complete with TS of 21. Up to
Chap. 3 changes to Pinyin in copies
2-4 with John M. So far one
afternoon a chapter. (!)

Wednesday 27 October 1971

In chaps. 18-22 the problem of time becomes
insoluble.

(1) chap. 18 (貴妃有親) takes place on
    五月十五

(2) chap. 19 鳳姐 spends 'two or three days' clearing
    up afterwards. In those two or three days are Pao-
    寶玉's visit to 花宅 & its sequel and
    湘雲's arrival. Then there is 寶玉's quarrel with
    張道 about using his girls' room + the will
    reconciliation. All this would take us to about
    五月二十

(3) Chap. 21 (p.274) mentions 大姐儿 first sickening for smallpox. [crossed out] We are told that the disease takes 12 days to run its course. [crossed out] On the twelfth day 贾琏 rejoins 凤姐 + discussion with her (Chap. 22, p.249) re: plans for 宝钗's birthday on 正月二十一 (!)

(4) After the birthday celebrations + the guessing one of them, 元春 sends in 灯谜 and is dearly made into 贾母 saying「明日正是节呢…明日晚上再玩罢」 i.e. an obvious lead to 正月十五 [crossed out] !

<u>Note</u> Chap. 23 in 脂砚 started:
「话说贾元春自那日幸大观园回宫去后 …」
The 乾隆 抄本 had this, but inserts 人母次日彻颁众人过节,那 preceding Chap. 23 on say, must have been a 'floating' section written before the internal bridges between it + chap. 18 had been worked out.

p.252 "Naked and carefree through the world" is perhaps all [crossed out] right for 赤條條无牽掛; but as the line later on (p. 254) makes him burst into tears "Naked and friendless…." is better, though less accurate.

Thursday 28 Oct. 1971
Second thoughts.
  Chap. 21 (p. 238) 「四人面面相覷」
Second to Chap. 22 (p. 256) 「忽然报
娘娘…… 四人听说, 忙出来至
贾母上房」
  Skewed to presumed 240 「湘云仍往
代玉房中安歇」——— 243 「且下回分解」
         = ch. 21.
    chap. 22 woolen end of 凤姐终觉不自.
This val. give a better version. But this
can't possibly be pieced. (脂砚 has the same as
today's). ——— In any case I don't mark 二十一/十二.

Friday 29 Oct. 1971
  p. 253 紫鹃却知端底
       乾隆抄本 (suspicious unconnected section of
MS) has this.
       脂砚庚辰 has 袭人 and a comment
on 袭人

p. 254 Bao-yu's 「大家彼此」is quite
unaccountable in printed text.
  脂砚 has 「你别隐私岂不大家彼此。」
in 袭人's lot. which makes Bao-yu's reply
wrong comprehensible.

30 Oct. 1971

p. 255 「便拿了回房去。次日和宝釵湘雲同看、宝釵念其詞曰…」

脂庚辰C. has 「便携了回房去令湘雲同看、次日又令宝釵看…」

乾隆抄C. has 「便拿了回房去次日和宝釵湘雲同看人念其詞曰…」
　　　　　　　　　　　　　　　　　　　　宝釵

庚辰 is obviously a much better text here

─────────────

255) 最能**移性**

This is almost certainly the 疑相 (yixing) of 北京语语汇. (?)

《尤须询》 writes 侬性.

= 误解 etc.

═════════════

Monday 1 Nov. 1971

p. 258. 雲丫忙遣雲環和个女人将雲兰唤来

Where has Jia Huan come from? And what happens to him afterward? Perhaps it should be 丫環. No. (庚辰)「雲環与兩个婆娘」. Corrected to 丫環. Probably just two tall old women each.

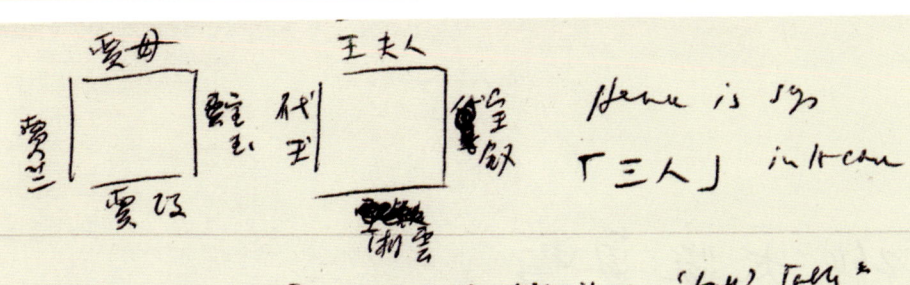

Here is sgn 「三人」 in it can

of the third talk, since it wasn't a "full" talk. Also, when it says that [crossed out] 雲母命 他 (Jia-tou) 在身边笑了 it seems imply that there was no fun place at the top table, & that he turned aside beside the old lady on the side.

Wed. Nov. 3 1971

257. 一带好雲环雲兰等纷来一齐玄拖 心机猜了.

宝鉴 has this too. It seems absurd that 雲兰 should be old enough to ~~insinuate~~ sober & write riddles.

Thursday 4 Nov 1971

Dorothy notes 18-20 ④

Friday 5 Nov. 1971

p. 199「十二个小尼姑小道姑……」
p. 210「幽尼女道」
p. 262「一班的十二个小沙弥十二个小道士」
「又小和尚小道士」

Also: (p.262)「文官等十二个女戏子」
No 女戏 other than 龄官 has so far been mentioned by name.

p.264 太監 夏忠
p.172 六宮都太監夏秉忠
Also the distribution of rooms in the 大觀園 given in this chap. doesn't tally with chap. 37 et seq.

	chap. 23	chap. 37
迎春	綴錦樓	紫菱洲 Amaryllis Eyot
探春	秋掩齋	秋爽齋 Autumn Studio / Snug-in-autumn Studio
惜春	蓼風軒	藕榭 Lotus Pavilion

Probably it would be safer to alter 23, as it would only cause confusion to stick to the text.
Names in 37 are:

宝釵: '蘅蕪君' ~~Lady~~ Lady Allspice
代玉: '瀟湘妃' ~~H-Sistery Lady~~ River ~~Sprite Queen~~
迎春: '菱洲' Amaryllis Islander
探春: '蕉下客' Plantain Lover
惜春: '藕榭' Lotus ~~Habitu~~ Dweller
李紈: '稻香老農' Farmer Sweetrice
宝玉: '怡紅公子' Green Boy
湘雲: '枕霞舊友' Cloud Maiden
(Crab flower club)
醉寳玉:「雪威侵竹冷、秋爽帶也凉」
陸游:「地偏身飽閒
　　　秋爽睡珠簧」

秋爽

p.462 祝隱路住 Keinbay Friend
（立湘雲） Cloud Maiden

代王's joke consists (for purposes of masked) owing at Plantain Lover by stages.

(1) "If I rain I'll call ~~you~~ myself sometimes "Under the Plantains".

(2) ——— 代王's deer-meat joke.

(3) "All right, then. I'll call you "Plantain Lover".

---

9 Nov. 1971 (Tuesday)

Re 小沙弥 小道士 (See 5 Nov.)
This is not the only difficulty.

玉皇廟, 達摩庵 Clashes with 櫳翠庵 (p.500) — But perhaps the first two are not intended as proper nouns.

Monday 15 Nov 1971

Phonecall from Mary Tregear explains 煨蠟釘硃動起手來 in chap. 53. Sylladge Coats the stone with wax, sticks 15 characters in it & fixes the seal with vermilion in it fresh they before carving. Her informant, 'Miss Chen', types 天工開物 by 宋應星. Translation 'Chinese Technology in the 17 C.' in Ashmolean Far Eastern coll. library.

✶ Copy 3 of chaps. 21, 22 to Minford on Sunday 14.

Wed. 17 Nov. 1971

Re 太監夏忠. This is also text of 庚辰; but 乾隆抄本 (interestingly enough) has 夏守忠.

p.204. 呆了半晌、登時掃了興

乾：好似打了個焦，登時掃去興頭

庚辰：好似打了個焦雷、登時掃去興頭

Prev. 焦雷 is like 焦霹靂 = 旱雷

19 Nov. 1971

V. interesting textual difference concerning who stood up when Baoyu came into the room.

刻本：探春惜春和賈環都站起來

庚辰：惟有探春和惜春賈環站了起來

乾隆：惟有迎探二人及賈環站起來

Asread to: 探春惜春和賈環都站起來

Sat. 20 Nov. 1971

Perhaps 'Over the Rainbow' would be best for 枕霞閣 (p.458). The bridge leading to it may be thought of as a rainbow and the reflection of the sky in the water gives the 雲中 impression to those sitting in it. On the other hand Chap. 5 associates her with 'clouds' and her name means Cloud, so perhaps best stick to Cloud Maiden

Mon. 22 Nov. 1971

合德：飛燕外傳：「飛燕有女弟合德 姿宏 體, 始醇粹于信, 不能飛言比」

(墨憨齋) 古今小說 Old Gut Lowe's
Stories Old and New

Wed. 24 Nov 1971

Copy ② ⼄ 15-22 lent to Arthur Cooper.
To be returned by Christmas.

Thursday 25 Nov. 1971

鑌鐵鎗 (from 西廂, cited 代王 in 23)
No doubt 'pewter' is correct, but 'leaden' makes
better sense for the English reader, who might well think a
pewter spear a better weapon than a silver one. 'Leaden
counterfeit' sounds soft & useless. 'pewter counterfeit'
makes you wonder if 'spear' is a mistranslation or a
misprint.

It's clear from 庚辰 that the end
of 23 is meant to be a broken sentence
「原來望 —— 卻聽下回分解」
Previous copyists must misunderstood this.

26 Nov. 1971
Rough TS of 23 completed.

Monday 30 Nov. 1971
冰片 Borneol, Borneo camphor. (cf. Malayan, Barus,
or Dryobalanops camphor) from wood of 'majestic East Indian
tree' - Dryobalanops aromatica. Hence Mathews 'Baroos
camphor from Barus'.

29 Nov 1971.

㉔ KYTT has 涎脸; 嫌脸 (xián liǎn) [北京话语词汇]
= 惹人烦厌, etc.
But: 小说词语汇释
gives 涎瞪, 涎脸, 涎脸涎皮, 涎皮赖脸
all = 嘻皮笑脸
不就重之欲

Tuesday 30 Nov. 1971

p. 275 雲琮. Since 雲琮 comes first among the 玉輩 on p. 145 & apparently lives with 邢夫人 & is counted a「大家子念書的孩子」, it seems almost certain that he must be a son of one of 雲老爷's concubines — of whom we are constantly being told that there are a good many.

Sat. 4 Dec. 1971
21–23 sent to Price & received editing. Copy letter with typists for some days.

Wed. 8 Dec. 1971
Troy weight
for Gold, Silver and Jewels
20 pennyweights in an ounce
阿戍 11 2 dwt.

The 乾隆抄本, has a virtual monopoly of the whole 倪二 passage, presumably to make 倪二 less sympathetic. Better follow printed text, i.e. 15 xyears w. sequel.

＊ The small differences between the corrected 抄本 text on a [crossed out] 庚辰 text make it un essay outing that the 抄本 is forked.

Friday 10 Dec. 1971

Since Bao-yu scarcely knew Jia Yun by sight, it seems highly improbable that Jia Yun wd. have known 茗烟 by name. This passage was in my view invented by Kao O to explain 焙茗. ×掏小雀儿 is almost certainly the name of a game — probably 'tag'.××

Second thoughts: 在房簷①上掏小雀儿 suggests that they were, quite likely, looking for fledgelings (This is spring-time). But it remains true that 雲芸 is unlikely to have known 茗烟's name & that this whole passage has been 改壞了 to explain 焙茗. 雲芸 is vexed because no-one is expecting him. He comes in & finds a courtyard full of playing pages who ignore him until he shouts at them. The novelty opens the scene carefully.

—× Suggest keeping 'Tealeaf' throughout the book.

Both MSS ——— have 綺霰

庚辰 has 綺霰齋, 乾抄 has 綺
霞齋, 俞 has 綺霰齋
The 人民 綺散齋 can't possibly be right.

掃花 is likely to be the 掃紅 of chap. 9,
miswwritten.

綺霞齋 must be the correct version.

Saturday 11 Dec. 1971
    Problem abt. 綺霞 is that this is the name
of one of Bao-yu's maids, & it seems highly
improbable that he would name a study after one.
— On the other hand 綺霞 is a reasonably well-known
combination & the other two are simply unheard of.

    More pages: Cloudy 拂雲
                Stony 伴鶴
                Trickles 引泉

Tuesday 14 Dec. 1971   52/J66/6
    24/283 檀雲 unheard of elsewhere,
& supposed to be responsible maid. This passage
accounts, only one, for the absence of the
senior maids beginning with 襲人, the most senior.
晴雯 That 檀雲 should be 晴雲 is
deducible from the order 襲人, □, 麝月.

and from the form of the characters (雲)
Thus 庚辰 has 檀雲, like the rest,
乾隆 does in fact have 晴雲:
「晴雲又因他母親的生日接出去了
射月又現在家中養病」

Thurs. 30 Dec. 1971

Chaps. 15-20 (Copy 2) arr. back
from Arthur Cooper, who later rings to
explain that 21-22 retained through
oversight.

Wed. 5 Jan 1972

As to whether or not 晴雲 had a mother:
in chap. ~~80~~ 78 (p.1013) on the night of her death
we are told 「一夜叫的是娘」. This was
in delirium; but she must at least have had a
mother to remember.

Thursday 6 Jan. 1972

25/289 「命他去抄『金剛經呪』唪誦」
There appears to be nothing of this name. There are
various treatises or Dharaṇī called '金剛' something or
other. The likeliest of them to have been ~~written~~
copied as an act of merit is the short 金剛

壽命

陀羅尼經 (full title: 佛說一切諸如來心光明加持普賢菩薩延命金剛最勝陀羅尼經 — No. 1136 vol. 20) which or may refers to the merit of copying it 抄寫 (unlike the others, which may refer to the merit of reciting it.)

「尔時佛告马天王言：若有眾生怖畏死難病苦夭橫，有如是苦。但書寫此經受持讀誦，或別持此陀羅尼，或畫普賢延命像……」
Perhaps "Life-prolonging Dharani Teaching of the Immaculate Diamond".

乾隆抄本, reveals that「正过薛姨妈院中坐着」was inserted by Kao O, presumably to explain why 王夫人 wasn't in her own room at the time. But this doesn't help matter at all, because in this hour to hear 凤姐 telling her tale or what she would undoubtedly have heard along for 薛姨妈. Much better orig* that 王夫人 is with 贾母, 贾环 comes back from school & reports to 贾母 & 王夫人 sends him to her room. Then when 凤姐 gets back she reports to 贾母 (薛姨妈 for if this an opulent) & she and 王夫人 go off to 王's room to talk about it. — Thy wonders have observed much is pred of 雯𡆥 because the Old Lady was evidently hostile.

However, 庚辰 makes it seem as if 王夫人 was in her own room all the time, which also present problems.

※ This doesn't work, either. 凤姐 & 宝玉 must have got back together. Why should 王 + 凤 come for it when he visited later if 宝玉?

庚辰 makes 王夫人 run when 贾环 is being objectionable. he just says 「因见王夫人在又说话」

庚辰 has 狗肏器闷塞
　　　　　不识好人心

Sunday 9 January 1972

25/29: 「寄名的乾娘」
寄名 (1) 认他人为义父母
　　 (2) 认僧尼等为师而不出家以祈长寿
'godmother' seems closest.

Tuesday 11 January 1972

Dorothy in Oxford. Give her copy of
20-24. Note: I hold no copy of
21-22 at present. copies as previous.
① Price ② Cooper ③ Minford ④ Liu.

Thursday 13 January 1972

The major diffs. in Kao/Ts'ao text of 趙姨娘; 馬道婆 scene: big arg? for 費 text is that it makes 趙 an illiterate — which she surely must have been. Then

(2) in Cao text ~~she has~~ 賈 doesn't tell Zhao 'what to do' — instead of dg it herself

(3) it seems much more likely that 馬 wg would have been looking for 賈 — not for 趙 — + 脂硯 remarks on the fact that ~~he~~ her 紙人 were all 現成.

Hard to see why 高 altered.

+ Curious that 庚辰 showed how 青面白髮鬼。乾抄 青面紅髮鬼

人 (4) It's never explained in the Ep 6, exactly what is to be done with the paper figures.

Sunday 16 Jan 1972   with 室 & son.

The point of 趙、周's enty/ is completely lost if 高's version is followed

Monday 17 Jan 1972

Sometimes 高 is not altering for country. E.g. 「只見趙姨娘的兩個人近來...」 庚辰 has 「只見趙姨娘和周姨娘兩個人進來」

where even the subsequent text of 庚抄 shows its its pre-corrected text must have been erroneous.

Thursday 20 Jan 1972

端公 (chap. 25 庚辰 has 「请端公送祟的」 where 印刻本, my have 「送祟的」

Only Anchoshi replaces its un, citing 明律 礼律 禁止師巫邪術 a:「自号端公太保、師婆及妄称彌勒佛、白蓮社、尊明教、白雲宗等会、一应左道乱正之術、或隱藏圖像、燒香集眾、夜聚曉散、佯修善事、煽惑人民、为首者絞」

The pass about 王子騰 is quite unsavoury. (NO) ?See 家 a 夫人 has evidently dropped out. All the other visitors are women. Kao O has wrongly omitted 眷属 after 親戚. It should read 「刑夫人弟兄並各親戚眷属」, i.e. the wives of Lady Xing's brothers and the wives of other marriage relations. Men didn't go sick-visits on boys and women.

Saturday 22 Jan 1972

Doré Chinese Superstitions vols. 1-3

II. p. 158

"At the present day, charms bestowed by the 'Heavenly

master', 天師 (D.H. Descendant of 張道陵) every be obtained at all Taoist monasteries. These magic writings are suspended in the principal apartment of the house & are reputed efficacious for warding off any evil influence..."

清嘉錄「今俗人家以道院所送天師符, 黏貼廳堂 謂能鎮惡, 崇拜燒香」

Id. III p.vi. "Imperial orders in China are issued under seal, written on yellow paper & marked with cinnabar or vermilion pencil. Taoists hen even if initiated, their dignity, & issue their charms under the seal of 太上老君 or that of 張道陵"

Demon-expelling Charm

張天師天昱怡明七星掌腸心肝魚(二鰲)

Deann... expelling chown employed of Taoists

[sketch of a talisman/charm with characters 右 敎 門 inside]

教門 張道陵
右 三教 勅令
曰門 取勝吉

Clarence Burton Day Chinese Peasant Cults
p.50 張道陵 (天師) greatest jmy of
exorcism ... and demonic waters.
(5/5 expiring malignant time) see chp. 24.
Centre on 龍虎山 until 1927.

 Re 庚辰年「有的又藉玉皇閣的張
真人種子宣騰子」

There seems to be no consensus on 庚辰子 宣騰
KYTT 「= 宣①」 would have to mean 「= 瑄」, which is clearly impossible. Perf. a misprint for ③ (諸后王之任召)

mōtōki: 「① 上京をのべ付へる」 seems like it, not 「② 土地を殷かにする」.

The 脂硯 version seems better. The 張太郎 holds in saying one of the 3 things proposed (眾人七言八語) whereas 「曾……」 is what they actually did + about adventitia. "But it was no good……".

⊗ 王子騰:
庚辰: 「日落王子騰夫人告辭 去後 次日王子騰也來瞧, 问 接洽小史後家……」
Looks as if it can't be 王子騰夫人 who comes next day.

But 王子騰 was definitely not in the capital. He died without even reaching. (…不久奉旨擢內閣大學士 即行來京……離京只二百多里地了 感冒風寒…死了」 — 人亦糊塗的).

Better leave it out.

Mon. 24 Jan 1972
庚辰夾批 p.580 「補明趙姨進怡紅

為行法也」 is silly whichever way you understand it. If 為行法也, silly because how can it be said of 賈環? If 行法 means now, it overlooks the fact that 寶玉 is not in 怡紅 but in 王夫人上房.

Wed. 26 Jan. 1972

ch. 25. p.298. Kao O's alterations make a very big text here. How do you understand 「在外間聽消息」 if the recovery is a gradual one? At what point did the news reach them?

p.298 代玉先念了一声佛
cf. p.295 「該！阿彌陀佛」
Ruined, as usual, by Kao O.
See 庚辰 w. note by 脂硯:
「念了一声阿彌陀佛」
脂注:「針對病竹一声」

Friday 28 Jan 1972
大奶奶 = 李紈 is confirmed
p.546 「平姑娘，过来，我声替你大奶奶姑娘们替你赔个不是」
Pres. 璉 is 二爺 because 子珠.
宝玉 is 二哥. Is he our 二爺 as well??
Yes. p.214. 茗烟 calls him that.

p.176 尤氏 calls 賈璉「二爺」
p.181 凤姐 calls 珍「大爺」
p.132 尤氏 is referred to by 凤姐 & her own servants as「你们奶奶」,「我们奶奶」
p.270 贾敬 is「大老爷」 贾郝(「那边大老爷」)
p.128 贾敬 is「大老爷」

賈母 老太太

賈敬　　　賈赦、邢夫人　　　賈政＝王夫人
大老爺　　大老爺　　　　　　老爺　　太太

賈珍＝尤氏　　賈璉＝凤姐　　賈珠＝李纨　宝玉
大爺　奶奶　　二爺　二奶奶　大奶奶　　二爺
　　　　　　　　　　　　　　　　　　　二哥

Sun 30 Jan 1972

Can't find any observations on the inconsistency of the two 仙人 reappearing in chap. 1

「你我不必同行, 就此分手各干營生去罷, 三劫後我在北邛山等你, 会齐了同往太虛幻境……」

but reappearing together in chap 25.
脂硯齋 says「僧因風道因玉一绿不乱」, which plumbs depths of fatuousness [unusual?] even in C.H.C.

Better excise Taoist altogether. He adds nothing to the scene, & in fact creates other difficulties, quite apart from inconsistency w chap. 1 — How can 贾政's 内方 above boundary of garden *wonderful if he is trying to both?*

Mon 31 Jan 1972

The word 26 Nth on 該, 阿羅陀佛
'God, sees you why' is so much
better than the above translation, that it seems
best to keep it & lose the rather diffy point
(along lines of Mos O, in any case).

Tues. 1 February 1972

Noon. Best TS of chap. 25
finished. Insert 'and grandmother'
in monk's directions. The text as it
stands seems needlessly puzzling.

Chap. 26
佳蕙
Bernard Read <u>Chinese Medicinal Plants</u>
134a gives Melilotus (indicus and arvensis)
for 蕙草. 'Melilot'

Wed. 2 Feb. 1972

309 兔鶻 ('goshawk') They may not be
allowed, but goshawks are flown copying at
rabbits. etc.
Changed 'Mt. Retribution' to 'Iron Net Mts.)
Better so, as site of hunting expedition (with
many days.
Chap 24 Altered 'proceed' to 'came' on last page
between 'paused', closer with the other excerpts,
esp. 25 init.

Afterthought All this arose from initial failure to remember that 明兒 doesn't mean 'tomorrow'. 11.2.72

Thursday 3 Feb 1972

Chap. 26 beginning. The time all wrong again.

紅玉 and 賈芸 「相見多日」 after 芸 moves in to 筆更.

But 「和兩 …… 來過, 用不着 …… 男人、賈芸 卻去了」

Chap. 25 says this was 「第四日」; so 多日, 漸漸 etc. can only refer to 3 days!

And when is 佳蕙's visit supposed to be? Since it appears to occur in the same day as 芸's conversation with 寶玉 in 怡紅院, it must be 33 days after 芸's & 紅's days together. But a month seems rather a long while to be thinking keenly about her handkerchief. And 佳蕙 says 「你這兩日 ……」. It was the another case of Our Careless Author, like so many others.

The last indication of season or date before this whole section is in ch. 23 (p. 268) 「那日三月 中浣」

ch. 26 p. 309 紫英道三月二十八日去的, 前兒才就回來了, 寶玉道:怪道前 兒初三日先我在沈世兄家赴席不見 你呢。

This is (by the way) 五月初二

[p. 307: 出因明兒 ㊋ 五月初三日是

我的生日 !!!)

乾隆 庚辰 冯云 前党又就回車了（即寄回）
乾挣: 前日初六才回来

Suggest amend 吴 赠佩蛇 鸭's bday
date 七五月初九 (n 初十)

Chap. 27 (313) 今 飲日乃是四月二十六日
原来这日未时交芒種節.

KYTT Sys 芒種总在六月七或八日!
(other texts have got this)

Oucle Monboshi's xxx-jiw 五月
Pretofy 四月二十六日 should be   ✗ No.
㊄月二十六日

In that era what about Chap. 31
十五日正是端陽佳節

4/26 is a perfectly plausible date for 芒種

chap 31 端午与 Pleix OK.

Better 之后 33天至17天
and her 鸭's bday on 四月初九
Actually 3×3 gives best result.

33 is too long.

Friday 4 February 1972

Suggested timetable for chaps. 23-31: ✗

(23) 268   3/15 葬花. Bao-yu's invitation to 贾芸「明兒来找我」

3/16 贾芸 visits 凤姐 and waits for Bao-yu

3/17 贾芸's 2nd meeting with 凤姐. Gets job. Waits for Bao-yu. Bao-yu whom fun 北静王 & told by 小红 about 贾芸's visit.

3/18 贾芸 begins work in garden.

3/19 王子腾夫人's birthday. Bao-yu burnt 3 candle.

3/20 Visit 了 马道婆

? 3/22 Bao-yu's illness begins. 贾芸 and 小红 thrown together.

3/28 潇湘 3/25 Visit 了 和尚
贾芸 sees in
party scene   4/3 end 了 3×3 days' convalescence
                4/3-4 Bao-yu visits 沈世兄 on '3rd' or '4th'.

4/6 冯紫英 returns from hunting expedition.

4/8 薛蟠's party

4/9 薛蟠's birthday

✗

Preceding no good.

chap. 27 (313)   4/26 芒種節
                        馮紫英's party.
" 28 (337)   4/27 次日天明方醒
" 29 (343-4) 5/1   清虛觀做好了
" 29 (351)   5/2   次日 代玉病
" 29 (355)   5/3   过了一日至初三日
                     乃是薛蟠生日   ⊕
" 30 (356–) ? 5/4   宝玉等打面一笑
" 30 (366)   "   '明日是端陽節'
" 31 (369)   5/5   这日正是是端陽佳節

If the intercourse in the 馮紫英 passage remains 薛蟠, all problems of date disappear. Thus —   But 初三日 still needs   Otherwise

3/28   馮
4/3·4 沈世兄's party   馮's return to try ago.
? 4/16 馮 returns from hunting exp:
4/22   End of 33 days
4/25   薛蟠's party
4/26   芒種節. 馮紫英's party
4/27   次日
5/1   清虛觀
5/2   代玉病
5/3   薛蟠's birthday

But see over for final

chap. 23	p. 268	3.10	(三月中浣) 代玉埋花
24	274	"	Bao-yu meets 贾芸
24	279	3.11	(次日) 贾芸 visits 凤姐
"	281	"	meets 小红
24	282	3.12	(至次日) 贾芸 meets 凤姐 r is given job. Waits for Bao-yu. Bao-yu returns from 北静王 in eving r told about 贾芸's visit by 小红.
25	288	3.13	贾芸 begins working in garden.
25	289	3.14	(过了一日) Bao-yu burned by candle.
25	291	3.15	(次日) Bao-yu sees 贾母.
25	291	3.16	(过了一日) Visit of 马道婆
25	294	3.18 (?)	(这日) Bao-yu's illness begins.
25	296 (?)	3.21	(至第四日) Visit of mad monk
26	309	3.28	冯紫英's hunting exp" begins.
26	309	4.3 } 4.4 }	沈世兄's party.
⟨26	309	4.6	冯紫英 returns from hunting⟩
26	300	4.23	End of 33 days.
26	307	4.25	薛蟠's party
27	313	4.26	(至次日乃是四月二十六日…… 交芒种节) 冯紫英's party.
28	337	4.27	(次日)
29	343	5.1	單表到了初一这一日 Visit of family to 清虚观

29	351	5·2	(次日) 代玉病了.
29	355	5·3	(过了一日至初三日) 薛蟠生日
30	358	5·4	(因此日夜间闷)
〃	366	〃	(原来明日是端陽節)
31	369	5·5	(这日正是端陽佳節)

Perhaps it's best to leave everything unaltered & merely assume that Bao-yu had sufficiently recovered to be allowed out occasionally before the 33 days were over, although he had to go on sleeping in his mother's apartment.

<u>Saturday 5th February 1972</u>
Re proposal to leave everything unaltered: Best omit 「初心」 found in 乾抄, , since it would mean that 馮's black eye would have to last nearly a month.

<u>Wednesday 9 February 1972</u>
Arthur Cooper returns Chaps. 21–22 (copy 2)
<u>Note</u> These copies require corrections found in (9 thsis) copy 4 now with David.
AC reads (overnight) & returns 23–25.

<u>Thursday 10 Feb. 1972</u>

The weaves most closely identified with silk are taffeta, satin, chiffon and crêpe
(EB)

Under "Satin" the Commercial Press Compilers
E–C Dict'y gives (1) figured satin 花緞
(2) white satin 白綾

<u>Friday 11 Feb. 1972</u>
p.305 李璟 庚辰 and 乾抄 both have 藏蕤

小說詞語匯釋 p.643「萎靡不振,提不起精神來的樣子」
Cf. p.392
「方才雨村來了要見你,那半天才出來! 既出來,全无一点慷慨揮洒的談吐,仍是葳葳蕤蕤的。我看你臉上一团私慾愁悶氣色!这会子唉声吹氣,你那些還不足,還不自在?終故这樣是什麼原故?」

(乾抄, here has corrected 葳蕤 ~~的~~ to 委瑣
庚辰 has 葳蕤)

305 Bao-yu's remark
「磕了牙,那時候才不演呢。」
is presumably a sarcasm.
庚辰 has
「把牙栽了那時才不演呢」
乾抄, rejining had
「把牙栽了才不演習呢」 neither but
altered this to:
「磕了……」
Nobody seems to know what 栽牙 means.
(Perhaps Kao O didn't)

Monday 14 Feb. 1972
26/307 老胡老程他們 this is a 高 com.
庚辰 has 古董行的程日興他。See 乾抄.

Tuesday 15 February 1972
Actually 高's conv. 子程日興 is an improvement. Xue Pan only lies out of self-interest, never from malice; so when he says 「除我之外, 惟你配吃」 he really means it. Then why are 詹光, 程日興, 胡斯來 and 單聘仁 all present at the party? The answer must be because they are all four donors of the ~~gift~~ feast (perhaps one of the four items comes from each of them). Hence 「老程和老胡他们」 best translated 'old Hu and old Cheng <u>and a couple of the others</u>'.

Chaps. 23-25 (Copy 3) to JM. After speed-jo on chap. 12 with him (copies 2 + 4)

~~Tuesday 22 February 19~~
Monday 21 February 1972
Rough TS of ch. 26 finished.

Tuesday 22 February 1922
Work on chapter headings.

Wednesday 23 February 1972

26 p.306 Although the 油葫蘆 quotation from

西廂記 doesn't, in context, really say anything about love, but its context & (particularly) the chapter-heading — 葬花情 — seem to make it pretty clear that this is [an?] account to a declaration of love. So I think it has to be translated this by: 'a drawn-out [avowal?] [dream?] of love'.

Preface

① Page headings:

| THE STORY OF THE STONE | CHAPTER XI |

Chapter headings (cf. Modern chaps. xi)
Initial ital ital ;
and ital ital ital pp.

② 1. Notes on spelling
2. Intro.
3. Contents
4. Text of Book.
5. List of chars
   Tables.

③ Table of Contents

CONTENTS

       CHAPTER I   PAGE
Ital 1

Suggested subtitles of ~~Parts~~ volumes.

Volume One	The Golden Days
Volume Two	The Crabtree Club
Volume Three	The Warning Voice (973)

Chapter-heading slips attached to all copies in my binding this evening. (23-2-72)

Tuesday 29 February 1972

"Best" typed copy of (1) Chapter headings (Contents)
(2) List of characters
(3) Note on spelling

now all completed.

Copy 3 of chap. 26 and of Contents r

Write to Dorothy & Vellacott asking for TS. back.

Saturday 4 Mar. 1972

周世昌 新澄 179   quote 蝶戀仙
史諱幸 insupper 了不上 一月 instead 了不上

一年 in chap. 12. He says 蝶薌仙史
icover claims support of「旧钞」for this emendation
He says that [crossed out] all 旧钞 G. citations of 蝶薌
compared with 脂硯, but doesn't appear by all
抄本 have 卒 here. Seems a pretty obvious bit of
special pleading.

Earliest ref. to 蝶薌仙史 is 一粟's
红楼梦目录 on p.67
　　增评加批金玉琢图说
　　　王郁庵, 蝶薌仙史评. 光绪三十二
年 (1906), [crossed out], 上海桐蔭軒石印
本 一函二十卷
Can't find any ref. to 蝶薌仙史评㊙
　　Still this is in 風月宝鑑時字
周 conveniently overlooks「倏又臘盡春来」
✗ Not exactly — see p.180 But he reads a
year into chap. 13
　　He says 这年冬底 shd. b「夏末秋初」

Chen 182　襲人此時至少，不过十七歲
This makes his earlier remarks on chap. 6 seem pretty
silly ("two innocents...") In fact, it made a
very nasty seduction scene of it.
183 周 goes into acrobatic contortions on 宝玉's being

Tuesday 07 March 1972

Copy 1 of Chaps. 1–23 returned by Betty Radice, Recorded Delivery.

Friday 10 March 1972

Decided to adopt the 「耳动本」 emendation 「不上一月」 in Chap. 12. It does seem to make an easier read (and it might be genuine).

Re 清钱五百串 in Chap. XVIII (which seems extraordinarily ungenerous in that context)

清代货币金融史稿 (杨端六, Peking 1962)

p. 11 「... 雨钱之市价, 钱之名称, 亦因此私钱混杂之多少而大分别, 曰大钱 (参制钱也), 曰清钱 (同上种)...」

「制钱」 is defined as 「各省官局筹出之钱」

So there are "500 strings of unmixed Imperial Mint copper cash" which perhaps makes it a little bit more exciting.

(The 三百 of the modern printed edition — 俞平伯's 八十回校本 has 一百串 — is quite mystifying. 亞东 has, uncorrected, 伍百, which is even dearer, & even 王　　's printed edⁿ has 五百)

Wednesday 15 Mar. 1972

Found necessary to redo chap. 1 p.7 putting in the titles 紅樓夢 and 石頭記

Also change 'Nanking' to 'Kinling' on 1/7, 2/8, 5/9.10 —— It's too confusing to the reader to be told that the 賈 family are all living in Nanking.

Monday 17 April 1972 10 p.m.

Rough TS draft of Introduction completed. (Phew!)

Monday 24 April 1972

Copy 1 and Copy 2 of <u>The Story of the Stone</u> vol. 1 posted in 2 parcels to J.P. Letter sent separately with corr. for Intro.

Friday 28 April 1972

Acknowledgment of letter & parcel from Jennifer Around.

Thursday 25 May 1972

Cheque for vol. one (£600) received.

Thursday 29 June 1972

ch. 29 p.343 代王's maids
扮乞, han 春讖, not 觀哥
覵哥 and 覵哿 or presumably
one & the same person.

Friday 30 June 1972

p. 353 香薷 Xiang-ru
Bernard Read CMP p.31
Elscholtzia cristata 'Lepechin'
简明 中国植物图鉴 p.186 calls it
Elscholtzia patrini.

Monday 3 July 1972

The Dryad's House to
The Naiad's House: Contents:
  chap. 26,

Chap. 18/16/28   Also
  "   18/5   瀟湘妃子
  "   20/29   bellows
Chap. 23/10/6   ('River Sprite')
  ——— /21   ?
Chap. 24/1/15   on second thoughts
Chap. 26 ——— Title   'River Queen'
  ——— 12/25   perhaps better 15/9/72

───────────────

Tuesday 19 Sept. 1972
<u>Culin   Chinese Games of Dice & Dominoes</u>
RSL Soc. 19982.d.17 (1898)
(Smithsonian Report US Nat. Mus. 1898)
doesn't help very much with 骨牌副
  Combs. of <u>dice</u> (but doms. generally the same)

② ⊡⊡ 天   ⊡⊡ 板櫈   Duplicated pieces
  ⊡⊡ 地   ⊡⊡ 虎頭   in 32 domino set:
  ⊡⊡ 人   ⊡⊡ 紅頭什   1/1, 1/3, 1/5, 1/6
  ⊡⊡ 和   ⊡⊡ 高脚七   2/2
  ⊡⊡ 梅   ⊡⊡ 高脚六   3/3
  ⊡⊡ 長三   4/4
         ㊍   5/5
         ⊡⊡ 三鶏   6/4, 6/5, 6/6

                                P.T.O

But in chap. 40 錦屏 seems to be used for [domino image]
This is more understandable if the set has bicoloured sixes [domino image]

4. 牙牌舞燈詞 in 清 劉蓮陸's 牙牌參禪圖譜 (O.I. 9100, GJDJ. 4 [觀目日齋叢書 (4)])

四六: 偎偎為錦屏索笑
四六: 在錦屏相對

For 「二六:
    雙瞻玉座引朝儀」

cf. ib. 「二五:
    又瞻玉殿」

For further confirmation of 錦屏 = 4:6
see also ib. 四季結同心

4/6, 最又:「錦屏人」
For 「六:橋梅花香徹骨」
  cf. 北, 五六:「方兒六,橋梅蕊」
This "同心圖" also has 「金釵十二」for 長六.

Another 金屏 in 乞巧詞
  「四六:
    錦屏風透不住斗牛宮」

骨牌副 in ch. 40 end of 中.

① 贾母 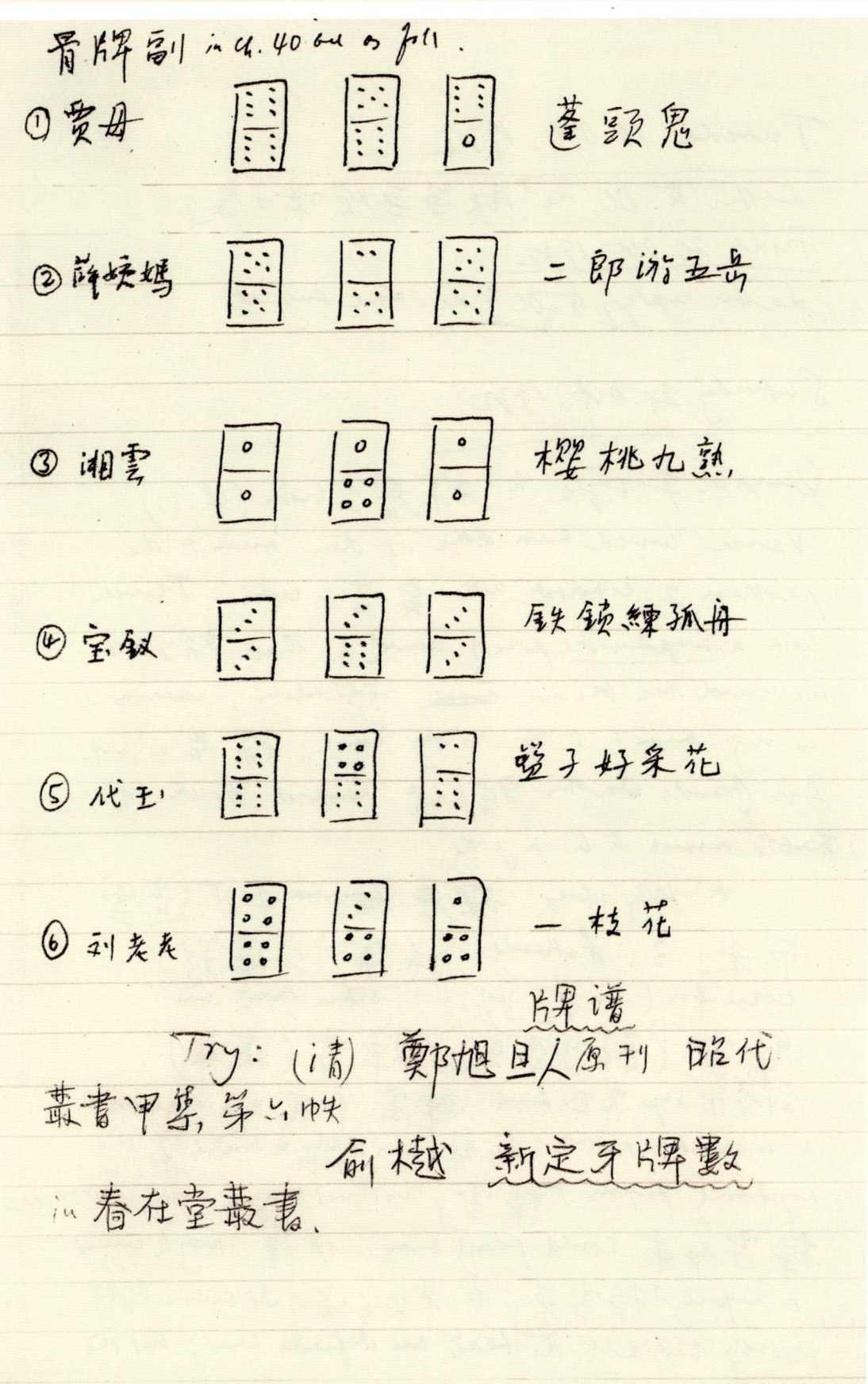 蓬頭鬼

② 薛姨媽　　　　　　　二郎游五岳

③ 湘雲　　　　　　　　樱桃九熟

④ 宝钗　　　　　　　　鐵鎖練孤舟

⑤ 代玉　　　　　　　　鳌子好采花

⑥ 刘老老　　　　　　　一枝花

Try: (清) 鄭旭旦人原刊 牌譜 昭代
叢書甲集, 第六帙

俞樾 新定牙牌數
in 春在堂叢書

Tuesday 10 Oct. 1972
Letter to DC re「鐵笛無煩說子房」
Friday 20 Oct. 1972
Letter replying to DC's on same subject.

Saturday 21 Oct. 1972

Question of style in 探春's letter (ch. 37). Verse would have done if there weren't the problem of contrast with 雲芸's letter. Trouble with a euphuistic piece of verse be that 探's letter too would then become comic ridiculous, whereas it is only meant to be mildly comic. 探春 is not Don Armado. In this 雅/俗 contrast it's the 俗 that's meant to be a joke.

　　* Why does 探春 speak of「造雪而來」? Actually '造雪' is 高鶚's emendation (see 乾抄): other texts are 綽雪 (乾抄原文), 掉雪 (庚辰), 俞平伯 says 有正 had 綽雪 (my copy n.a. just now — a misprint or a misquote: 俞校 can seldom be trusted), + mysterious prepares「掉雪」without saying why, or what 掉雪而來 could possibly mean. 伊藤 may be correct in referring「掉雪來」to 東山之會. It seems highly probable that all the texts are defective here; but the

meaning is doubtless what GY implies: 'Come & join us girls in a poetry club' (NOT 'come & talk to me about this').

Monday 20 November 1972

Work begun on prose translation of Vol. 2

In 小红's rejoinder on p. 318 五奶奶 will have to be arbitrarily identified with 卜氏 ('五嫂子' in chap. 23 p 263), 舅奶奶 with 王子騰's wife (this may in fact be intended, since she is evidently out of town — have 帶信, 順路, etc.) & 姑奶奶 with 王夫人, the great dispenser of pills & potions.

Tuesday 21 Nov. 1972

花神 is presumably female.
月令廣義: 「女夷為花神 .... 花姑乃為花神」

Wed. 22 Nov. 1972

On second thoughts 花神 is probably general. Every flowering tree & shrub has its own carrier, presumably for the use of that particular flower-fairy. Centering this interpretation on accords much better with Daiyu's Flower Burial, which ends this chapter.

Thurs. 23 Nov, 1972
Trio of actresses:
* 齡官 Charmante (Fu 齡 = 寿 see 16/4/73)
* 文官 Élégante (→賈母)
* 宝官 Trésor [小生 (p.366)]
* 玉官 Topaze [正旦 (p.366)]
　葵官 Althée (→湘雲)　大花面
*（药官 Pivoine [死了的藥官¶58/746] [小旦]
　芳官 Parfumée (→宝玉)　正旦
　蕊官 Étamine (→宝釵)　小旦
（藕官 Nénuphar (→代玉)　小生
　荳官 Cardamome (→宝琴)　小花面
　艾官 Artémisie (→探春)　老外
　茄官 Aubergine (→尤氏)　老旦

宝釵（四兒）
Osm PNYE and
Mockashi gin
"王夫人也水清序"
of saving this
afterward, but can't
find any such form
by 王熙凤.

Charmante
Trésor
Topaze

※

Friday 1 December 1972

Chap. 27 Lost section (代王 on the meaning of 种芷节 — 人民 ed. p.320):
The largely new-invented paragraph put in here to explain the '昨日' references would need to be excised & rewritten in any edition which did not begin a new volume at chap. 27.

別的姐妹 does seem to mean 'the other girls', whatever it may or may not mean in modern 口語 Chinese.

北京… 鞋踢拉襪塌拉 = 人衣履不整
(e.g. 你这么……的, 怎么见人?) Presumably
鞋搭拉襪搭拉 is called the same expression.

小說…sp 鞋塌拉襪塌拉 = 鞋襪敝舊.

Monday 4 Dec. 1972

The end of chap. 27 seems to prove that 庚辰本 is a draft. It's still of help as are 脂本 & 程本.

Tuesday 5 Dec. 1972

Chap. 27 rough-typed.

Wednesday 6 Dec, 1972

清虛观 (338) All the 清虛's in 琵琶记 and 长生殿 refer to the moon:「清虛境」,「清虛殿」, 清虛洞天,「清虛洞府」all mean「月宫」, acc. to Morohashi.

紅麝香珠: 红楼梦索引 (王梦阮), 沈瓶庵撰、中华 Shanghai 1916):
卷6, p.41:「红麝香珠、至今京市有鬻者、初出宫製、非止费不易得也」

Thursday 7 Dec, 1972

平安醮, cf. p.146 (ch.13)「九十九位全真道士 打四十九日 解冤洗業醮」
'ninety-nine Taoist priests of the Quan-zhen sect were to perform ceremonies of purification and absolution …'

紫金錠 was made out of 紫藤香 = acronychia laurifolia or 'laka wood'

錠子藥 = 錠剤 Moro:「主薬に乳糖・アラビヤゴム等を加へて、小さな円板形、円錐形等に固めて作った薬。タブレット。」

鳳尾罗 'maidenhair' chiffon (?)

Sunday 10 Dec. 1972

Chap. 28 「试想」──「在耳东西」
Something very peculiar about this passage.
The style is that 于注文. 「试门」(123, 130, 171, 190) and 「想」「想罢」「忽想」「细想」
(216, 250, 277, 362, 378, 415, 431, 436) common in 批文. Note that 乾隆高抄本 didn't have 「因此一而二」to「在耳东西」, which was inserted later. Also「反覆推求了去……」was curious like the 眉批: 「反復推求鳴悲。」

But ~~会式~~ 「昨䜴批葬花吟之客……
But 不言鍊句……」.「想景,想情,想了,
想理」does seem to refer to 「试想……」
?? it does it. — In any case, it isn't written over that bit in earlier version.

It certainly looks as if
「~~鹅鸣~~」「蠢物! 杳不所知! 逃大造,
出塵網便可解释這段悲伤!
石兄……」
must be comment.

Surely there can't be anywhere else in the whole book which begins someone's thoughts with「试想」
Perhaps 曹 had sketched this out in 又 prints expans. but never got round to tying it up??

Monday 11 Dec. 1972

Compare with 俞校本, p. 176 (in chap. 17–18)

「此時自己回想……且說已經為是」
This is obviously 原文, but it is at the same time
'石頭自註' (Stone's Note to itself). The style is
exactly the same.
 Y. also 177, where the passage「按此一字……
大相矛盾了」is exactly in the style of this passage.
And note that the 作者答曰 bit which follows
has 蠢物 (待蠢物將原委說明) just
as here he calls himself 蠢物.
 Probably some mispunctuations. It shd be

「……反覆推求了去,真不知此時此際欲
為何等。——蠢物!杳無所知!逃大
造,出塵網便可解釋這段悲傷!
——不是:……」
 Note that 脂硯 refers to 'yesterday's guest' as
「寶玉之化身無疑」
Perhaps the 寶玉 家 supplied a bit himself?

高抄's corrected version is

「……又不知寄屬誰姓,因此一而二,二而三
反覆推求了去,真不知此時此際如何解釋
這段悲傷、不是……」
 From this it looks as if

「何等蠢物!杳物所知!逃大造,出
塵網便可解釋這段悲傷!」

ch. 18　庚辰「此時自己回想當初……」
　　　(正文)
　　　甲戌「此石頭記自敘：想當初…」
　　　(双批)

I suspect that「此石頭記自敘」should be「此石頭自敘」and「此時自己回想」should be「此石自己回想」— though perhaps the latter not so likely, with several 批語 refering to「此時」.

Wednesday 13 December 1972

It was a gross blunder to translate both 宝哥哥 and 宝姐姐 as 'Cousin Bao'. Better say 'Cousin Chai' or 'Miss Xue' for Xue Bao-chai.

ch. 28　p. 328　人形帶葉參　三百六十兩不足
　　The 三百六十兩不足 must be 批文. It may belong at the side of the words 方子.

*Friday 15 December 1972

28. (宝玉的方子) 上用大紅紗‧ 磨搗is the only text which makes sense of this passage. It wants 「罩那乳鉢研麵子呢」
庚辰, ~~~~ has 乳鉢乳了隔麵子呢
明 ——　　　　　乳鉢乳了會 ——

Saturday 16 Dec. 1972

「她不吃飯了」etc. (Daiyu & the maid).
Again 高抄原文 is better than anything else.

Sunday 17 Dec. 1972

28 馮紫英曰. Once again, 高抄 has the best text「你們令表兄弟」. 庚辰 & printed text all have「令姑表兄弟」or「令姑表弟兄」, 俞校, as usual, quite useless.

Monday 18 Dec. 1972

紫金錠
紫金散
錠子藥
錠劑
左归 (医学) 張景岳、治肾水不足、營衛失養等
右归 (医学)「右归丸、張景岳方、用大熟地八两 大肉桂 etc. etc. Principles for stomach disorders
紅麝香珠
紫藤香 (藥)「即降真香之古籍別名」
降真香 also called 雞骨香
何首烏 Polygonum multiflorum root.
茯苓「古謂乃松之神靈伏結而成'故知'」
係生於截斷松樹根部下之一種菌類菌屬物

益母草 Leonurus sibiricus (Siberian motherwort)
Chief ingredient in 八珍益母丸

八味地黃丸「參看腎氣丸」(鳶)
天王補心丹 醫方「世醫得効方・寧心丸」
茯苓 Indian bread, Lycoperdon, Tuckahoe
(SOED)

Thursday 21 Dec 1972
The 人民 annotators seem wrong (p.337) in explaining 松花色 as a kind of green? Moro. gives 'brown' understandings: 「うすかきいろ」, 「とびいろ」.
Cf. Ch. 35 (p.424)
「松花配桃紅」
　　蔥綠配柳黃
犹 (p.392) has 「うすかき」 in furigana beside the 松花 in ch. 35. This, too, seems wg. 桃紅 and 'pale orange-brown' don't make a contrast at all. Suspect 松花色 is the colour of 松花蛋. Dark brown + pink is in fact a v. good colour contrast.
— On the other hand 脂硯 (in the 批本 in 甲戌G.) evidently thinks it's a kind of green:
「紅綠牽巾是這樣用法，一笑」
Better stick to green. One feels ought to be a cloudier green than the '雅淡' 蔥綠. 'Viridian'?

Friday 22 December 1972

Ch. 27 「晴雲, 綺霞, 碧痕, 秋紋, 麝月, 侍書, 入画, 鶯兒」

戚本, 甲戌 have
「晴雯, 綺霞, 碧痕, 紫綃, 麝月, 侍書, 入画, 鶯兒」

庚辰 has 紫綃 corrected to 紫鵑
(N.B. This is not in the copyist's hand. The copyist wrote 鵑. This correction is 鵑)

吾抄 ~~has~~ (curiously enough) has simply:
「晴雯等」 with 「綺霞」 inserted between 雯 and 等

Actually the narrative makes it seem unlikely that 紫鵑 could have joined the others by this stage. She is later ~~face~~ being told by Dai-yu to put the room in order.

Probably this is meant to be a list of maids from the apartments of 寶玉, 三春 & 寶釵. (chess has been accounted for elsewhere) The correction to 秋紋 seems wholly inexplicable. For a similar problem, see Tues. 14 Dec. 1971 where 檀雲 suddenly emerges in a list of Bao-yu's chief maids, never to reappear.

That being so, it seems probable that 秋紋

is intended in Chap. 28 (338 9)
「说着，便叫了紫鹃来「拿了这个到你们姑娘那裏去…」紫鹃答应了…」
where 庚辰 has 紫綃 in both places with 綃 altered to 鵑 only in the first and 林姑娘 instead of 你们姑娘. The「你们」appears is 馬折 as an alteration. (Presumably to square 「紫鵑」)

Itō is surely right to reject 紫鵑, but his reason for keeping 紫綃 seem silly.
Better say 秋紋.

Sunday 24 ~~September~~ December 1972
1.30 p.m.   MS of Chap. 28 completed.

Tuesday 26 ~~Sept~~ December 1972

p.345 贾芸、贾萍、贾芹: Cousin Zhen's juniors in the generation below him
    贾璉、贾璃、贾瓊 (Lian, Bin, Qiong) his juniors in his own generation.

p.343 代玉的丫头：婴哥 is unnecessarily confusing here. Better keep 春纖, although she doesn't seem to appear elsewhere. CXQ seems deliberately to have coined some new names here (cf. 文去) to support what he had said earlier about even the skivvies being allowed to go.

But perhaps it wd. be better to scratch this problem out & put all of Cheng's "Parrot" in vol. 1 ch. 3 to 'Nightingale'. 'Nightingale' appears as Daiyu's chief maid in ch. 21 without prior introduction, where as we know (ch. 97) that Nightingale was given by GJ to Daiyu & that she was devoted to her from the start.

p.1254 「李纨…道：可真呢，林姑娘私这丫头又是前去的缘法完！倒是雪雁是他南边带来的他倒不理会…」
p.1472 紫鹃 becomes a nun (with 惜春)

Thursday 28 Dec. 1972

p.344.「出门的媳妇子们」 in 俞校本 (302) this is 「出门的家人媳妇子」. This seems to confirm the view that 家人媳妇 in chap. 14 means only women servants.

Friday 29 Dec. 1972

344「那街上的人…」etc. It looks as though

One has to choose between this & 诸本.「贾母等……」etc. It doesn't seem possible to take the best of both. Under the circumstances seems best to choose 诸本, because 程乙 seems to involve a misunderstanding of what 「前头的全副执事摆开」really means.

Tuesday 2 Jan. 1973

345「一手拿㸃蠟剪跪在地下」

庚辰「还一手拿㸃蠟剪跪在地下」

But in 戚抄本, the「一手拿着剪烛」was inserted late. It wasn't in 原文 — ? know whether from oversight or because the 戚本 didn't have it can't be known. Certainly it makes better sense without it. It is always said that he dropped it & left it on the ground.

Thursday 4 Jan 1973

人民:「那子孩子总说不出话来」
俞本:「那孩子通说不出话来」
庚辰:「那子孩子痛说不出话来」(later corr. 通)
戚抄:「那子孩子痛的说不出话来」
(cm. 通抄)

Present text seems to be part of the consistent editorial effort to make Xi-feng less 利害. No reason to suppose that 痛的 wasn't the author's original text.

Thurs. 4 Jan 73 cont'd

(345) 人民「並雲璉,雲瑤,雲琼等…」
     俞本「亦且連 雲璉,雲瑤,雲琼等…」
     庚辰「亦且連 雲璉,雲瑞,雲琼等…」
     (『瑞』'corrected' from 『瑤』)
As usual, 高揚, had the best text:
「並且連雲瑤,雲瑞,雲琼等」
(altered to「並雲璉 ……」)

Wed. 10 Jan. 1973

346「榮國公的替身」
cf. ch.18 p.199「買了許多替身」
H. p.29 "proxy novices".
Presumably he was bought by 榮國公賈源 as
a 替身 for 賈代善 when the latter was a child.

Thursday 11 Jan. 1973

346「果真不在家」. Hawkes assumes that this is a lie;
but Bao-yu really is out — at Feng Zi-ying's. The
flower-fashion business took place very early in the day &
Bao-yu went out very soon after lunch.

Sunday 14 Jan 1973

Ch. 29 國公爺 etc. Why does 張法官 say 不知
連大老爺二老爺尤記不清楚了? Hsiao

good saying that 代善 must have died when his boys were big, because 賈政 (in ch. 33 <p.398>) specifically refers to 賈政's upbringing by his father: 「當日你父親怎么教訓你來呢!」. It looks as if this is one of those Cao/Gaomulian confusions which no amount of reasoning will explain away.

4月 25日 薛蟠's party
4月 26日 芒种節: 馮紫英's party.
4月 27日 p. 337
5月 1日 p. 343 ⟨ 5月 2日 p. 351
5月 3日 p. 355 薛蟠's birthday.

Sunday 28 Jan 1973

pp. 273-5 Since Bao-yu's 通靈寶玉 is represented throughout as being attached to a cord (穗子), it must be supposed that 「往地下一摔」 meant holding it by its cord & dashing it on the floor like a conker, so that 「才奪下來」 refers to the jade (still in his hand), not to the object he was using to hit it with, & 代玉's 「奪過去」 on 354 presumably means snatching it from Bao-yu, who had been holding it all this time. — Hence her remark about the 穗子, which is actually in her hand when she makes it.

Tuesday 30 Jan. 1973

「嚥氣」(ch. 29, p. 355) (yàqì) =「斷氣」:
cf. ch. 13,
 「繞嚥氣的人、那裏不乾淨」

Friday 2 Feb. 1973

Ch. 30, p.358:「前兒」referring to the quarrel of 五月二日. This is 五月三日 (?). ✱
So 前兒 has to mean 'yesterday'.

30/360/1 「藕合紗衫」: cf. TS 3/33
 (3/38/3「一頂藕合色花帳」) 'lilac-coloured'.

汪皮賴臉的
cf. 嘻皮笑臉 etc. 輕佻 'cheeky'
 (was clear) (joke) 'fool around'

✱ Perhaps a day is meant to elapse (on p. 355)
between「也哭起來了」&「誰知這個說
In that case 明兒初五 does mean
'tomorrow' and 前兒 does mean 'day before yesterday'.

4月25日　薛蟠's party, 代玉 shut out 于怡红院

4月26日　芒种节、埋花吟、冯紫英's party. Meets w/ 琪官.

4月27日　Reconciliation 于宝玉 and 代玉. 宝玉's oath about 金玉

5月初一　Visit to 清虚观

5月初二　Big quarrel about 金玉.

5月初三　薛蟠's birthday, 贾母's complaint.

五月初四　Reconciliation (arranged 与凤凤) 金钏's dismissal, 龄官 in the arbor

五月初五 p.366
Saturday 3 Feb. 1973
p.366 原来明日是…… "Next day going to…"

Monday 5 February 1973

薔薇 rosa multiflora (polyantha)
Read: 'rambling rose'
Gillies: 'The wild rose of Northern China, Korea and Japan. Flowers small, white, in branching panicles.'

花鸂鶒 qī.chi ? Casonca rutila (ruddy sheldrake) ?

Tuesday 13 February 1973

30/359 「便咬着牙，用指头狠命的在他额上戳了一下子，哼了一声…」
q.25/289 「咬着牙，向他头上戳了一指头…」

TS 25/3: 'Sunset clenched her teeth. She stabbed the air above his head with her finger.'

Saturday 17 Feb. 1973

p.362 「从贾母这里出来往西走过了穿堂便是凤姐的院落」
So all texts. But no amount of ingenuity will square this with 周汝昌's 贾家府第想像图. Chou's plan is a pretty useless object at the best of times, but this seems to rule it out altogether. Unless —

PART II

February 1973

August 1975

紅樓夢

February 1973 —
August 1975

Saturday 17 Feb. 1973 (cont'd.)

— Unless 「这裏」 means the east (garden) side, and he is supposed to go the long way round to the door out of the north side of GJ's apartment

[diagram: floor plan with red arrows showing a route; labels 凤姐院落, 王夫人處, 穿堂, 这裏, door (门), and a "NO!!" with compass mark]

— but this seems to make nonsense of 「便」
「西走过了穿堂(便是)凤姐的院落」

Sunday 18 Feb. 1973

TS 12/2 (Jia Rui's assignation)
'You can slip into the gallery west of this gate.'
p.139 「悄悄在西边穿堂兒等我」

TS 12/3 'The gate at the end of the alley-way opening on to GJ's quarters had already been barred; only the gate at the east end remained open"

p.137 「賈母那边去的門已倒鎖了，只有向东的門未閂」

So far this, all fits 周's plan, Ch.3 however doesn't seem to fit

TS 3/23 'Passing along a verandah which ran beneath the eaves of the hall they came to a corner gate through which they passed into an alley-way running north and south. At the south end it was traversed by a narrow little building with a short passage-way running through its middle. At the north end was a white-painted screen wall masking a medium sized gateway leading to a small courtyard in which stood a very little house.....
.... Lady Wang now led Dai-yu along a gallery running from east to west which brought them out into the courtyard behind Grandmother Jia's apartments. Entering through a back entrance ....

p.3「...由後廊往西、出了角門，是一條南北甬路、南边是倒座三间小小抱廈廰、北边立着一个粉油大影壁，後~~~~~ (It's at this point that 周's plan goes wrong)，後有一个半大門，小小一所房屋....王夫人遂携代玉穿過一个东西穿堂、便是賈母的後院了，於是進入後房門....」

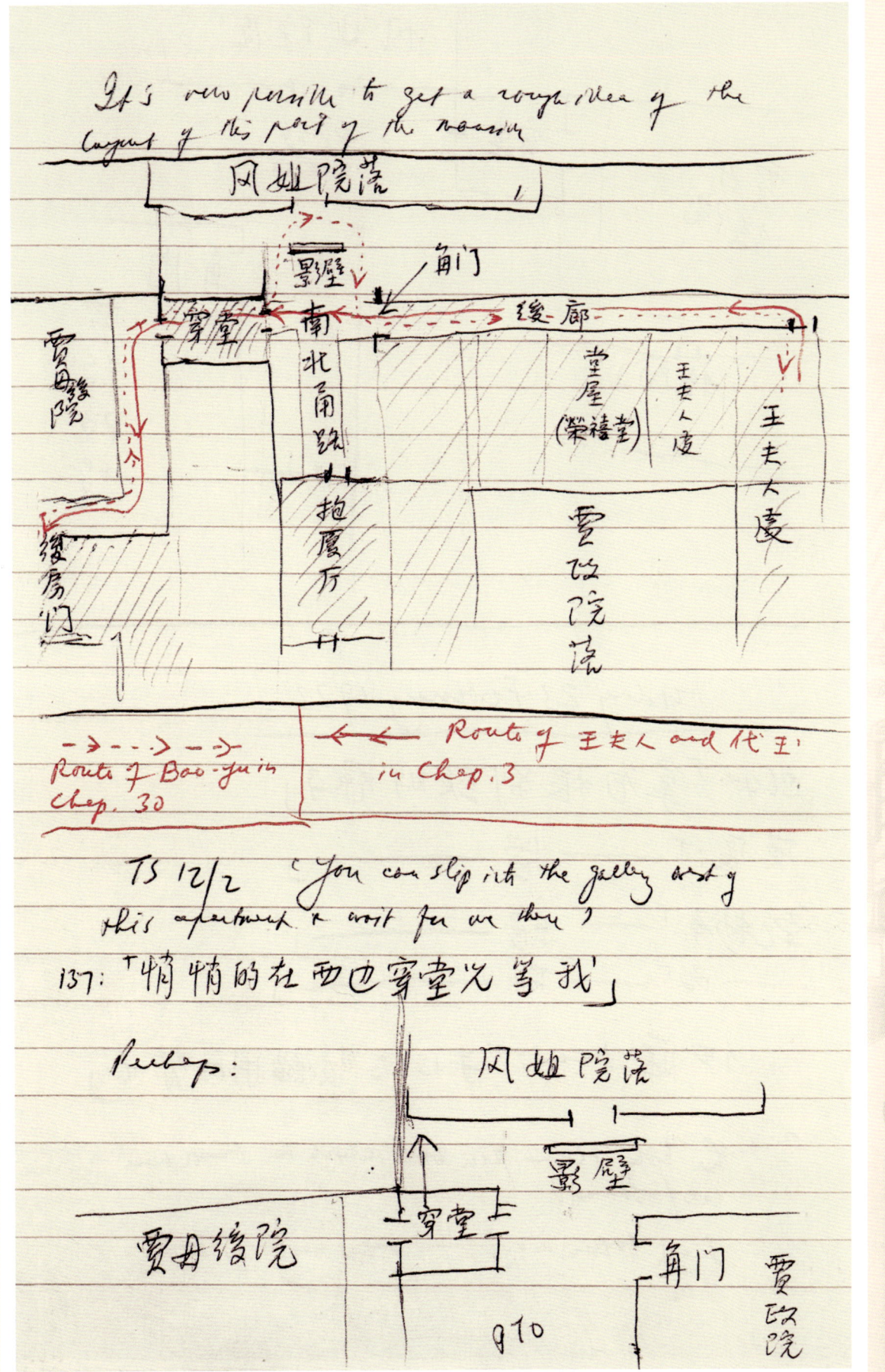

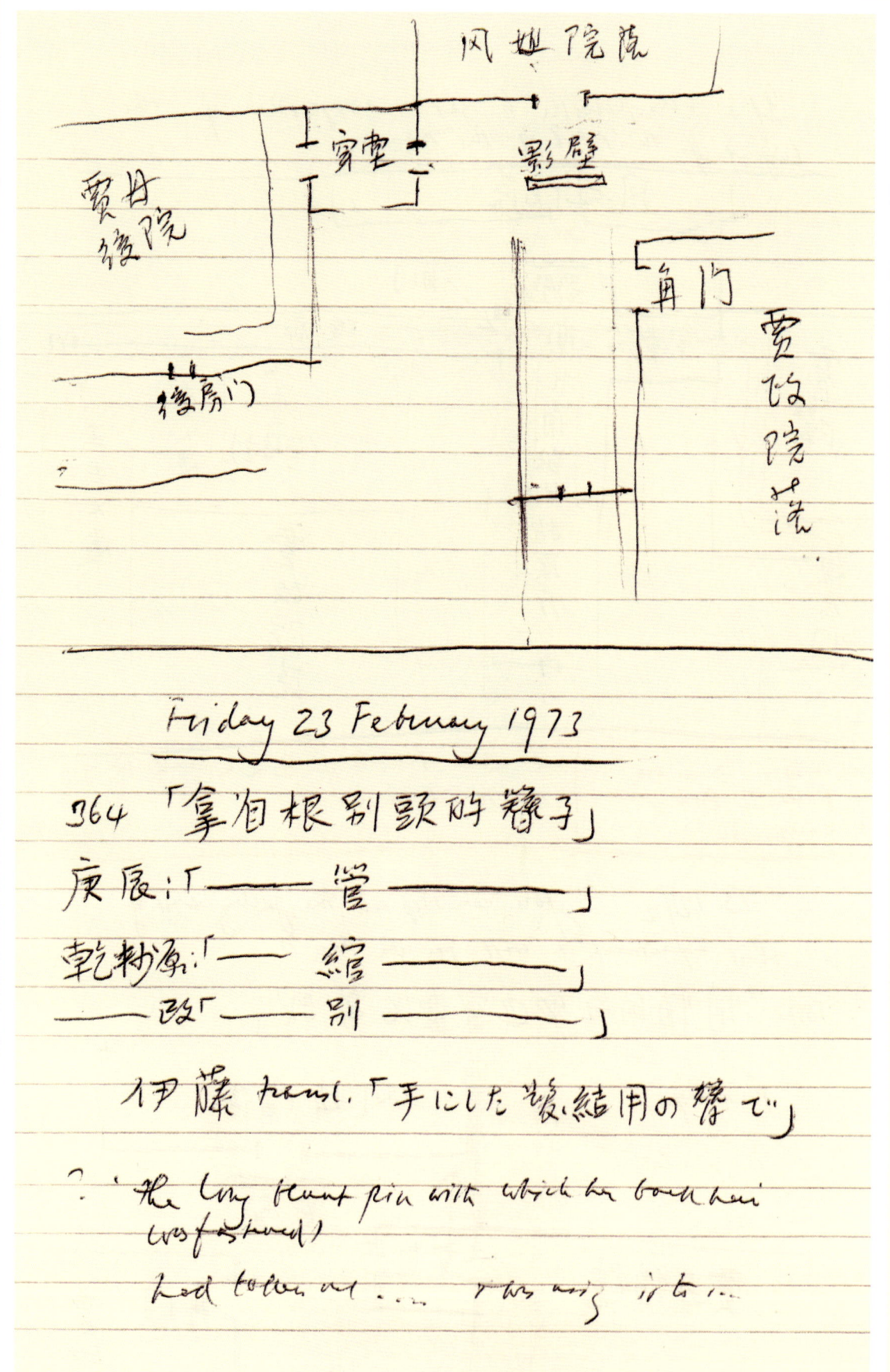

Friday 23 February 1973

364「拿泊根別頭的簪子」

庚辰:「————簪————」

乾粉序:「————繪————」

———政「————別————」

伊藤 transl.「手にした髪結用の簪で」

? 'the long blunt pin with which her back hair
(was fastened)
had taken out ... r has mrg it to ...

charmante

Saturday 24 February 1973

The little actress (齡官, ~~elegant~~) whom Bao-yu watches in the arbour is said to be very like Dai-yu ("...嫋嫋婷婷,大有黛玉之態"); but it is not *Charmante* who is referred to in Ch. 22 as being v. like Dai-yu. Ch. 22 makes it clear that this is a troupe bird from outside (hence Xi-feng's jokes about Granny Jia's supposed stinginess). Also the two players who are referred to optionally are the 小旦 and 小丑 & *Charmante* appears as a 貼旦 — though this last seems not v. important.

薔薇架

Chap. 17: p.179 怡紅院 has 海棠 and 芭蕉 in forecourt, being Youril stalage effect in this comedy, is it not?

(197) 「院中滿架薔薇」
But if ~~this~~ it is is past the 後院 that he sits, how is he looked out in Ch. 30, p. 366

(..."一氣跑回怡紅院去了"......」
「把院門關了」...)   ??

(for 'garden full of powder roses' (rose-trellis) see TJ 17/25)

p.179 on the way to 怡紅院「穿過竹籬花障編就的月洞門,俄見粉垣環護,

Is one meant to believe that 怡紅院 was completely surrounded by pigsties?

Sunday 25 February 1973

364「一直到底、一画、一桌、一句的看了去」
庚辰 is obviously much better:
「一直、一画、一桌、一句的看了去」
this, uncorrected, is the very 乾抄。

Since all texts say 十八画, it must be assumed that CXQ wrote 蓋. Curiously enough 草書「蓋」does 蓋 onto the bottom in this way.

Monday 26 Feb. 1973

「敷衍」v. 莊子,天運 (14為)
集成 p.228.

(1) 橫一 (al. 画)
(2) 点丶   (6) 捺㇏
(3) 撇ノ   (7) 剔 ㇏
(4) 直丨
(5) 弯 ㇈

推掯
from 韓子賈島
(題李凝幽居詩)
大韓愈布衣空
很待記了40兩

Wednesday 28 February 1973

伏中

「伏天：夏至後 ~~四庚日起~~ 第三庚日起 三十日內 謂之伏天 …… 為夏季最熱之時期」

「夏至：陽曆六月二十一/二日」

Dog-days: "In current almanacs the dog-days begin July 3, and end Aug. 11."

Thus making '三伏' and 'dog-days' approx. equivalent. CXP is surely wrong to ~~call~~ speak of early 五月 (陰曆: i.e. early June) as '伏中'? But the whole of this ~~passage~~ ~~??~~ section of the book seems premature in its description of the weather.

Thursday 1 March 1973

Roles   '.... parts'

丑   comic
正旦   ~~female~~ leading lady
小旦   soubrette
小生   male lead ←
大花面   ~~lead~~ 'painted face'
小花面   secondary 'painted face'
老外   old man
老旦   old woman

Friday 2 Mar 1973

Perhaps 'Principal Boy' better for 小生, meaning

The more strongly visual overtones, (Lesbianism)
— 小旦 seems to be the same as 貼, (女孩子)
— so 'soubrette' is OK for either.

Tuesday 6 March 1973

MS of Chap. 30 completed and first-corrected.

Monday 12 March 1973

「羊血山黎峒丸」

黎峒：黎民所居之山、在海南島中、環黎母山而居、各

中國醫學大辭典：p.4076 黎峒丸：
牛黃、冰片麝香各二錢五分、阿魏、雄黃各一兩、生大黃、孩兒茶、天竺黃、麝三七、瓜兒血竭、乳香、沒藥、藤黃、各二兩、山羊血五錢。

羊血was one of several optional ingredients, so perhaps 羊血山黎峒丸 simply means 'Li-dog pills with 羊血' — Though 'Hainan kid's blood pills' comes better off the tongue & prob. the best rendering for here.

Thursday 15 March 1973

369 「蒲艾簪門、虎符系臂」

東京夢華錄

端午 「…自五月一日及端午前一日
賣桃、柳、葵花、蒲葉、佛道艾，
次日家家鋪陳於門首，以糭子、五色
水團、茶酒供養，又釘艾人於門上，土庶
遞相宴賞」

艾 mugwort common artemisia
菖蒲 acorus calamus (calamus)

See also 繁勝錄 (p.118)

See also 五月 in 夢粱錄 (p.156 sq.)
「…以菖蒲或通草雕刻天師馭虎像
于中…」

See also 武林旧事 (p.379)

虎符 pro¹ connected with 天師.

Friday 16 March 1973

370 懶懶的 Not in KYTT. 北京话语汇
gives làn de (懶怠)「不乐意做某一件事」
Perhaps it's this.

370 (扇)骨子 : the radials y fans are called
'sticks' and 'guards'

「縐臉子瞼」 'gin so, a nasty look' (?)

Great deal of 「散」 in ch. 31. 「喜散不喜聚」, 「橫豎有个散的日子」

燕京歲時記
　「小虎 ... 繫於小兒之背」
抄本 has the correction 背 → 臂

372. 「你也不怕臊了他！就是他認真要去...」
抄 / 原.2 has 「你也不怕臊了便是他認真要去...」

Tuesday 20 March 1973

p. 375 Shi Xiangyun's 「二嬸娘」 is her 'Aunt Shi' (史鼐's wife)

p. 376 「新大紅猩猩氈的斗篷」 cf. ch. 8 「大紅猩猩氈斗笠」, the same. 'red felt.' Perhaps 'scarlet felt'

ib. 「縧紋石」 undiscoverable. Probably an agate ('ribbon agate') a veined agate

p. 377 樓子花　伊藤 says 「花冠が高く著く品種」 of the 薔花 and 「二階」 of the 石榴花,

Math. has 脈氣充足 'a good constitution'.
Any source for this?

双星：牽牛、織女 = 夫妻。

Friday 30 March 1973
Servants addressing their master often say
'我们' as a sort of humilific (a period slang?)
1st person singular. Cf. expressions like '娘儿们'
meaning 'a female'.

Sunday 1st April 1973
p.372 「二哥哥 ~~你不告诉我~~ 」: 你不告诉我...」
庚辰 has the obviously right text here:
「二哥哥不告诉我，我问你就
知道了」. This is the text in 俞's
八十回校本. (p.326)

Monday 2nd April 1973

374) All texts have 「起来讓我洗澡去」
but this surely ought to be
「讓我起来洗澡去」?
She's the one who has to get up, not Bao-yu.

Thursday 5 April 1973

377. 縹冗 'Fishy'

Saturday 7 April 1973

p.379 「心裏不知怎麼一動，似有所感」
庚辰 「只是默默不語，正自出神」
乾抄 { 原文「只是默默不語正自出神忽」
      改文「心裡只是一動 似有所□忽」
「正」 is partly lost in the photograph and 「感」 almost completely lost. 「忽」 was crossed out by mistake and then added again.
胡程乙本:「心裡不知怎麼一動 似有所感」

「在階下繫橙……連忙迎下來」
is a bit puzzling

Sunday 8 April 1973

p.379.「寶玉因問道」 如胡乙本,
庚辰 and 俞校本, both「笑道」
高抄 原「笑」改「問」. Inexplicable alteration.

MS of ch. 31 completed.

Monday 16 April 1973

House rules etc… recd from Frances Balfour.

椿齡 is presumably 齡官's full 名 (a 字!). 'Charmante' is therefore, strictly speaking, a 'mistranslation' (「椿齡」: 祝人壽考之辭 KY77); but (a) 'Vivace' is sure to convince the knowledgeable reader that you don't understand French (soubrettes are thought of as vivacious rather than longeval) and (b) 'Charmante' is at once sympathetic as French and understandable to the monophone English reader. Better keep Charmante. Seems a pity to give away her identity in the chap. heading when it's carefully concealed in the text. — Perhaps better not name her in the Chap. heading.

Wednesday
~~Tuesday~~ 2 May 1973
Copy 3 of Chaps. 27–31 sent to Dorothy Liu, 22 Castlebar Park, W5.

Thursday
~~Wednesday~~ 3 May 1973
胡程乙：襲人聽了驚疑不止又是悄又是急又是臊連忙推他道這是那裏的話你是怎麼有了還不快去嗎
庚辰：襲人聽了這話 唬得魄消魂散只叫神天菩薩坑死我了 便推他道這是那裏的話敢是中了邪還不快去
乾抄：襲人聽了 ~~這話~~ 唬得魂飛魄散只叫神天菩薩 ~~坑死我了 便推他道這是那裏~~ 話敢是中了邪 還不快去

胡程：接了扇子一句话也没有竟自走去
庚辰：夺了扇子便忺忺的抽身跑了
乾抄原文：夺了扇子便扭身忺忺的跑了
…… 改文：接了扇子一句话也没有竟自走去

他（近来，如今..） 越发……
'he's getting so……'

~~Thursday~~ Friday 4 May 1973
p.389「说不得我只好慢慢的累去罢了」
cf. ch.8 p.104:「说不得束荆西凑恭恭敬敬封了
　　二十两赘见礼」

5月4日 金钏's dismissal
5月5日 Lady Wang's party. 晴雯撕扇子.
5月6日 午间 史湘云 arrives. 金钏撅井, 宝玉挨打
「前日」 is the day before yesterday.

Saturday 5 May 1973
389.「忙向王夫人处来」
　庚辰,乾抄,原文,「
「忙向王夫人处来道安慰」
有正（俞校）
「忙向王夫人处来安慰」

乾抄改文:「忙問王夫人处去」
This is a good example of Gao's editing.
A line or two later we find that Bao-chai doesn't in fact say anything:
「獨有王夫人在里[間]房內垂有古淚, 宝釵便不好提这了」
Surely the 便 implies a change of mind, so perhaps the 原文 is better. Even so, the editing is much more intelligent & well-meaning than is generally allowed.

381:「後來我們太太沒了」
This surely can't, as 伊藤 seems to think, mean Xiang-yun's own mother? Perhaps 史鼐's first wife. Or his mother? Think I should say 'my uncle's first wife'.

Sunday 6 May 1973

伊藤 can't be right in saying that the 沒了 的問題 is 疑惑.

381 你还记得那幾年
This 小乾抄改文. Good editing.

Tuesday 15 May 1973
'Bad' words for housecats:

癡・抽身・風流・知己・生分・
薄命・造次・

387 「今日胆大說出來，就是死了也是甘心的」

A crucial passage.
Presumably "I can go to hell you now", not
'Now I have told you', etherthis otherwise the
irony of his ever declaration being made to the wrong girl
by mistake is lost.

✗ Not necessarily. Aroma is made to suspect more
than has actually passed — if you read this the other way.

Wednesday 16 May 1973
Ch. 28 p. 333
「悔教夫婿覓封侯」
Already quoted in 西廂記 5/1 浪裏來
煞 (落ding折)
Original is 王昌齡 青樓曲 二首其二
— First thoughts better than
2nd thoughts. I don't think it fits here really.

Thursday 17 May 1973

~~xxxxx~~ p.387 「驚人呀了…」 See Thurs. 3 May.

程乙 version 「又兒…又兒…」 is a feeble + inappropriate imitation of p.385 「代玉呀」 兒…兒…兒…」 Sung Brome's easier on bas subtle + less daring of such elaborate analysis.

Thursday 24 May 1973

See 15, 16 May. ~~Third~~ Fourth thoughts better than ~~second~~ third thoughts. CCWg agrees with this reading. CXQ too fond of a document not to know it this way. Y, les enfants terribles

Friday 25 May 1973

393 (33) 長府宮 cf. 161 (14)
    'Chamberlain'
('the chamberlain of his household')

Sunday 27 May 1973

For 曹寅綾 曹綸 see 清朝續文獻通考
卷 242 p. 9864, 9866.
 Also 裕瑞.

Sunday 3 June 1973

The dialogue of the Stone and the 二仙 in Chap. 1 which appears in 戚序本 and 靖batch MSS is a loss; but there is a good reason for its editing out — which is certainly earlier than 程 because 亁抄 程乙 is already without it — This is the inconsistency of the information given by the 一僧一道 later in the chapter that the Stone had already been a free-moving agent before they met it, with the earlier picture of it as a static rock that had lain at the foot of 青埂峰 ever since it was rejected.

Wednesday 6 June 1973

亁抄 early Chap. 32 + begin of 33 (程乙) seems to be unique.

Monday 11 June 1973

LAI SHENG, LAI DA.

Wu Shichang On the Red Chamber Dream p.240 implies that the alteration of 來昇 to 賴升 was a piece of wanton arbitrariness on Gao E's part. An examination of the texts suggests rather that it was a conscientious and much-needed editorial improvement.

chap. 7
- 胡「大總管賴二」
- 乾「大摠管賴二」
- 戚「大總管賴二」
- 庚「大總管賴二」

chap. 10
- 胡「賴陞」
- 乾「來昇」
- 戚「來昇」
- 庚「來昇」

chap. 14
- 胡「都總管賴陞」
- 乾「都總管來陞」
- 戚「都總管來昇」
- 庚「都總管來昇」

chap. 16
- 胡「只憑賈赦…賴大賴升」
- 乾「只憑賈赦…賴大來昇」
- 戚「只憑賈赦…賴大來昇」
- 庚「只憑賈赦…賴大來昇」

彩明　　　　　　　Chap. 14.
　　甲戌回前總批：
「凤姐用彩明，因自識字不多，且彩明係未冠之童」

　　甲戌，庚辰眉批：
(1) 寧府如此大家，阿凤如此身分，豈有使貼身丫頭与家裏男人答话办事之理呢。此作者忽畧之處。
(2) 彩明係未冠小童，阿凤便于出入使令耳。老兄並未前後看明，是男是女乱加批駁，可笑。

Chap 45.
賴姑〈...笑道...昨兒妳又打發彩哥兒賣東西 (庚辰)
乾抄 some but 彩哥 (no 兒)

批書者 seems to be right in saying that 彩明 is a boy, but way in suggests that there are male servants among them for their ads etc. 5 wife.

Ch.14.「至次日卯正二刻...寧國府中婆娘媳婦...」

Wednesday 27 June 1973

Corrected galley-proofs of vol. 1 sent to Penguins (First Class letter: £1.36) Covering letter to Miss Hoppen.

Wednesday 4 July 1973

宝玉自知不能讨饶... and all the subsequent Baoyu's swears & cries are absent from 庚辰 and are added in 乾抒. It seems pretty absurd if all the time he is gagged. Forum MS.

Also, anon, 乾抒 is much better than 旋抒.

Fu the better reading

「宝玉急的跺脚、正没抓寻处...」, rather than 「急的手脚正没抓寻处...」

Cf. Ch. 1 「急得士隐惟跌足长叹而已」

Sunday 8 July 1973

Either way, much is unexplained. Why did they bring a rope but not tie him to the bench? Why did they not gag him if tied to do so? And if they did gag him (as the MSS imply), why is no mention made of anyone taking the gag out?

Wednesday 8 August 1973

Work recommenced after long break.

Friday 10 Aug. 1973

胡~~~~ 滅程乙本 ineapliedly reads
「迎探姊妹兩个」coming out with the rest when
王夫人 goes to rescue Daoyu.
庚辰 and 乾抄, both have 「迎春姊妹」

Saturday 11 Aug. 1973
Page-proofs (2 copies) received from
Penguins (~~late~~ First Class Letter Mail. £1·53
p.m.? 10/8) To be returned, with
galleys + copy; by Aug. 31.
Copy not in parcel.

25 Aug 1973
(Page-proof corrections)
Chap. 24 「檀雲又因他母親的
生日接了回去」
檀雲 must be for 晴雲 — otherwise
where is 晴雲? Yet chap. 77 is at great
pains to show that 晴雯 lost both parents in
infancy. Prob. Our Forgetful Author. Better say
'cousin' on p. 483. — Not at all satisfactory

but *faute de mieux*.

On this day corrected page-proofs (with galleys and copy) returned to Penguin (FCL mail, え1.53)

Tuesday 4 Sep. 1973

庚辰「經心扶侍 問他端的 且聽下回分解」

乾抄「經心扶侍 且聽下回分解」 「細問要知端底究竟好麼」

Fruit-dy 為他 is obviously wrong. ??

Wednesday 5 Sept. 1973

MS of 33 finally completed.
Note, Translated as it stands, the last para of 33 implies that ay the servants Tall 寶玉 to 怡紅院, yet it is clear from 34 that 賈母 + 王夫人 came too, — so this has to be inserted in the translation.

Chap. 34
庚辰「冥冥之中若不怕死自怕, 所謂 糊塗催鬼業矣」 Looks like Recycled consuel. NO See 14 Sep.

「惟恐宝钗沈心」
胡本   do.
庚辰「————do.
But 乾抄 has 嘆 can't 存 !!

Is CXQ just courteous in is 襲人 lying
when she ~~would~~ tell 王夫人 that Baochai's
medicine has been used?

Sunday 9 September 1973

p.405「又不許叫喊」refers to the
fact that he was gagged & therefore makes
nonsense of the 高本 alterations.
    (p.396「堵起嘴来」....「乱嚷
乱哭」)

Monday 10 September 1973
ch. 34. p.
「我時掌辦有嘴兒...」胡戚程乙本
「我常乙辦有口兒...」庚辰
「我長長辦有嘴兒...」乾抄
    Cheng them all 'mis-spellings' of
「拌嘴」(彼此口角)

乾抄 34/4a a lot of corrections here or from a text diff't from both 程本 and 庚辰.
(e.g. 「只是这几次有事就混忘了」
庚 has 「只是这几次有事就忘了」
乾原 has 「只是这几天有事就忘了」

30/11/12 藥子
    搭赸、乾原 had 搭擂
Explanation (curious) not in K&TT but in 或语
「搭訕！谈话时用不经意的话
敷衍他人、俗称搭訕」

Tuesday 11 Sept 1973

乾 34/4b「左思右想一时七情
怒将五内陣然炙起」
5 winged chars. found it no other text.

Wednesday 12 Sept 1973

乾原文 best here:
  「大家都是一半截夺一半掷实
  竟让举星她说的」

410 一个不防头的人 (=不留神)
        y. p. 88
Note on 8 Sept「冒失、粗心没顾忌」

「犯舌」 乾原如「絞舌」= 拉老婆舌頭
（住搖人的私語，挑撥是非）

Friday 14 Sept 1973

「冥冥之中若不怡然自得
豈可謂糊塗鬼崇矣」

Cf.「余二人如大快遂於九泉矣」
「冥冥之中」and like「冥中」(=陰間)

Monday 17 Sept 1973

「要想什麼吃的玩的…」
弘原文子乾抄 but 以为 庚辰．

Sunday 23 Sept, 1973
  ch. 34

檀雲 again.

  胡藏程乙本「悄悄的告訴晴雯，麝月，
秋紋等人」
  庚辰本「悄悄告訴晴雯，麝月，檀雲，
秋紋等」
  乾抄本「悄悄的告訴晴雯，麝月，香雲，
   秋紋等」

[cf. 25 Aug. 73, 14 Dec. 1971, 30 Dec. 71., 5 Jan. 1972.]

YPB 353/11 Apparatus (iii 178), as usual, quite useless. However, one can presently deduce that 「戚本」 (which is his 底本) was the same as 庚辰. 「晴雯, 麝月, 檀雲, 秋紋」

N.B. In chap. 24 晴雯 is absent from an enumeration; here 碧痕 is missing from an enumeration.

Thursday 27 Sept. 1973
Ch. 34
The corrections made to the interview of Aroma with Bao-yu, particularly at the end, seem designed to suggest that LW is fully A that she is a benevolent to be Bao-yu's 屋裏人. On the whole A becomes if anything nastier in the later version. She is slightly more presumptuous in the earlier one — but that's another matter.

Monday 1 Oct. 1973
p.410 「真合壓倒桃花」: 『壓倒桃花』 is presumably a quotation. Can't place it. (Not in 曲 Arts of west, as far as I can see, is 西廂記」

Thursday 4 Oct 1973
Re 七―二,―五 (cf. 11 Sept 1973)
Only ex. I can find at the moment of this common device is in 倩女離魂 三折: 十二月/堯民歌 which have 1—9 and 10—1. But of course, this is quite common.

Saturday 6 October 1973
  MS of chap. 34 completed.

Wednesday 10 October 1973
  415 代玉's comment on 西廂記「脫布衫」 not very apt, really, since the passage in question describes 張君瑞's circumstances, not 鶯鶯's.

  418 「你姨娘可憐見的、不大說話、和木頭似的，公婆跟前就不獻好兒」
The problem is that 王夫人 hasn't got a 公婆. One feels that this ought to have been 「你大嫂子可憐見…」 But in that case why does Baoyu preface it by 「我說大嫂子不大說話…」 as if he were introducing a new subject?

  Actually I think it must be Li-wan who is meant throughout. She is the only careful person not there.

(See p.414 李衎......去过之後, 一起一起的敬尽了)

424 松荘y, Thurs, 21 Dec. 1972

Thursday 11 Oct, 1973
㉟
伊藤 seems to make no distinction between
打 辮子   and   打 络子

{ Natalie Rothstein   V&A (Textiles)
{ ? Edmund Caper.

Tuesday 16 October 1973
㉟
俻膳, 呈樣
~~According to...俻膳...~~ 佩文韵府 has an entry for 呈樣:
西湖志餘:「行都官酒庫每歲清明前開煑 中秋前賣新 先期諸庫 ~~~~~~~~ 呈樣 點檢 所 以呈府 筵中擇日開沽」
"To submit a sample/specimen (for testing)"

For 俻膳, 佩文韵府 quotes 南史

(南史 35) PNP 卌九.

劉湛傳:「廬陵王義真出為車騎將軍南豫州刺史、湛又為長史太守如故、義真既居武帝憂 便帳下備膳、湛禁之」

Wednesday 17 Oct, 1973

~~Sept~~ 伊藤's ~~would not think it Yauchin~~ ~~volatile some~~ understood 呈樣 defining *cing*. 呈樣 implies that it was made principally for some other purpose, & the foung-ying 'had a look' or 'sampled' it. Perhaps before any was sent to 貴妃 in the palace — if 初 is right & understood 備膳 in this way. Presumably it ought not to one shed offerings.

It's a question really of finding some ref. to ~~settle~~ rules governing contacts between Emp., concubines and their families.

欽定宮中現行則例 (光緒中定本)

大清通礼

內務府慶典

欽定總管內務府現行則例

乾抄 原文 seems to be unique here again:
「姨媽那里曉得這是舊年（預）備膳的，他們想的法兒不知弄些什麼麵印出來，借省清湯的味道做出來也罷了究竟沒意思 誰家常飯吃他呢 那一回呈樣的做了一回……」

庚辰 is same as 程乙 (more or less):
「媽媽那里曉得、這是舊年備饍他們想的法兒不知弄些什麼麵印出來、賣新荷葉的清香全仗省好湯究竟沒意思、誰家常吃他了、那一回呈樣的作了一回……」

乾抄 seems the better text here. What does "這" mean in "這是舊年…"? 庚 + 程 require it to mean "小荷葉湯", but how can it? 手 has to mean the 銀模子, which could be used to make many kinds of soup (小菊花湯, 小菱角湯, 等.)

Thursday 18 October 1973
On second thoughts, all these shapes must be for the one kind of soup — unless 30/40 means 30/40 of one shape on each 銀模

No. Merely (1) chrys. (2) lotus (3) plum (4) caltrop. Passage badly-written (?)

Tuesday 30 October 1973

Wed. 10 Oct's remarks re 418「你姨娘」etc. Not v. apt, since Bao-yu's「大姨子」definitely a fresh subject. The explanation prob. that「公婆」used very loosely here — in effect = 'me'.

420「(賈母)和薛姨媽分賓主坐了；寶釵湘雲坐在下面」

Later:

「上面兩雙是賈母薛姨媽，兩邊是寶釵湘雲的」

Presumably then on the same positions:

```
  薛        賈
      炕
  釵        雲
─────────────
     地下
```

Monday 5 Nov. 1973

p. 424

The 大紅 and 松花 汗巾子 must surely be the pair exchanged by Bao-yu & Bijun. In effect he is ordering one 绦子 for Aroma, one for Bijun and (?) one for himself.

For 紅汗巾子 cf. p. 394. That's what the 戏子官 calls it.

Saturday   10 Nov 1973

Xi-feng's managers seem to take no account of Tan-chun & Xi-chun.

Monday 12 Nov. 1973

※ 36/430
「七个大丫头, 八个小丫头」
All texts the same.
This seems to imply that Bao-yu has 16 maids — twice as many as Grandmother Jia! In fact, the 贾府人物系统图, which includes all the maids Bao-yu ever had (several didn't stay: e.g. 茜雪 got sacked quite early on in the novel), can produce only 14 names! Probably there were 4 of each, or 凤姐 is still lying abt both brothers (Bao-yu and Jia Huan) — Though this, too, is strange, since Jia Huan is never mentioned as having maids of his own, only 小厮. Is one to regard this as another lapse of the forgetful author or as another example of 凤姐's crookedness & mendacity? (Perhaps 宝玉 was supposed to have 7/8 maids but the money for them was all embezzled).
If (4)3 : 4 is right for Bao-yu, it would be —

at this juncture —

天 (襲人): 晴雯(1), 麝月(2), 秋紋(3)

刃 ? ?
— No, it doesn't una.

晴雯, 麝月, 琨痕, 秋紋, 倩霞 (5) 6/1/74 Doubt about this comma too

Sonej keh the some strokes?

36/432 也配使三个丫頭
  MSS 兩三个丫頭
Xi-feng's outburst appears to be directed against
赵姨娘, as CC was aware. The '兩' is
essential to this interpretation, in view of
「姨娘們每位兩个丫頭」 above.

胡程: 也不想想自己也配使三个丫頭
乾原: 也想一想是什麼阿物兒 也配使兩三个丫頭
改文: 也不想想巳也配兩三个丫頭
  N.B. 乾原 and 改 both have the
「們」 missing before this.
庚辰: 也不想一想配人是奴寶兒 也配使兩三个丫頭.
有乙: 咱們 也不想一想是奴纔、也配

俅雨三个丫鬟

Notice that this is really directed at 赵姨娘 reinforced J comparison w. chap. 60 (see 伊藤) where 芳官 enrages 赵姨娘 & says:

「梅香拜把子——都是奴几呢」

◎ Thursday 15 Nov, 1973
The point is, who cut the maids' wages? '外头', 执事, ~~赵姨娘~~, or 凤姐?

Perhaps we should understand 「如今裁了丫头的钱」 ~~specially~~ as impersonal with 「外头」 as the understood agent. This leaves it open to the reader to suspect that Xi-feng was of being held back the money. Surely 赵姨娘 wouldn't complain to 王夫人 if she'd done it herself?

The punctuation 「就耽误了咱们」 favoured by some (人民, 伊藤) implies ignorance of the Pekingese idiom. 「你们耽误咱们」 is an imperative. YPD is right. 咱们想一想 means (in effect) 'you'd better'. (cf. Tyler Sergeant-Major 'we'd better smarten up a bit, hadn't we?')

Sunday 18 November 1973

Chap. 36 has no continuity with ch. 35.
「见宝玉好似一日」「今日缘了这句话」「不过每日……」「十分清闲日月」「如今且说……常来着教他」「这日又见」436「一日」Seems to imply a passage of perhaps several weeks.

Tuesday 20 Nov. 1973

36/428 星宿不利, 祭星

(1) 宿命智陀罗尼经　　21/1383
(2) 宿命陀罗尼　21/1382
(3) 文殊师利菩萨及诸仙所说吉凶时日善恶宿曜经 21/1299
(4) 宿曜仪轨　21/1304
(5) 七曜攘灾决 * 21/1308
(6) 七星如意论秘要经 20/1091
(7) 七曜星辰别行法 21/1309

viz. 20/1091 and
    21/1299, 1304, 1308, 1309,
1382 and 1383.

Wednesday 21 Nov 1973

Of these it's (7)   (1309)
七曜星辰別行法 which seems most
relevant.
Perhaps 'an unlucky conjunction in the
constellation of his nativity.'

Sunday 25 Nov 1973

彩鳳 'SUNBEAM' appears to be a
hapax phenomenon in ch. 23 p. 456
Only the 程 texts have this, 乾 and 庚
both have 彩霞. It will be necessary
to alter p. 539, 540 so that SUNBEAM disappears.

SUNCLOUD }
SUNSET } maids of Lady Wang

SUNSHINE page employed by .....

(小霞 caused by SUNRISE)
? a MOONSET
a MOONRISE

Monday 26 Nov. 1973
In Chap. 30 (p. 363) all texts give 彩雲 as
the maid Jia Huan was flirting with; in Chap.
61 all texts agree that 彩雲 stole things for 賈環;
and in ch. 72 all texts agree that 彩霞 was the one

who was expected to become 賈環's concubine. It's hard to believe that there isn't a mistake here.

Tuesday 27 Nov 1973

Perhaps it would be best to turn the 彩雲's in 30 and 61 into 彩霞's — i.e. translate as 'SUNSET'. It depends on whether or not 彩雲 makes any significant later appearance.

Wednesday 2 Jan. 1974

1519. 甄士隱 tells 賈雨村 his daughter's fate:

「產難完劫、遺一子于薛家以承宗祧」

which can't, under any circumstances, be squared w. chap. 5.

Monday 7 Jan 1974

The key-word in chap. 32 (385) is 知己. Perhaps 'true friend' rather than 'true love'.

知音 p. 1121 and 1155 is a different problem.

Thursday 10 Jan 1974

All texts seem to agree that GJ has 8 senior and Bao-yu 7 senior & 8 junior maids, however unlikely this seems. Perhaps Xi-feng is meant to be lying. In fact it looks as though GJ, 王夫人 & 宝玉 all had 4 senior maids in XP's original plan (not counting 婆人):

鴛鴦	金釧	晴雯	賈環 had no maids.
鸚鵡	玉釧	麝月	江樓夢人名辭典
琥珀	彩雲	碧痕	has no justification what-
珍珠	彩霞	秋紋	ever for ascribing 彩霞

to 賈環.

Sunday 13 Jan 1974

Chap. 4 (p.49, Pp. 121) 「咱們東南角上梨香院」All MSS have 「東北角」胡程乙本 etc, have 東南, i.e. a very late alteration of East (& wrong, as it happens).

Wednesday 23 Jan 1974

36/436 葵官、药官. Evidently introduced by Gao E (see 乾扰.) MSS had 宝官, 玉官 (cf. 30/366). It's a bit hard to see why he made the alteration, unless he simply wanted to introduce some more ones of the 12. Alternatively he may have reasoned that 玉官 was a 正旦 & therefore the proper person to try the 步步娇. But Bao-yu was ignorant of such matters & perhaps CXQ intended this. Any way, seems better to keep 宝官 & 玉官 from a 'story' point of view. They show a 小生 + 正旦 going around company (like 芳官 + 药官 ?)

Note: for ROLES see 1/3/73

Saturday 26 Jan. 1974

贾蔷's bird appears variously as

玉顶 (程本)

玉顶金豆 (庚辰) and

毫翅梧桐 (乾原) (!)

36/437 蔷's「贾蔷…不觉站起来」

is pretty silly, since there's no reason to suppose that he was sitting down. MSS 「慌起来」obviously preferable.

Sunday 27 Jan 1974

36/438「自此深怀人生情缘各有分定,只是每每暗伤,不知将来葬我洒泪者为谁」

乾库 had none of this. It is inserted in 乾改

庚辰 on the other hand has it all + adds:
「此皆宝玉心中所怀也,不可十分苑(苑)凿」 ※ No Def see 28/1/74

I suspect that all from 自此 to 妄凿 is 诖文. On the other hand it ought to fund to one. (且说)

Monday 28 Jan 74

36/438「我昨儿晚上的话」isn't consistent with 36/436「一日」
Better say 'the other night'.

Referring back to 「自此...」(27/1/74): Perhaps this is all 诖, 且说 implies an digression of some kind — perhaps it.
                                    PTO

Perhaps it is better to treat 「自此一」 as conn. betw. 妄擬? Stone?

Wednesday 30 January 1974
Rough TS of Chap. 36 completed.
(「自此一妄擬」 omitted in TS)
Viz. 36 took 3 months (interruptions)

Thursday 31 Jan. 1974
(Chap. headings)
ch. 32 手足耽耽
Pres. for 耽耽 (虎視眈)
Fu 手足 = 兄弟 cf HHS 「兄弟当左右手也」

ch. 37
乾原文 begin.
「却說宝玉每日在園中任意……」
(Nothing abt 賈政)
庚辰 begin
「这年賈政又点了学差，擇于八月二十日起身，是日拜过宗祠及賈母起身諸了宝玉諸子弟等送至洒浃亭。却说賈政出门去後外面諸了不做等記学差……」

趙岡 ~~suggest~~ Roing out that there is no certainty between 35-36. But this is equally true of 36-37.

Monday 4 Feb, 1974

4/25 薛蟠's party
4/26 芒神節、馮's party. 琪官
4/27 Rec. of 宝玉 and 代玉
5/1   Visit to 清虚觀
5/2   Quarrel w. 代玉
5/3   薛蟠's birthday
5/4   Rec. of 宝/代. 金釧 dismissed. (龄官)
5/5   Lady Wong's party. 撕扇子
5/6   湘雲 arrives. 金釧投井. 宝玉挨打. 襲人 & 王夫人. 代 and hawks. 宝釵 in w.w. 怒
5/7   Silver + 宝玉. O'tide and 宝玉.
       × × × → 八月

37. Re 賈政's appointment (not in 乾抄 原文)
賈政 appears not to be present at the ouverhead sovereign where are 賈敬 attends in ch. 53
His father's return mentioned in ch. 70
p.902「當日眾姐妹皆至房中侍早膳畢，便有賈政書信到了……說六月准進京
Unquestionably the passage about 賈政 is a addition 37.

Wednesday 13 Feb. 1974

37/450 Gao E's 「这是等我取去…」 is an improvement on MSS 「这话你是等我取去」. 晴雯, as subsequent exchange shows, is eager, not reluctant to go.

Friday 15 Feb 1974

37/452 「白海棠和韵」 No title in 庚辰 and title in 乾抄, chiang added as an afterthought.

Thurs. 21 Feb. 1974

白海棠 can't, after all, be begonia. Begonia is never a 'mass of blossom' or 'tear-soaked with tears'. Suggest Malus theifera (茶海棠)

NO. All this 'autumn' stuff makes it even unlikely that we have to do with a spring species famed for out-of-season flowering.

Friday 22 Feb. 1974

MS of 37 completed?

Friday 1st Mar. ~~29 Feb~~ 1974
___

藕香榭 description here sounds exactly like
that of 滴翠亭 in ch. 27 — not at all like
a dwelling-place. (Except that one might deduce that
滴翠亭 is in the middle of the water & 藕香榭 nearer the
middle of the water.)

藕香榭的水亭子   40/488

Perhaps 'the position from which Xi-chun's
brushwork drawing took its name'? Obviously
she didn't like it in middle of the water.

Suggested plan:

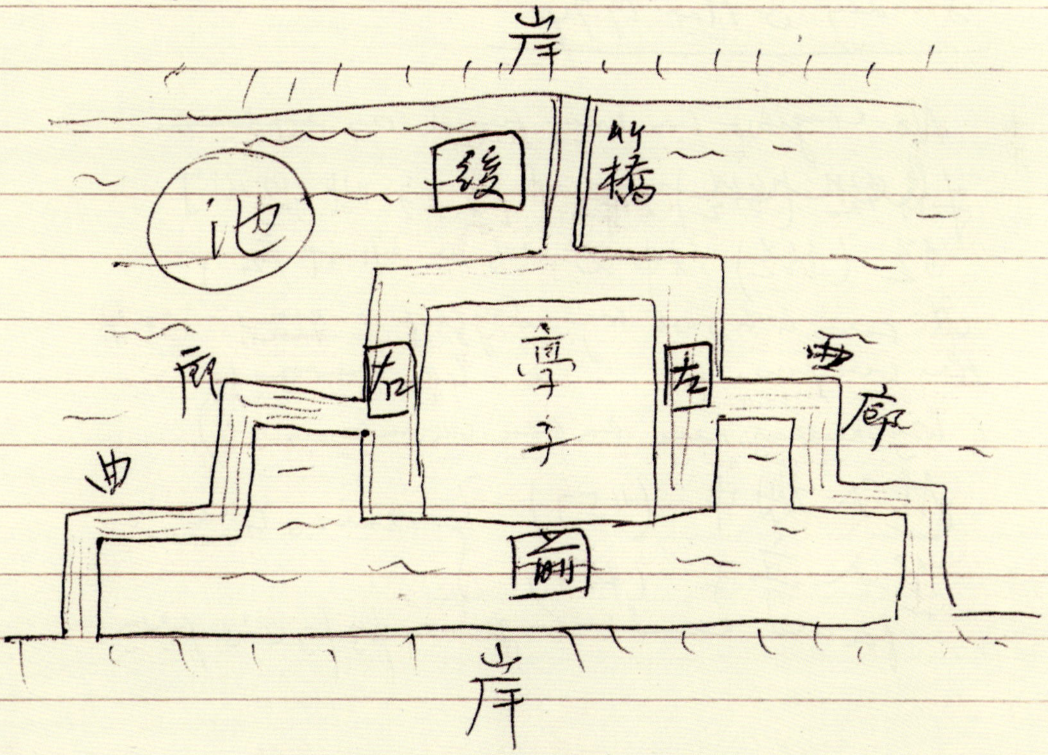

[diagram of a pavilion plan with labels: 岸 (top), 池, 後, 竹橋, 廊, 門, 亭子, 門, 西廊, 曲, 前, 岸 (bottom)]

Bk 23/266
「迎春住了綴錦樓…
惜春住了蓼風軒」

Fu 綴錦樓 'The Painted Chamber' see
18/206 (T. 364)

Fu 蓼風軒 'The Smartweed Loggia' See 16.

Bk ch. 37/443
「他(迎春)住的是紫菱洲,
四丫頭住的藕香榭」

Sunday 3 Mar 1974

No exegetist has volunteered an explanation
[慌慌張張] 神 「沒的叫他們
慌(慌) 神兒似的作什麼」
It seems to be quite any. Suggest it means 'as if
they were possessed' i.e. like automata.
('Why, needlessly, make them behave like automata??')

住入棚中 (457) } seems to call
住入亭子 (458) }
for an emendment of 1/3/74's prev.

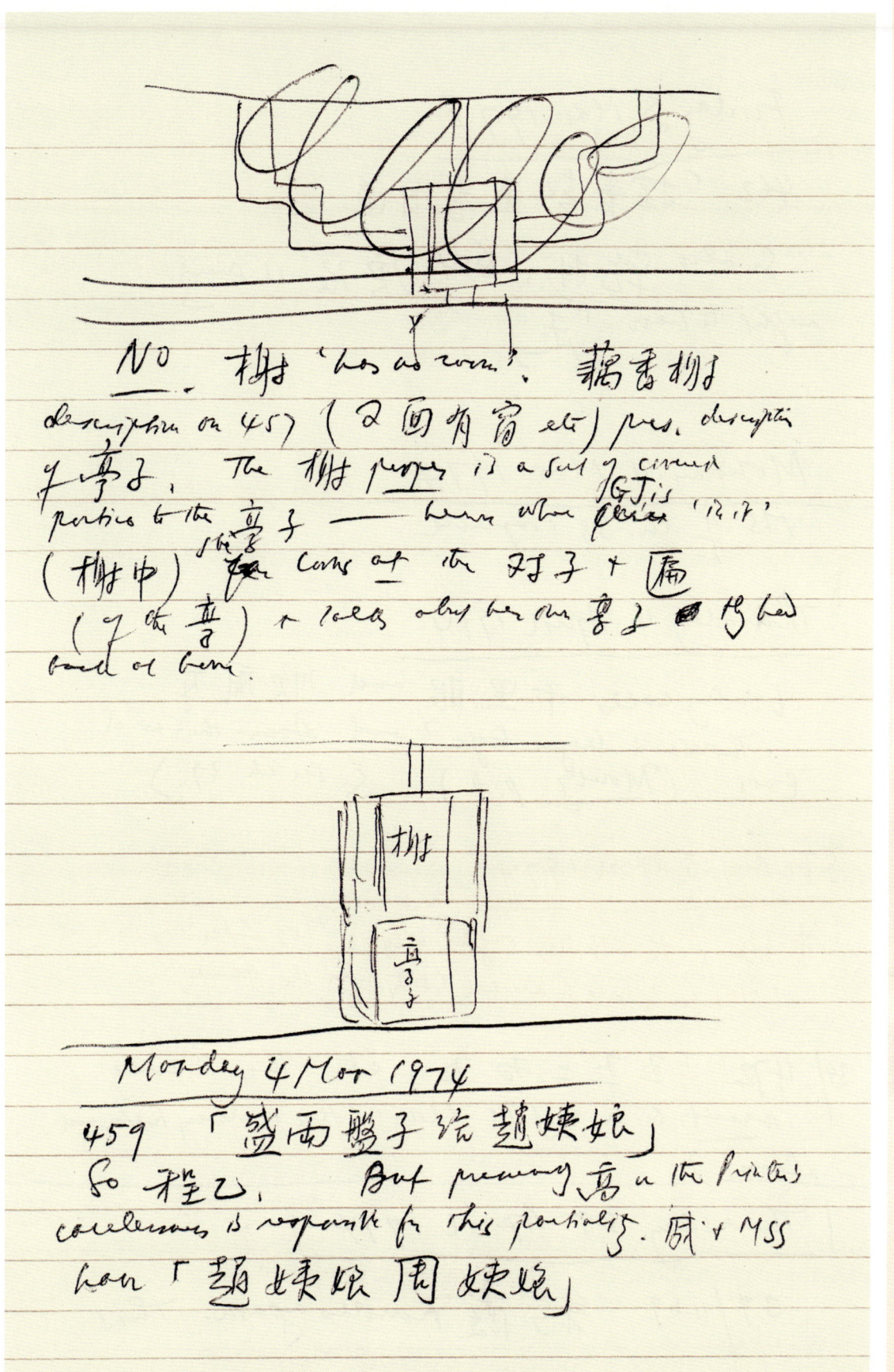

NO. 榭 'has no room'. 藕香榭 is description on 457 (是面有窗 etc) pres. description of 亭子. The 榭 proper is a sort of covered portico to the 亭子 —— hence when q[uote]s 'is it' GJ is (榭中) shd [?] come at the 对子 + 匾 (of the 亭子) + lady observer on 亭子 [?] has back of beam.

Monday 4 Mar 1974

459 「盛两盤子给赵姨娘」 so 程乙. But presumably 喜 in the Printers carelessness is responsible for this partiality. 戚 & MSS have 「赵姨娘 周姨娘」

Friday 8 Mar 1974

462 「探春起来看旧道:」
So also 乾抄, but 庚辰 is surely
right to have 「走」.

Monday 11 Mar 1974
MS of ch. 38 completed.

Thursday 4 April 1974

Waley calls 千里眼 and 顺风耳
'Thousand-league Eye' and 'Down-the-wind
Ears' (Monkey p.11)   (see ch. 29)

Friday 5 April 1974

李纨 / 大奶奶 ought to be 'Mrs Zhu'.
'Mrs Li' will be needed later for the Huas.

39/ 472 「五五二两五」etc. This is surely
meant to be a joke (like 'ten + eleven, twelve and
eleven')

Thursday 25 April 1974

39/469 彩霞 trouble again. This

makes it look as if 彩霞 was No. 1 after 金釧's death. If that were so, it seems a bit unlikely that 旺兒 (Chap. 72) would ask for her & 王夫人 yield her up without comment. Also, the character here given 彩霞 subs 彩雲, who is 王夫人's great standby all through the latest part of the novel. And it would be slightly indelicate for Bao-yu to comment like this about someone he had made a pass at in ch. 25. So all in all it seems likelier that 彩雲 is meant here. Better say 'Suncloud' for consistency.

<ins>Friday 10 May 1974</ins>

MS of ch. 39 completed.

<ins>Thurs. 23 May 1974</ins>

「李氏站在大觀樓下，往上看有．命人上去開了綴錦閣．．．．」
 Elsewhere called 綴錦樓 (18/206, 23/266); but 18/206 shows that it is in fact a gallery (東西飛樓曰綴錦樓，西面斜樓曰含芳閣). Here it is evidently

used as a storeroom. Ch. 23 (266) unaccountably makes it the home of 迎春; but as she is elsewhere shown inhabiting 紫菱洲, T.459 alters to 'the building' on Amaryllis Eyot, to avoid any clash)

Friday 24 May 1974

A. Charbonnier: L'art de la laque, les techniques chinoises et japonaises retrouvées
 Gazette des beaux arts 6 ser. 15 i (1936) 95-104

M. Jourdain & S. Jenyns: Chinese export lacquer of the 17ᵗʰ-18ᵗʰ centy. Oriental Art I (1948) p. 143-8

E.B. Price Secrets of the Chinese lacquer shops
 Asia 32 (1932) p. 418-9

W.P. Yetts Chinese Lacquer Burlington Mag. 48 (1926) p. 258-64

V. Rienacker Chinese lacquer Apollo 40 (1947) p. 53-6

Sammy Lee.

Tuesday 28 May 1974

40/491

「上面左右兩張榻……」
Something v. peculiar abt. this whole passage.

戚程本, 乾原, 庚辰, 俞校 (戚本) all different.

乾抄 gives 王夫人 a 榻, & this 一榻一凡 seems to contradict both what is said in the 一个一个 bit & what is said at the beginning of the chap. where 李紈 has 二十多張 moved out. And the 下面...里王夫人的 seems to clash with the 東边 刘姥姥 etc that follows. Suggested reading:

上面左右兩張榻 ~~榻之~~ ~~~~ 東边刘
姥姥, 刘姥姥之下便是王夫人, 西边
便是湘雲, 第二便是宝釵, 第三便是
代玉、第四迎春、探春、惜春挨次
排下去宝玉在末, 每一榻前兩子
雕漆几之有海棠式的 之有梅花式的
之有荷葉式的 之有葵花式的 之有方的
之有圓的其式不一

PTO

31/5 No. see SV 31.5.74

上面左右兩張榻是賈母薛姨媽坐也劉姥姥刘姥姥之下便是王夫人西也便是湘雲第二便是宝釵第三便是代玉第4便是迎春探春惜春挨次排下去宝玉在末 ~~東邊設楊妃榻~~ ~~~~ ~~~~ ~~~~ 榻上都鋪錦裀蓉簟每一榻前兩張雕漆几×有海棠式的×有梅花式的×有荷葉式的×有葵花式的也有方的有圓的共式不一、一个上面放自炉并瓶一引攅盒一个、一个上面空設烟歌備放人所喜食物。攅盒式樣隨几之式樣、每人一把烏銀洋鏨自斟壺一个十錦琺琅杯、李纨凤姐二人之几設於三層榻内二層紗榻之外。

[flower drawings with labels: mallow 葵, crab apple 海棠, plum 梅]

Friday 31 May 1974

40/479 The problem of the party seems to begin with Bao-yu's anachronistic proposal:

「我有个主意…」 It looks very much as if something is missing (all texts the same).

After agreeing GJ gives the following order (乾庚):「明日就揀我們愛吃的做了，按人數裝了盒子來」

乾改文子 40/491 is worth considering:

「上頭放着一分炉瓶一个攢盒。」

The 空設 有 but isn't much use, because it seems evident from the text that follows that the food is already there. Suggest:

上面左右兩張榻、榻上鋪着錦裀蓉簟，每一榻前兩張雕漆几，一个上頭放着 (炉瓶一分)，一个上頭放着攢盒。上面二榻四几是賈母薛姨媽，下面一榻兩几是王夫人的。餘者都是一椅一几。東邊劉姥姥，他之下便是王夫人，西邊…寶玉。再末、李紈鳳姐二人之几設于三層檻內二層紗橱之外。几也有海棠式的，也有梅花式的…其式不一，攢盒式樣亦隨几之式樣，每人一把烏銀洋鏨自斟壺、一个十錦珐瑯杯。

On 479 Baoyu's「再一个什锦攒心盒子」
the 再 is heavily inked over an indecipherable 原文 in 乾挍. It is about eating way.
Having the food go in the 攒心盒子

40/483「这个薄片子还说是闷造上用的呢, 竟连这个官用的也比不上呵」
Seems to be ~~beautiful~~ a reproach levelled at the author's own family.

Monday 17 June 1974

Lee Yu-Kuan Oriental Lacquer Art
~~Tokyo~~ Weatherhill 1972 (recommended to me from Roy Tregear 10 June 74)

直漆 'direct lacquering'
泥子 'lacquer putty'
堆彩 'embossed coloured lacquer'
夹纻 'fabrics'
脱胎 'hollow-body dried lacquer'
塑像 'mud-body lacquer'
木胎 'wooden-body lacquer'
磁胎 'porcelain-body lacquer'
金属胎 'metal-body lacquer'
剔, 刻 'U- and V- shaped carving'
毛雕 'incision technique'

剔花, 魚子紋 'chisel-carving' / 'fish-roe pattern'
攢生 'lacquer soaked cloth structure'
桂妝 'cassia-juice coloring'
平脫 'Submerged and polished-out design'
鑲嵌 / 百寶嵌 inlay
帖金 / 金箔 gold foil
戧金 / 戧銀 gold & silver needle engraving, Fu technique in 輟耕錄 30.
素鬘 'white colour-enying'
綠漆 'green lacquer'
剔红 'carved red lacquer'
印板刻子 'pasted-on design with carving'

___

In 戧金 technique design was engraved in black lacquer ground with a needle & engraved lines filled in mixture of 彭羅 & cypress & then with gold dust.
Variation of 戧金 are 泥金 (painting w. thick gold lacquer); 描金 (painting w. thin gold)

Pl. 133 彩漆圓食籠 'a square food box of glazy brown lacquer & fine basketwork.' coloured lacquer decorates on top. Basketwork painted w. gold lacquer.

Pl. 134 編竹也描金漆長方盤 (rectangular tray w. basketwork sides) 描金 gold-painted decor on red-lacquered ground. Basketwork sides.

Pl. 127 - is a 朱漆戧金圓碟

Pl. 119 剔紅漆秋海棠華式盤
(four-lobed oval ... dish)

Pl. 111 is a 戧金漆茶托
'gold-filled engraved design'

Pl. 103 編漆張盒 'basket with sacrifice box'
Parts of basket with a side of cup box and lid

大捧盒 'food box'

Pl. 99 編竹边彩漆绘方盒
Square wood box w. lid + woven basket sides.

p. 16a (a wan-tzu or fylfot design signifying 长寿 - 21 shd
be asked. 14, 15 wan-tzu a key fret pattern is 对 fu - -

Pl. 71 珊瑚紅戧金 罩峰鋼漆硯盒

Pl. 62 編漆倦盒

Pl. 61 朱紅漆戧金 彩粧盒

Wednesday 19 June 1974

綴錦樓 is E of 大觀樓.
Seating order is (opposite) N-facing:

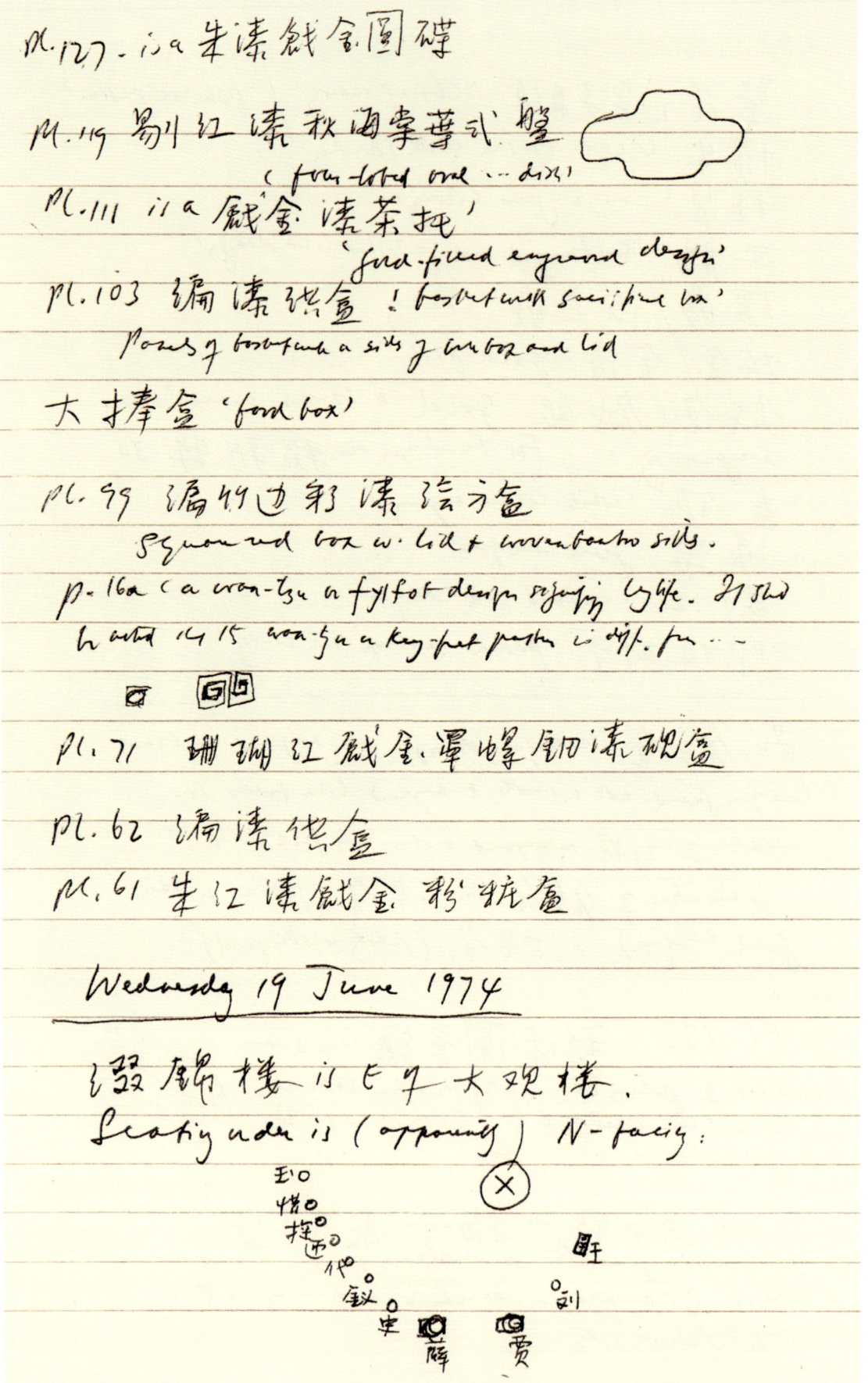

Presumably 李纨 and 熙凤 (& subsequently 晴雯) must be somewhere near ⊗. The water must be N. of 大观楼. See ch. 18 & ch. 17. In ch. 17 贾政 &co. walk from 蘅芜院 to 大观楼. In ch. 18 元春 goes to 花溆 by boat before being carried to 大观楼.

Friday 21 June 1974
End of 40 probably lost:

庚辰:「乘人大笑起来只听外面
　　　乱嚷」

程乙:「乘人听了由不的的大笑起来
　　　只听外面乱嚷々的不知何又且
　　　听下回分解」

戚本:「乘人大笑起来、只听外面乱
　　　嚷、且听下回分解」

乾抄 (supposed to be copied from 程本!):
　　「乘人又大笑起来、要知以後、
下回分解」

No mention of 乱嚷 in ch. 41.

N.B. G&G seems in his version of the end of 40 to be preparing for the 阁声大笑 of 41; but there's no particular reason uy 劉姥姥 heavily shd, think this anam so tediously funny.

MS of ch. 40 finished this morning. Letter to Doming re 綴錦樓 etc.)

Wednesday 26 June 1974
Rough TS of 40 finished.
彳順領 means (anticlockwise), 綴錦閣 must face water.

Thurs, 27 June 1974
1) 五畝園小志/志餘/題詠   謝家福
    望炊樓叢書
2) 雲間第宅志 王湾 藝海珠塵土集
3) 山陽河下園亭記 李元庚 小方壺齋叢書 三集
4) 武林第宅改 柯汝霖 武林掌故叢編第十二集
5) 春草園小記 趙墨 ——— 八集
6) 風木盦園題詠 丁丙 ——— 二十四集
7) 陳氏安瀾園記 陳璜鄉 培煙畫事堂 小品圓明園記
8) 竹墭小志 阮元 靜園叢書
9) 江邨草堂紀 高士奇 昭代叢書乙集六軼

武林掌故 9100

Monday 12 Aug 1974

41/500

櫳翠庵

cf. 17/195

「或山下得逢尼佛寺
或林中藏女道丹房」

T.344: 'a tiny temple nestling beneath a hill
a nun's retreat hidden in a little wood'

'Green Bower Hermitage' makes a sort of
proof-ref. to this.

Thursday 15th Aug. 1974

The 茄脂 recipe in 戚本 etc. is
much better than the one in 程本. The
程本 version makes 刘老's remark about
the chicken pointless.

Tuesday 27 August 1974

Receive copy of Itō's 中国古典文学大系
'Kōrōmu' (Heibonsha). Posted in Japan June 17th.

Saturday 31 August 1974

41/502 「代玉函…」「宝鈔知…」. The
variant on the latter raises the question whether but

showed to 代王 a both obd. to 宝敍. (Obviously one of the two most he way). Chap. 25 shows that Daiyu was *** fang indifferent to the quality of tea (25/294)

Saturday 7 September 1974
Best MS copy of 41 completed.

Friday 13 September 1974

Benjamin March: *Some Technical Terms of Chinese Painting* Waverley Press 1935.

Sunday 15 Sept. 1974
Chap. 40/483：「再找一找、只怕还有、要有，就都拿出来，送这刘亲家两匹，有雨过天青的，我做一个帐子挂上。……」

Chap. 42/510：「这是昨日你要的青纱、一匹、……」

Obviously Chap. 40 passage should keep the 抄本 text:

「再找一找、只怕还有青的、若有时都拿出来、送这刘亲家两匹、做一

个帐子我挂…」

(N) 兩匹 is too much for a dress & this
※ passage 不通. I think it should read:

「若有時，都拿去单，一匹送至刘
頡家，兩匹做一个帐子我挂…」

Tuesday 17 Sept. 1974
Letter to Dudy about 「養不去那阿物…」

Sat, 21 Sept 1974

42/508 「八月二十五日」. Evidently the date of chaps. 40-41.
A day seems to be lost in the text or has
昨兄 (人民 p.508 and 俞校 p.443) seems to be right. GJ and 大姐 are owning to have developed cold and fever within an hour or two. Yet as the text stands the 「大逛大觀園」 took place not 'yesterday' but on the same day. The difficulty can be overcome by supplying 次日 ... similar after the 「起說」 of the first text.
✗ No, this produces so many more problems. To have a lost day in which nothing happened is

even more puzzling than referring to today's events as 「昨兒」. Better just emend 「昨兒」 to 「今兒」

Sun. 22 Sept 1974

42/508 姑奶奶 is what 刘姥 calls 凤姐 (q. 6/75). 王夫人 is curiously omitted from the list of acknowledgements which includes, apparently, even the maids.

程乙:「大姐固为我找你去」
俞校:「大姐兒固為找我去」 (and 庚辰)
No. see 24/9/74   Both don't make sense.
Shouled b 「大姐固为我去……」

程乙 has 「八月二十五日病者東南方得之有縊死家親女鬼作祟又遇花神用五色紙錢……」
~~俞校 庚辰 omit~~
~~It's very hard to believe that Gao E put this in.~~

俞校、庚辰 omit 至有……祟又」
It's very hard to believe that Gao E put this in — which can only mean that he is using an older text. Presumably this means that 程甲 is based on a pre-1760 text.

Tues. 24 Sept 1974

Notional timetable of 8 ⼋ 25 日
(chaps. 40, 41, 42 init.)

    8 a.m. 寶玉 gets tasks. G.J, G.L (flowers)
9 - 9.30   Naiad's House (芳官 etc.)
    9.45 Lunch in Paulownia Room (Autumn Studio)
(N.B. Patience at home)
      Boating
10.45 - 11.15   Alpine Court
11.30 - 12.30   Farewell Church (chandelery)
12.30 - 1   walk. Callers
1.15 - 1.45   Hermitage
    G.J. returns to Smithstone Village
2 - 2.15   walk.
2.15 - 3.15   GL in Green Delights
3.30 Return to morning Cot etc. Return of
    Y-z folk to garden
4 p.m. Dinnertime
5 p.m. GL with XF

This leaves a good 2 hours of daylight for the events of the beginning of chap. 42. It therefore seems certain that 8月25日, 8月25日, 8月25日 is a mistake.

「大姐固然我找你去」

Sunday 29 Sept 1974

42/513 Impossible to make much sense of the passage describing GL's departure from 「又命了一个老婆子…」 onwards. (How many boys did extras, & in what order did they do it?) It's symptomatic of the general sloppiness that 板儿 appears to have disappeared altogether from the story!

Tuesday 1 October 1974

42/514
「这并不是书误了他、可惜他把书遭塌了」

This seems to be better than the 俞校 text:

「这是书误了他，可惜他也把书蹧蹋了」

Hō (uncharacteristically) seems to have followed the 程 text here — without saying so.

N.: Actually 俞校 can be made to yield quite good sense.

Sunday 6 Oct 1974

42/517 詹子亮 is 詹光 (elsewhere so called). Better stick to Zhan Guang.

Tuesday 8 Oct 1974

42/518 「就是配這些青綠顏色...」 probably does mean 'get them for you', 'supply you with', in spite of the subsequent order of 石青 and 石綠 + the student part to use 乳 to make them own colors. The subsequent statements represent a change of plan in the light of Xi-chun's admission that she has virtually no materials to start with.

× No. Why 「這些青綠」?

(and why only 「青綠」)

Friday 11 Oct 1974

Rough T/S of chap 42 completed.

Tuesday 15 Oct 1974

43/523 「帶了平兒、襲人、彩霞等」(and 麝月) seems to imply that 彩霞 is 王夫人's chief maid. Better stick to 彩雲 for chief maid and 彩霞 for 賈環's girl friend.

Thursday 31 October 1974
43/529/2-3 「就蓋起廟來供奉」 appears to be misplaced. The natural order would seem to be:

「這都是當日有錢的老公們 和那些有錢的愚婦們 聽見有個神、也不知那神是何人、因聽些野史小說 便信真了 就蓋起廟來供奉」

Wednesday 6 Nov 1974
Rough-typing of ch. 43 completed.

Thursday 7 Nov 1974
44/~~530~~534 穿堂, 穿廊, 雙院子的 台階 etc

Sat 9 Nov 1974
「新蓋的花廳」 must be in 賈母's 後院 (Non-existent in 周汝昌's plan of the house). See plan on next page for probable layout of 穿堂, 後院, etc.

Perhaps in 43/531 Silver is still where Xifeng counts it in 44/534

在賈母's 後院 see Y 3/20/11.

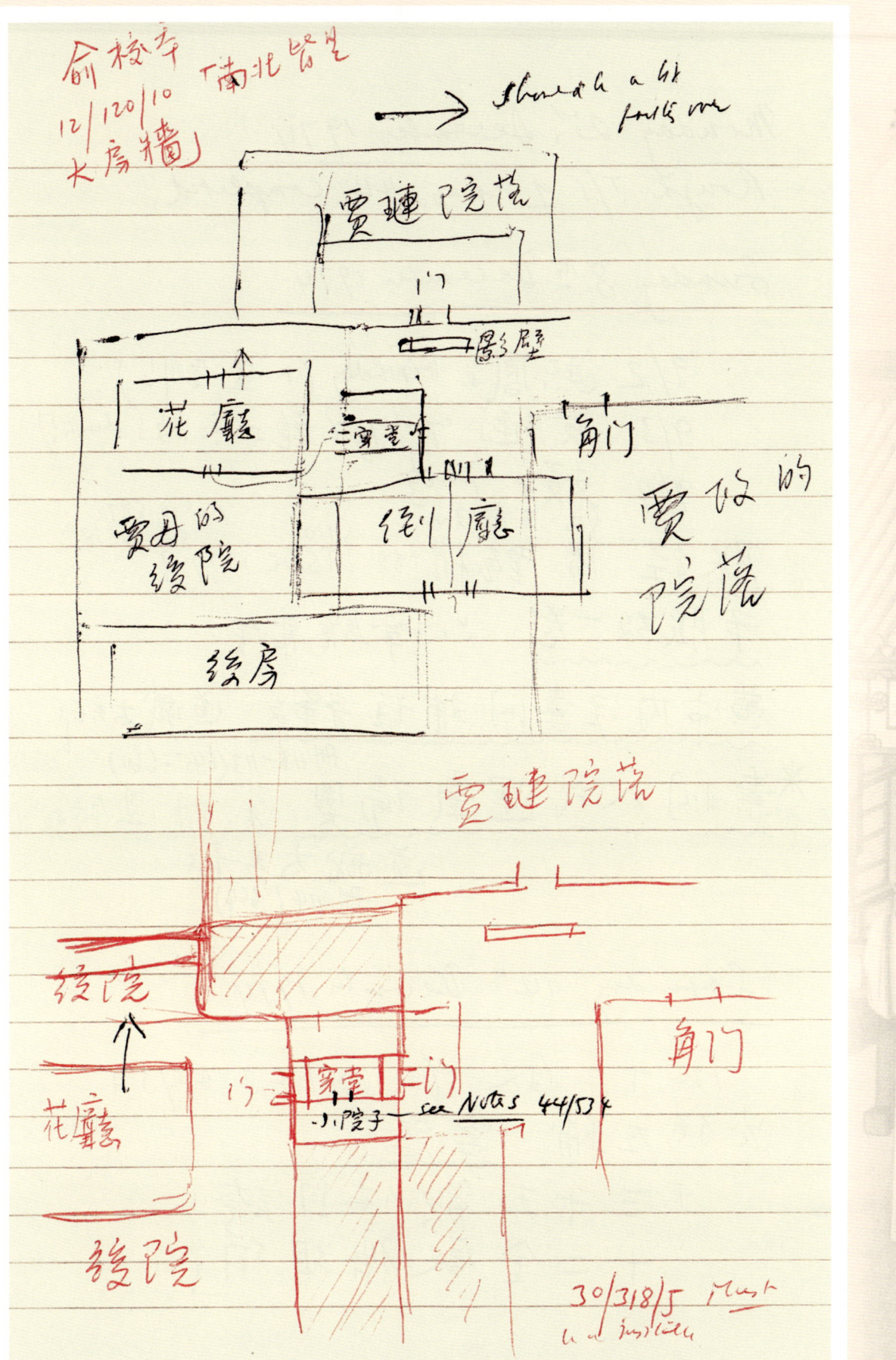

Monday 2nd December 1974

Rough T/S of chap. 44 completed.

Sunday 8th December 1974

9/2 熙鳳's birthday (+ 金釧's)
9/3 賈璉's apology (鮑二家的's death?)
9/14 賴's party
　　(晉·王叔和
脈經　晉·甄權 撰　TSDC 1377?　(9100　(also SBTK
　　　　　　　　　　　　　　　　　　　　　5工 BOX 38
乎脈訣一卷　二·譯館叢書

黃帝內經素問補註釋文　道藏太玄部
　　　　　　　　　　　　　冊 113-113 (645-660)
※素問入式運氣論奧　宋·劉溫舒撰
　　　　　　　道藏太玄部
　　　　　　　冊 114 (664).

Saturday 14th December 1974

Fn 十二釵 of. YFCJ 42/5A
長孫左輔　宮怨
「三千玉貌休自誇
　十二金釵獨相伺」

Wednesday 18 December 1974

45/546 「替寶玉打抱不平忿」 Doubt this is intentional. 李紈 (whose 風趣) doesn't normally go in for this sort of thing.

Friday 27 December 1974

45/548 「画的……那圖樣……」 No one has mentioned to her that there are wanted. How does she know? 「老太太」 is a mistake — possibly Gao E's. See 42/518/3 where it says 「你和太太要出來」

Tuesday 31st December 1974

Receive best T/S of chaps. 81, 82 from JM. Give JM copy of chaps 32–38.

Tuesday 7th January 1975

45/551/11 「然後他三人去了」 Our Fugitive author. 賴嬤嬤, 賴大家的, 周瑞家的, 張材家的 make 4. None of them has been off the stage up to this point.

Wednesday 8 Jan 1975

Mention of 史湘雲 in ch. 42 (broken chair p. 516)
Doesn't seem to be mentioned by name after that until p. 601
「誰知忠靖侯史鼐又遷委了外省大員，不日要帶家眷去上任。賈母因捨不得湘雲，便留下他了，接到家中，原要命鳳姐兒另設一處與他住。史湘雲執意不肯，只要和寶釵一處住，因此也就罷了。」

This seems to imply that Xiang-yun moved in from outside. She's not mentioned in Bao-chai's dormitory arrangements in chap. 45 (p. 552) so can surely not have been around all the time. She must be assumed to have gone left between end of 42 & beginning of 43 (an ill-fitting hinge)

Friday 10 January 1975

45/552/3–5 This paragraph doesn't seem to belong anywhere. It looks more like a note for a scenario.

553 「我長了今年十五歲」
Bao-chai was 'fifteen' in ch. 22.

Sunday 12 January 1975

45/554/9 「我明日家去和媽媽說了」
In fact she did it that same evening. There are

three possibilities: (1) Bao-chai said and meant 'tomorrow' but subsequently changed her mind; (2) Cao Xueqin wrote and meant 'tomorrow' and then forgot about it and failed to correct it. (3) 明日 means 'next time' or 'some time', in which case there is no problem.

Tuesday 14 January 1975
MS of 45 completed.

Wednesday 15 January 1975
Titles of chaps. 41–5.

Thursday 16 January 1975
Rough T/S of ch. 45 completed.

Friday 31st January 1975
41–45 best-typing & final processing completed.

Friday 14th February 1975
p. 569 「邢夫人 ... 方才明白」
The passage of time is not properly carried out. Probably just careless writing. 邢夫人 「晚上」 informs

贾赦 of her mission's failure. Then

(1) Jia Lian is called for and dismissed
(2) Jin Wen-xiang is called for, ~~and dismissed~~.
(3) " " " leaves after ƒ the time in which you could eat 5 or 6 (Got to significance of allus. to "five or six") meals.
(4) After further delay Jia Lian goes home.
(5) 至晚间 Xi-feng tells him what it's all about.

— Or is there some subtle difference of meaning between 晚上 and 晚间?

(Examination of the half-dozen examples in 索引 doesn't suggest that there is any substantial diff.)

Monday 17 February 1975
MS of ch. 46 completed.

Monday 10 March 1975
ch. 47 庚辰 has a curiously corrupted text for the passage describing the seating arrangements at the card game;

下一时死央来了，便坐在贾母下手，死央之下便是凤姐儿、红毹洗牌告么、五人起牌鬭了一回

(actually this is an omission of the 2 chars. 鸳鸯下)

Monday 10 March 1975

MS of ch. 47 completed.

Wednesday 12 March 1975

Rough T/S of chap. 47 completed.

Saturday 22 March 1975

John Minford brings translation of chs. 83, 84.

Monday 24 March 1975

48/592 「一日」 present certain difficulties. If it really means what it says & is not a mistake for 「次日」 (which Bao-chai's 「昨夜」 on p.594 might perhaps suggest.), it must bring a lapse of at least ~~November~~ a month.

    10月14日 Xue Pan leaves; Caltrop enters garden & has first poetry lesson from Dai-yu.

    ? 11月14日 '一日' Caltrop's first attempt at writing poetry.

    ? 11月15日 Caltrop's 3rd poem. Arrival of more cousins.

? 11月16日 ('明兒十六，咱們可該起社了')

49/605 ? 11月17日 ? ('昨兒的詩日己自己了')

49/606 ? 11月18日 ? ('到了次日清早')

50/624 ? 11月19日 ? ('次日雪晴')

51/637 ?　11月20日？（'至次日起筆'）

52/650 ?　11月21日？（'至次日'）

53/659 &　12月初（'當下已是臘月'）

53/664　12月29日（'已到了臘月二十九日了'）

53/668　正月11日

53/668　正月十五日
　　　This is still the date of the end of ch. 53
　　　　　　　　(i.e. end of vol. 2)

✗ See 1 May for second thoughts.

<u>Saturday 29 March 1975</u>

MS of chap 48 completed

<u>Monday 31 March 1975</u>

Rough T/S of ch. 48 completed.

<u>Thursday 3 April 1975</u>

Gao E's alteration of 保齡後史彝 to 忠靖後史彝 is an example of 'posthum' edd?

<u>Saturday 12 April 1975</u>

49/603 '此時...' This pass. is a hopeless mess. There are 11, not 13, people living in the Garden.

And even if you extend the sense of 'living' to mean 'spending a good deal of time there' (but that 'even that' is true of 凤姐), how can 凤姐 be included in the category of 'young people of chapters 15, 16 & 17'? And what is said about ages & dates/times of birth might be meaningful in speaking of 2 or 3 hundred people, but in the case of a bare dozen is plainly ridiculous.

Wednesday 16 April 1975

蘆雪奄   It's necessary to alter 'rainy night' in 18/365/5 to 'winter snow'

Saturday 19 April 1975

MS of chap. 49 completed.

Sunday 27 April 1975

50/613 Who takes over the writing when Li-wan goes? And when does Li-wan return? (She is back by 50/617「夠了 夠了」). Presumably it's Bao-chai, though this is not said, who takes over the job of copying. This is why she orders 寶琴 to 耶兒. She would hardly be willing to work 寶琴 copy, however much she may have considered herself in loco parentis. But if Bao-chai takes one from Li Wan, Tan-chun has evidently taken one by 617/7. (617/7 precludes TC being [crossed out] taken one when LW left, however).

Tuesday 22 April 1975

50/617 「沒有社社擔詩的…」
The three instances of BY's inadequacy were, in fact,
(1) Writing poorly because he lacked fixed rhymes (限韻)
(2) Failing to turn up (on Golden's birthday)
(3) Not being any good at limited rhymes.

韻險, whatever its 'real' meaning, must refer to (1).

Thursday 1 May 1975

Is March 24 calendar affected by
50/623 「這才是十月」? Certainly this is the text of 庚辰 etc.
It seems safest to stick to this and amend
? 一日 in 48/592 ?
NO Stick to Mar 24 plan: otherwise there's a lost month. Better amend 「這才是十月」
to 「這才是十一月…」

Friday 2 May 1975

The decision [?] is [saying God's?] continual ref. to the fact that "New Year is at hand". This would surely be impossible in mid-tenth month?

Monday 5 May 1975

All texts are hopeless over the 10A — 12A dates.

(1) ~~Dai-yu [?]~~ Caltrop goes to Dai-yu on ~~[?]~~ 10/14 to learn about poetry & reads 王維 all night.

(2) "(一日)" she comes back [?] to change her book. She writes 2 poems & composes a third in her sleep that night.

(3) Next day there are a lot of reunions. Jou-yu says 〈明兒十一〉

(4) A day or two later (?) Li Wan says 〈昨兒的 正日巳日过了〉

(5) ch. 50 (1.623) 賈母 says 〈這才是十日 呢 誒 場 雪〉

(6) Before and after the 詩社 meeting, we are told that New Year is "near".

In the long run it seems best to preserve the elevated haste of Caltrop's bid to learn poetry of a single view & allow 十一日 to [be?] unaccounted for. This is probably the way [Tsao-yin?] wrote it. The dates are almost an afterthought — perhaps actually inserted [?]. Certainly (一日) looks like an afterthought to 'make time'. (明兒十六) is merely a mistake.

※ The trouble with the above is that the indicating 'that it's is near the end of it you are so persistent (Aunts really their annual celebrations etc.). It's hard to see how you could possibly call mid-Kent month '年下')

Wednesday 7 May 1975

There are two places in chap. 48 when Caltrop stays out of doors carrying party, without apparently wearing any extra clothing other than what she wears indoors. This can't be later than 十月 (Nov.)

Why?

Final proposals:

(1) Alter 「一日」(48/592) to 「次日」(i.e. 10/15)
(2) Alter 「明兒十六」to 「今兒十六」(i.e. 10/16)
(3) Assume that 「明兒的乙日」(49/605) is 十一月初二. (Snow falling on 11/4)
(4) Alter 「這才是十月」(50/623) to 「這才是十一月」

Friday 9th May 1975

MS of chap 50 completed.

Sunday 11th May 1975

Rough TS of chap. 50 completed.

Sunday 25th May 1975

Best TS of chaps. 46–50 completed.

Wednesday 4 June 1975

51/632
「这三件…都是老太太的」……「太太就绞了这件…」

俞校：「这三件衣裳都是太太的」…「太太就只绞了这灰鼠的」

「太太」seems obviously the right text, especially after so much fuss has been made about the gift of clothes in an earlier chapter (

Sunday 8 June 1975

51/634 「我这外边没个人」 「往外边睡去」
i.e. 'outside the 煖阁' (which 宝玉 sleeps inside of). Not 'in the outside room'. No one is sleeping in the outside room. They are all in the same room.

635: 「向燈壺中倒了半碗茶」
i.e. 'bent over to the pot & poured out a cup of tea'

Monday 9 June 1975

51/634 「一更」(庚辰本「二更」) is very useful to be right. 「初更」 is wrong for 'first watch'.

Re 「貂頷」of CB (SU 'MARTEN'): "The Yellow-throated marten (Martes flavigula) ranges from India & China to Java; it is light brown on the shoulders, becoming blackish on the rump & has on nape chest."

Wednesday 18 June 1975

MS of ch. 51 completed.

Friday 20 June 1975

Rough T/S of ch. 51 completed.
Letter from J. Needham & Lu Gwei-Djen re 肝火 etc.

Tuesday 24 June 1975

52/650/5 「才命秋故等出采」
Ⓨ has (566/6) 「才命秋故檀雲等出采」
(See Notebook Tuesday 14 Dec. 1971)
210 (p.183, note 11) says 檀雲 is mentioned altogether 5 times: ch. 23, 24, 34, 52, 78.
(1) 夏夜即事: 「室霭檀雲品御香」
(this is not a book)

(2) 24/247/1 「秋紋碧痕兩個去舀水、檀雲因他母親的生日接了回去……」

(3) 34/353/11 「襲人…便悄悄的告訴晴雯、麝月、檀雲、秋紋等說…」

(4) 52/566/6 「才命秋紋檀雲等進來」

(5) 78/900/8 「鏡分鸞別、愁開麝月之奩、梳化龍飛、哀折檀雲之齒」

———————

程本：

(2) 「…檀雲又因他母親的生日…」

(3) 「…晴雯、麝月、秋紋等說」

(4) 「才命秋紋等進來」

(5) 「哀折檀雲之齒」

Wednesday 9th July 1975

52/649 「此夕寶玉便不命……」 It seems rather probable that Cao had forgotten that this was the second night of 晴雯's illness. It seems unlikely* that she would have been tucked out on p. 645 on the first night. But better translate what we've got.

* —~~[crossed out]~~ 650 shows the fact 'destroying the evidence', so this is evidently a new argument.

Wed. 9 July 1975 cont'd.

Re 檀雲: perhaps this was a substitute for 綺霞 which didn't get consistently applied (the mysterious 'fifth girl' < Aroma, Skybright, Musk, Ripple, ~~[illegible]~~ Emerald, X}
On the other hand perhaps there shd. always be Aroma + 4 & the fourth should always be 碧痕.

Ch. 24 is really crucial (T 483)
At this stage of the rône it looks as if the situation is

1. 襲人 (Aroma)
2. 麝月 (Musk)
3. 秋紋 (Ripple)
4. 碧痕 (Emerald)
5. { 晴雯 ?
    綺霞 ?
    檀雲 ? }

晴雯's subsequent development as a 'chowetei' is prefigured in Ch. 20 (T. 402, 405), where, ~~evidently~~ however, 綺霞 rather than 晴雯 appears:
404: (襲人), 晴雯, 綺霞, 秋紋, ~~檀雲~~ 碧痕.
                                        麝月

Sunday 13 July 1975
52/654「明兒是他的日子」. The actual birthday. (Today) being merely the first day of a two-day birthday

celebration (cf. arrangements for 賈敬's birthday in chap. 10 (, T/223). Probably this is an oversight of the author's at this point to explain why the clock went he was next day. Since there is nothing to indicate it in the two earlier refs. in this chap. to the birthday (p.646, p.649). Any patching up explaining had better be done here.

Tuesday 15 July 1975
MS of chap. 52 completed.

Sunday 20 July 1975
Rough TS of chap 52 completed

Monday 21 July 1975
⊛ 53/661
「御田胭脂米」 No need to follow 彧 in preferring「玉田」. It is almost certain 御稻米 that's being referred to here. It is, in fact, somewhat pinkish in colour. This is what Cotton-rice is given in Chap. 42 (see 42/445).

Tuesday 22 July 1975
宝琴's presence in the Jia family temple, at first sight baffling, is presumably to be explained by the fact that she has been 'adopted'.
(53/664)

Friday 25 July 1975

53/659 「王子騰陞了九省都檢點」
cf. 4/48:「又听母舅王子騰陞了九省統制，
奉旨出都查边」

Looks like the same appointment duplicated by mistake — hence problem of absent 王子騰 who appears to be present.

20 pennyweights = 1 oz   一兩 { 10 錢
                                { 100 分
  1 錢 = 2 pennyweights
  5 分 = 1 pennyweight.

Monday 4 August 1975

53/658 「书去開了藥方進來」

Looks as if something may be wrong here. Doctors don't go out with a prescription & then bring it in. Either they go out with you, sit down with you, write their prescription & hand it to you (chaps. 10 ~~...~~ + 42) or else they are shown out, write a prescription outside which is brought back to you by the servant, & close.

It should probably read

「開了藥方(...) 藥方進來, 寶玉...」

  (...) would be something like ~~...~~ 「老嬤 &
栗將」   Haplography of 藥方 wd. explain this.

Wednesday 13 August 1975

53/664 「從大门、儀门、大廳、燈阁、内廳,

内仪门
「内三门/开内垂门直到正堂」
① and 抄本 hen
「从大门、仪门、大厅、煖阁、内厅、内三门、内仪门、塞门直到正堂」

乾抄 has a「花」inserted after the「垂」. Obvious something is wrong with this text. A likeliest explanation is that 「内仪门并垂花门」 is an incorporated gloss on the earlier unusual 「内三门」

② shared read
「从大门、仪门、大厅、煖阁、内厅、内三门直到正堂」
   No. Above supposes 仪门 to mean 垂门, but this can't be right. What is being described is a single avenue of lights all the way to the 正堂.

Second thoughts

仪门 is definitely a gate inside the main gate, cf. 3/30.「入一黑漆大门内,至仪门前方下了车」 and note (31/(2)) ad loc. Also (16.)「进入三层仪门 果见正房…」
And 4/52/654:「嫂子必定是在老太、太跟前当些体差使,成年家只在三门外头混…」
[strikethrough]
Possibly the 仪门 & 内仪门 does (in this

cooking) mean 旁門, and 內儀門 並 內垂花門
are infact a gloss on 三門.
正堂 is 内, like the
榮僖堂 of the
榮國府.

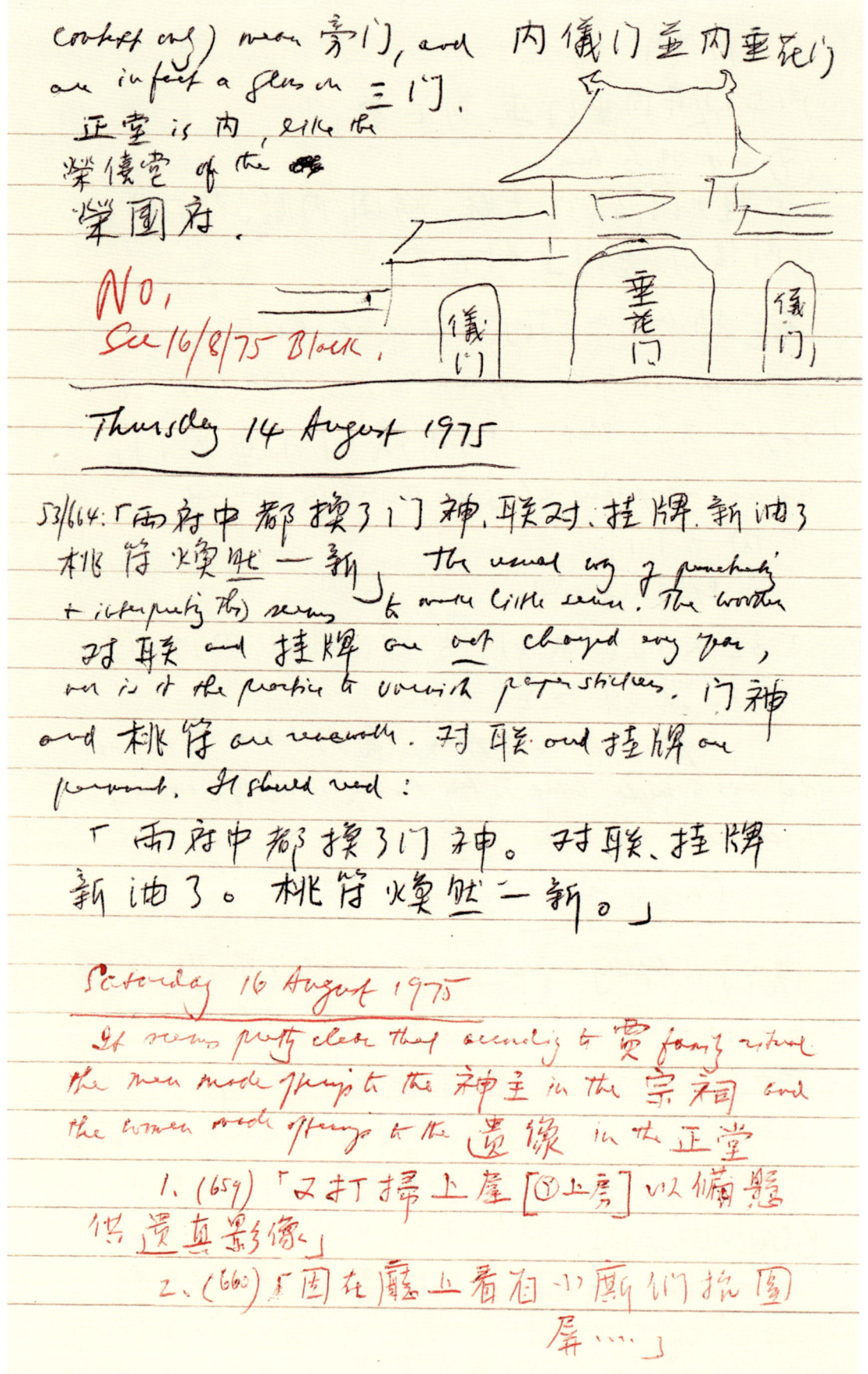

NO,
See 16/8/75 Block.

___

Thursday 14 August 1975

53/664: 「兩府中都換了門神、聯對、挂牌、新油了桃符煥然一新」 The usual way of punctuating + interpreting this seems to make little sense. The wooden 對聯 and 挂牌 are not changed every year, nor is it the practice to varnish paper stickers. 門神 and 桃符 are renewable. 對聯 and 挂牌 are permanent. It should read:

「兩府中都換了門神。對聯、挂牌新油了。桃符煥然一新。」

Saturday 16 August 1975
It seems pretty clear that according to 賈 family ritual the men made offerings to the 神主 in the 宗祠 and the women made offerings to the 遺像 in the 正堂

1. (659)「又打掃上屋[①上房] 以備懸供遺真影像」
2. (660)「因在廳上看着小厮們抬圍屏……」

Mr. François CHENG 程紀賢
17, rue A. Daudet 75014-Paris
tel. 535 36-70

3. (663)「賈珍看着收拾完備供器……令人
在廳柱下石磯上太陽中鋪了一个……褥子」

4. (664)「寧國府從大門……直到正堂一路大
門開……」

5. (665)「眾人圍隨賈母[母]至正堂上.
影前錦帳高挂、……上面正居中懸着榮
寧二祖遺像……」

For 內儀門 etc. (13/8/75) p. 665
「賈荇賈芷等從內儀門挨次站列,
直到正堂廊下」

庚辰 is different again from 程+戚
「內儀門, 內塞……」

Their probably the character between 「內儀門」
and 「直到」 are an incorporated gloss
(?垂花門) on 內儀門.

Missing parts of 乾隆拓本
supplied by copyist from printed
edition:

10/4 — 11/2

20/5 — 21/2

24 last page

40/6 — 51/4

60/5 — 61/5

71/1

80 last page

100/4-5

㉗	48
㉘	49
㉙	50
㉚	51
㉛	52
㉜	53
㉝	
㉞	
㉟	
㊱ (29/1/74)	
㊲	
㊳	
㊴	
½ ㊵ (Best Typeset 8/74)	
㊶	
㊷	
㊸	
⅔ 44	
45	
46	
47	

PART III

August 1975

紅樓夢

August 1975 –

Monday 18th August 1975

53/665: 「換次侍至階下賈敬手中」
胡藏程乙本「‥‥‥‥墀下‥‥‥‥」
Y and 庚辰 have「階上」 乾拷 has「下」
Must be wrong. 賈敬 can't be at one and the same time
「廊下」 and 「階下」

53/666 「左昭右穆、男東女西」
This seems an impossibility in terms of what is said above. NO. See diagram for explanation.

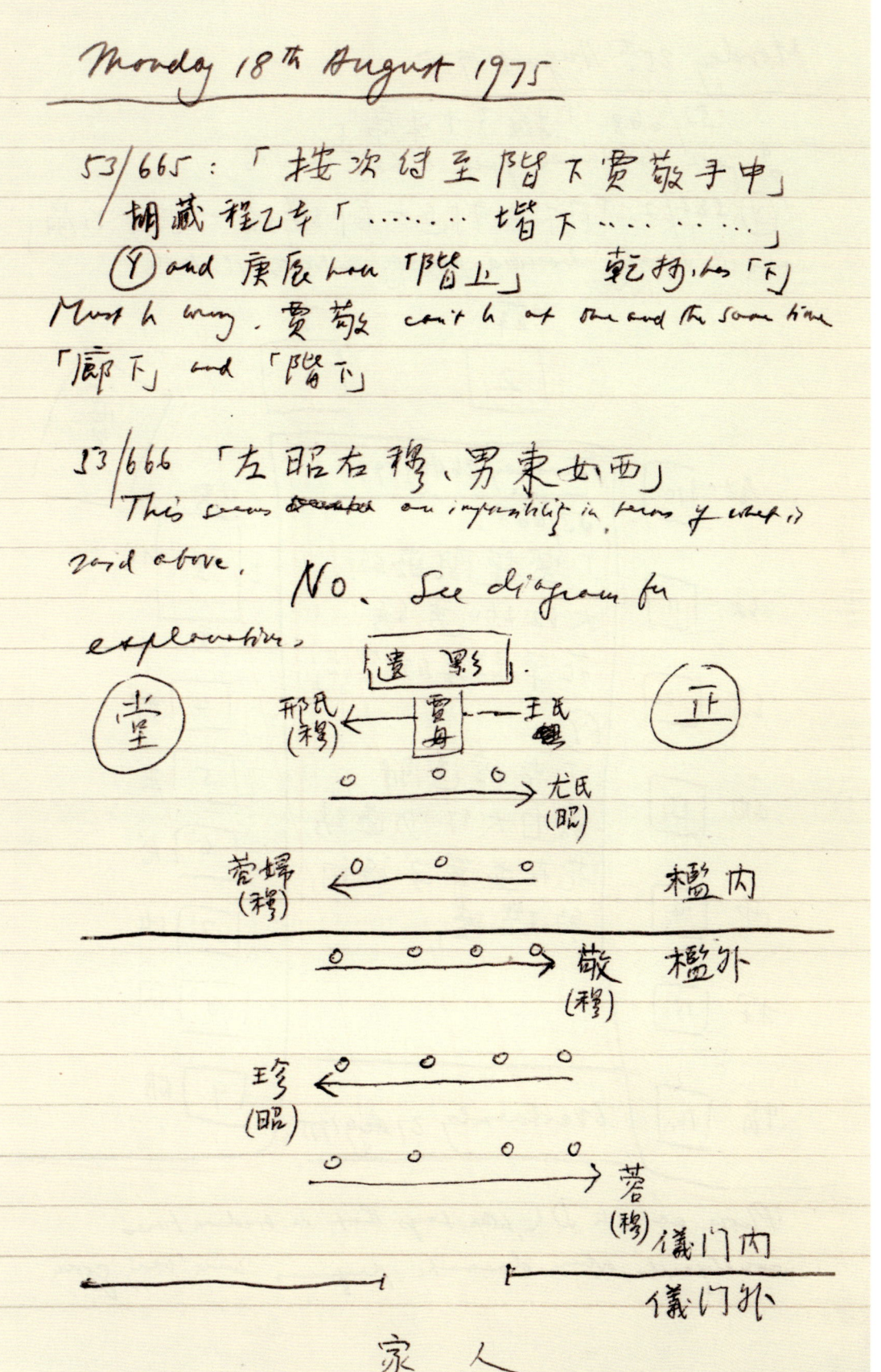

家 人

Monday 25th August 1975

53/668 「攏了十來席」
In fact there would appear to have been 16.
Ⓨ 582/2: 「目下只剩這一副璎珞 一共十六扇」
and the seating described probably indicates 16 tables:

```
            薛            李
            ┌──┐      ┌──┐
            │ 2│      │ 1│                ┌──┐
            └──┘      └──┘               /   │
                                        /  賈 │
                                       └────┘

 敘 ┌──┐                                琴
    │10│                                ┌──┐
    └──┘    Tuesday 26 Aug 1975      王 │ 3│ 代
            53/668:                     └──┘
 玫 ┌──┐    「紫檀雕嵌的                    雲
    │11│     大紅紗透繡
    └──┘     花草詩字的瓔珞」          ┌──┐
                                      │ 4│ 邢
 綺 ┌──┐    Ⓨ:                        └──┘
    │12│    「紫檀透雕
    └──┘     嵌著大紅紗透繡           ┌──┐
             花卉並草字詩詞            │ 5│ 王
 岫 ┌──┐     的瓔珞」                  └──┘
    │13│
    └──┘                              ┌──┐
                                      │ 6│ 尤
 西 ┌──┐                               └──┘
    │14│
    └──┘                              ┌──┐
                                      │ 7│ 納
 探 ┌──┐                               └──┘
    │15│
    └──┘                              ┌──┐
                                      │ 8│ 凤
 惜 ┌──┐                               └──┘
    │16│    Wednesday 27 Aug 1975
    └──┘                              ┌──┐
                                      │ 9│ 胡
                                      └──┘
```

Phone call to DC, who says that in modern times
courtyards above dramatic performances were being given

were inwardly partied over. Perhaps 「兩邊遊廊罩棚」 means not 'the roofs of the 遊廊' but 'the 遊廊 and the 罩棚' and 罩棚 means not 'roof' but 'awning'.

53/669 「乃望鑒珐瑯法信」
「信」 in the senses given by the dics. is a hapax legomenon. Perhaps it doesn't really mean that at all but either means in it an error for 像.
 The fact that Ⓨ has two 信's in fairly close proximity + apparently 5 its ceff'. seems to it highly suspicious.

~~Thursday~~ Friday 29 August 1975
53/670: 「賈蘭之母婁氏帶了賈蘭來」
Ⓨ has 「菌」 for 「蘭」 here. (Actually 蘭 doesn't exist in Ⓨ: the 'Jia Lan' in ch. 9 is 賈菌。) This is a better reading for the translation, as e.g. name Jia Lan involves awkward explanations.

Sunday 30 August 1975
MS of chap. 53 completed.

Thursday 4 Sept. 1975
Rough T/S of ch. 53 completed.

Thursday 11th September 1975

Best-typing of chs. 51-3 completed.
~~and further~~

Monday 29th September 1975

Vol. 2 Copies 1 and 2 sent in two parcels, Copy 1 to B Radice; Copy 2 to Will Sulkin.

Saturday 14th February 1976

63/807「日边红杏倚云栽」 This has already appeared in 40/493. TS must be revised to make fit this second context. Perhaps:
~~'Apricot makes the sun's ~~ petalled floor'~~
'Apricot trees above the sun's red-petalled floor'

Monday 16 Feb. 1976

63/807 MSS give the whole of 賞花時; 樵歌 gives only the first 2 lines. This seems to justify translating in its final body, down to 天涯. The second half is almost incomprehensible without the intervening dialogue.

Thursday 25 March 1976

芙蓉女兒誄

In the 歌 ll. 5 and 6 don't rhyme and are tough intelligible:
「駕鷖鷟以方比征兮 望舒月以離耶
聽車軌而伊軋兮 御鸞鷖以征耶」

乾抄 has 「臨」 for 「離」 here.
LS has 「前望舒便先驅兮 後飛廉使奔屬」
「前望舒以臨耶」 is perhaps the likeliest emendation.
The trouble is this means rhyg. iam and iang
Perhaps 「前望舒以駛耶」 is the answer.

Saturday 3 April 1976

79/1026 (Dai-yu quoting)
「紅綃帳裏，公子情深
　黃土隴中，女兒命薄」
This is 乾抄 改文. All other texts make her misquote these two lines:
「紅綃帳裏，公子多情，
　黃土隴中，女兒薄命」
Whether or not the misquotation is intentional, 多情
「薄命」 is retained in the subsequent 'corrections' in all texts.

「小姐」 「丫鬟」 better say 'miss' and 'maid'
'mistress' would have more 「份」 than 'young master'
　　　　　　　　　　　　　　　　(公子)

Monday 12 April 1976
Time-table for 「晴雯嚴命...」etc.
(1) 74/953 王夫人 summons 晴雯 and threatens her with dismissal.
(2) 74/954-5 晴雯's box.
(3) 15日「晴雯病勢甚重」
(4) 16日 王夫人 说:「快办了这一件 (司棋), 再办那一家的那些妖精」
(5) (16日) Shortly after 司棋's visit, 王夫人 arrives at 怡紅院 and has 晴雯, 蕙香 and 芳官 dismissed.
(6) 宝玉 goes with 婆子 to see 晴雯
(7) Next day (17日) Bao-yu summoned first thing to go to 上房 to see F+Maid to taken out 贾政 (有人请老爷赏桂菊) to make poems. (77/1005. Return 78/1012)
(8) The maid tells him on his return the story of 晴雯's appointment 「我今在未正二刻 (2:30) 就上任去了, 宝玉 须待未正三刻 (2:45) 才到家, 不能见面...」
(9) 宝玉「一人出园」goes to 前次看望之處... 竟为停柩之所. No one there, so he has to go back home.
(10) 老爷回家来了找你: 蜷螭将军诔

Sunday 2 May 1976
54/674「那贾琮弟兄...」So also 乾抄, but all 脂 texts have「贾環」. 贾琮, 贾赦's

son by a concubine, is presumably senior to 賈環, 賈政's son by a concubine, so 「賈琮」 is more 'correct'. This must be a correction made by 脂硯 or one of the other early 'editors'.

54/674 「八義中觀燈八齣」 and 54/682 「八齣八義」: Probably the first 8 齣 of 八義記 were known collectively as 「觀燈」.

Note that 八齣 「宣子勸農」 ends with very 'auspicious' words: 「須要殷勤教子孫, 莫嫌農事懶春耕, 非徒獨要倉廩熟, 還願诗州盡太平」. This would make a good ending for a festive performance.

675: 「你必想的周到」
Other texts, including 乾抄: 「比我想的週到」

675 「前駕碧的娘必死了」 Nothing about this elsewhere.

Wednesday 19 May 1976
54/682: 「命人將賈琮賈璜等自送回家去」
So all texts (except that 乾抄 appears to have 璜 for 璜 — no doubt a miscopying — and 等 crossed out after it). But 賈璜 wasn't in fact there (see 53/669 and 670 ¾ and ⓨ 582 and 583). Almost certainly this is a mistake for 環. 賈菌 is accounted for. 芹, 芸, 蔷, 菱 are adults able to look after themselves but too junior to

without an escort. This leaves only 環 and 玉釧, both of whom are 'in statu pupillari' and therefore have to be taken care of ~~because~~ before 珍 and 璉 can go off for a night on the town together.

Thursday 20th May 1976

54/682 「这些姑娘们比咱们家的姑娘…」
Who does she mean? If it is taken to include 宝釵 and 代玉, it seems a silly remark to make to actresses who ~~have been performing for 宝釵 and~~ arrived in the household even later than 宝釵 and 代玉; if not, who is there present but 宝琴 to whom this can refer?

ib. 「只用簫和笙笛, 餘者一概不用」
㊅ 「只提琴合簫管, 笙笛一概不用」(54/592/3)
乾抄原文:「只須用簫管笙笛一概不用」
—— 改: 「as 程」

Actually 庚辰 has a quite different text:
(1277) 「只提琴至管簫合笙笛一概不用」
This has been corrected to
「只要提琴至於管簫合笙笛一概不用」

Actually 乾原, is the only text that makes sense in the light of what 薛姨媽 says a few lines later.

On the other hand 庚辰 is corrected to read 「從沒見[有]用簫管的」. Perhaps the point about 楚江情 is that 'they don't have any wood-wind in the orchestra' because the 小生 is playing a 簫 in the stage.

Fn 簫管 as normal in 崑腔 cf. 余懷寄暢園聞歌記 (ap. 中國戲曲史(二) p.273) 「...至今雲仍不絕於梁懸矣. 合曲必用簫管......」

孟 Lucy says (p.274) 「北曲用絃, 南曲用管, 至崑腔, 則幾乎集管絃乐之大成」

南詞叙錄 says: 「今崑山以笛管笙琵按節而唱南曲者... 殊為可听」

顧曲雜言: 「今吳下皆以三絃合南曲而以簫管吹之」

客座贅語: 「...今則吳人益之拍板, 以洞簫月琴...」

<u>Wednesday 26 May 1976</u>

54 The order in the inner room must be

This can be worked out from what is said at the end of chpt 5 about Bk friendships:

賈母 hugs

	李	薛		代玉, 王夫人
	釵		湘	hugs 寶玉 and
		XF is omitted (all texts)	費	薛姨娘 greets, hug 湘雲. If
		The west side ends 尤/蘅/鳳	代	they are all sitting
		But perhaps the best solution is	琴	along together,
		釵/蘅/尤/鳳	那	this is only possible
			玉	if they are sitting in
			王	that order.

Since later 尤 joining attaches to 鳳.

Saturday 29 May 1976

Rough T/S of chap. 54 completed.

Monday 31 May 1976

End of 54 and beginning of 55: 程本 and 桉本 quite different. 乾原本 is unique.* 55 began

「話說剛將年事忙過鳳姐便小月了」

55 chiang shows 高鶚's insertion which prepares for this.

 Note in that 程本 and 乾改 are different in one particular at end of 54:

乾改：「親友來請赴席的」
程本：「親友來請，或來赴席的」

*有正大字本 is the same as 乾原文.

Tuesday 1 June 1976

55/692 巡海夜叉、鎮山太歲
Sound more like 水滸 than 封神.
 e.g. 阮小二 was '立地太歲'

Wednesday 2 June 1976

54 on tension between the generations (symbolized by tension between 丫頭, 孩子 on one hand + 媳婦, 奶奶 a tkdg greeding guns. 媳婦 begin to range as identifiable

people. Important to use everything which contributes to defining their statuses & pennings. For similar statues see 55/697「runs高低不知道」. For this reason perhaps the 扬舟 version of 54 and which refers to the reception of gown should be included.

高额 is surely missing an agreement in ending 54 with 凤姐's miscarriage. Yet if 54 ends with that, 55 must begin with that, which means that the 庚辰 opening of 55 with ref to visit of 太妃 is impossible. However, 58「谁知那表的那经是太妃已薨」has no reference if that is taken out. Possibly best solution is to put the 太妃 bit at the end of 54 chg with the 媳妇 parties and have the 小产 after that, at the very end.　　See Wu for 太妃 insertion.

Friday 4 June 1976

红楼梦人名辞典 has got 吴新登媳 and 吴大娘 as two people, but cf. ⓨ56/613「吴大娘和单大娘」with ⓨ54/596「二十一日便是单大良家、二十二日便是吴新登家」

Prob.「单大良家」shd be「单大娘家」
乾隆 looks as if it was「单大良」without the「家」
This is also the 庚辰 text. Better call her 'Widow Shan'

Sunday 6 June 1976

Ch. 55　程:(i) 便小月了不能理事
　　　　　(ii) 直孙三月间才渐上的.....

(Y) (i) 便小月了在家一月不能理事
    (ii) 調養到八九月間才漸～好…

乾原 is the same.
    In fact the narration in subsequent refs. makes
it quite clear that 凤姐 was still little if any better 用
了七月, so「三閒」is showing an erroneous 'correction'.
    cf. :—
(1) 61/776/28 李紈 and 探春 still managing & 凤姐
    still convalescent.
    ——/14「奶奶才進了藥歇下」
(2) 61/780 凤姐 has to be seen about the matter in bed.
(3) 62/783「回了李紈探春」. They are still in charge.
(4) 63/815/6「天氣炎熱」…「凤姐出不來」
(5) 64/820 Hot weather.   ⎫ late
    64/822「怪熱的」…「夏天有冰了」⎬ summer
         …「離暑月不敢用冰」   ⎭ early autumn.
    1823/11   「七月」

(6) 824「孫凤姐虛弱，又有許多遊子們回了
    畢…凤姐倚着門和平兒說話」
    …「又見姐～這兩日沒往那邊裏去，不知身上
    可大愈了…」
    「…雖說有三姑娘帮着辦理，也只好
    強扎掙着」
    i.e. she is not really better, but struggling to do what she
    can.   There seems to be nothing wrong until 八九月間

Tuesday 8 June 1976

園初「感序」章 has「單大良家」

Wednesday 9 June 1976

55/691「時屆李春」
  MSS「孟春」. Note that 乾抄, has
「孟春」 uncorrected.

Friday 11 June 1976

(1) 55/691 we are told that LW & TC spend from 6-12 at the office, returning 'about noon after taking their lunch'

(2) 55/692 WXD's wife comes to report Seming 'just as they are taking their tea' after completing their morning toilet + sending off Laoye Wang.

(3) 55/697 After the row with WXD's wife — which can't conceivably have lasted more than about 1½ hrs — they have their lunch (!)

Of course, lunch was prob. taken long before 12. It doesn't mean 'they left at 12, after finishing their lunch', but 'they left at 12, having taken their lunch at the office'.

cf T 14/273: 'At half past six I shall come over to hear the roll-call. At ten o'clock I take my lunch I should see people ... up to but not after eleven o'clock.'

For discussion of lunchy lunch times see 'Wed 17 Feb. 1971'
This has to be fudged over somehow in translation.

Friday 25 June 1976

Ch. 55/699 「那時趙姨娘已去」 A typical weakness in 曹's narration. One suspects that there was an earlier version in which he simply forgot about 趙 & this sentence was added later to account for her absence. But really, when could she have gone? And how? (By a window?)

Tuesday 29 June 1976
MS of ch. 55 completed.

Wed. 30 June 1976
Rough T/S of ch. 55.

Monday 5th July 1976

56/711/6 「我們太太多病 家務也忙…」
So 程(胡)本.
俞校「我們奶奶又多病多痛家務也忙」
乾抄原「你奶奶又多病多灾. 家務也忙」
改之「你奶奶又多病、家務也忙」
乾抄 is obviously the right reading.
Apparently 有正 had 「你們奶奶」 but 俞 (3/397)
(616/3行) has followed 康 etc. in printing 我們(!). ¥

圓初本:「你們奶奶又多病多灾」

(D746)   (姨媽)

KHHT = 大清會典
(康熙 ed.)

Tuesday 6 July 1976
 Schuyler Cammann
China's Dragon Robes Ashm. FE   CWt: Cam.
    4-clawed dragon = mang
  p. 115 'mang satins'
   p. 116 'Kiangning factory'
Satins (woven with three-cloud or five-cloud dragons)
 117 'bolts of satin + gauze for the Imp. dragon robes, & for all
other kinds of robes woven w. 4 or 8 five-cloud dragon medallions,
were counted to be small two (Ch.) ft broad & circa 20 or 40 ft in
length.'
 117 'The early Ch'ing sumptuary laws of 1652 mention
several kinds of satin to be used for robes. The list includes
3 forms of dragon satins: 3-cloud 龍緞, 5-cloud
龍緞, and 蟒緞; "decorated satin", chuang
tuan, either embroidered or having ornaments of gold and
colored silks sewn to it; "Japanese satin", Wo tuan,
which apparently did not actually come from Japan since in
1651 600 bolts of it were ordered from the Kiangning factories;
gold-brocaded satin, chin-hua tuan, having flowers or
other patterns worked in gold; & satin damask, hua-tu (花素)
tuan, self-figured, with clouds or other patterns.
 ... Magnif. ex. of chuang tuan in ROM

CWt:Pri <u>Chinese Textiles</u> by Alan Priest +
         Pauline Simmons   NY 1934
         (Small. Lots of good photos, line shots or cords)

CWt:Vui <u>Symbolism of Ch. Imp. Robe Rohs</u>
         Bernard Vuilleumier. Tournai of Bruges
         (many photos   Calls 刻絲 'silk gobelin')
         (There is a whole essay on 刻絲)
         The V. Collection is in Lausanne.

CWtC:New <u>Costumes from the Forbidden City</u> Alan Priest
                            NY 1945, Arno Press 1974
         Pictures. Not much info.

~~Thursday~~
<u>~~Wednesday~~ 8 July 1976</u>

程高	⟨命⟩國庚	乾扮
上用的粧緞	上用的粧緞	上用的粧緞
蟒緞 12	蟒緞 12	蟒緞 12
[上用雜色緞 12]	上用雜色緞紗 12	上用各色寧綢 12
上用各色紗 12	上用宮綢 12	上用宮綢 12
上用宮綢 12	宮用各色緞紗	上用緞 12
宮用各色緞紗	紬綾 12	上用紗 12
綢綾 24		上用各色綢綾 40
		These two are
		也 500

(50/712)

For the use of 档案史料 p.166
No.153 「…上用满地风云龙缎一疋
　　　　大立蟒缎 69疋
　　　　蟒缎 11疋
　　　　片金 14疋
　　　　妆缎 140疋
　　　　倭缎 20疋
　　　　……
　　　　宫绸 17疋
　　　　宁绸 68疋
　　　　又绸一疋 etc.

p.174 : No.159　　上用缎 28疋
　　　　　　　　　宫绸 30疋

Friday 9th July 1976

戚本	「皆不介意 56/715「独宝玉望个迂闷呆 公子的心性，自为是那四人 承悦贾母之词 忙至园中去看 湘云病去 湘云说他…」
上等的妆缎	
蟒缎 12	
上用元色宁绸 12	
上用宫绸 12	
上用缎 12	
上用纱 12	
上用元色纳纱 40	
xxxxxxx	

Must be something badly wrong with the text here.

庚辰本「後至蘅燕(芜)苑看湘云病去，
　　(改)　将这话告诉湘云说…」
(The person who made this correction omitted a short ditto marks of 湘云 which one needed in order to make sense).

Probably 「皆不介意」 is out of place
It should come after 「承悦贾母之词」
PTO

Note that the difficult passage is one in which the text suddenly changes into v. formal 文言:

「眾人都為天下之大，世宦之多，同兒女甚多；祖母溺愛孫者必古今所有常事耳。不足〔什麼〕罕事故皆不介意」他寶玉是個迂闊就公子的性情自然是那夕人承悅賈母之詞」

「眾人」...「不介意」is 批文.

Sunday 11 July 1975

56/704 「別叫別人的奶媽子的弟兄之子買」
Later 曹雪芹 says: 「要是... 使了奶媽子們，他們又就不敢說閒話了」
庚辰 says: 「另叫別人的奶媽子的或是弟兄哥的之子買了來」
乾隆 says: 「另叫別人的奶媽的或是兄弟哥的之子買了來」

「別人的奶媽」must be wrong. The punctuation

(1) 奶媽子的之子或是別人的兄弟哥哥

(2) 別人的 ── 奶媽子的，或是(奶媽子的) 兄弟哥的 ──
　　　　　　　　　　　　　兒子

56/704 「這有個原故...」
The repetition here looks as if it might have

been caused by incorporating both an original version and a correction of the text.

(1)「每月每處買辦買了令女人們分送我們收管」

(2)「外頭買辦總領了去，按月使奴按房分給我們」

Sunday 1 August 1976
Rough T/S of Chapter 56 completed.

Monday 2 Aug. 1976
57/719/3 「宝玉不信」
脂庚辰 and 乾抄「宝玉方信」obviously the correct text.
57/720 「頓覺一時恍惚…etc」 The 'corrected' text is inferior. 721/2 shows that Bao-yu had moved quite a long way from the place where he encountered Nightingale.

Thursday 5 August 1976
57/723/8 「拳心大變，更不免也有了他」
「更」in all 程本 and also in 乾抄, but 也 庚辰 ~~比戚乾上有王便~~ has 「便」
Acc. 俞校 408 (626/2) 戚序本 had「更」

乾原「舉止大便更…」
改文「舉止大變更…」

Tuesday 28 September 1976

57/722/14-15 「皆不知覺」 人民 and 俞 both put a semi-colon after this: he wasn't conscious that his eyes had a glassy stare or that he was drinking. This seems pretty silly. Much better a colon or dash — it was his zombie-like movements that he wasn't conscious of.

Tuesday 19 October 1976
57/729 邢忠 Elsewhere 邢德全

Friday 29 October 1976
MS of chap. 57 completed.

Sunday 31st October 1976
TS of chap 57 completed.

~~Wednesday~~ Tuesday 2nd November 1976
58/737 賈母 婆媳姪孫
康辰：入「邢王尤許」
威序：入「邢无人尤氏」
乾初：入「邢王尤許」 (uncorr.)

738 sq. 「十二个女孩子」 One presently learns that they were only eleven — 药官 had died, though we are never told when, & there is no mention of a replacement to make up the official number. This shed is [versions?] of the 「将表生子五人」 since only 3 (Charmante, Trésor & Topaze; 蕊官, 宝官 & 玉官) are unplaced.

Wednesday 3rd November 1976
Tōhō catalogue, curiously, gives as one title for 荷花 (dozens or other flowers): 清 楊鐘宝 筑荷譜

Friday 12th
~~Saturday 13~~ Nov. 1976
Write to DL re 踢踏.

Tuesday 16 Nov 1976
Something badly wrong with ch. 58. Apart from the fact that the 'twelve actresses' are in fact eleven, that only three, not 'four or five' elect to go home, and that the rest do not all go 'in the Garden' (two of them, 文官 & 茄官, go to apartments outside), there is a careful over-specification of the para. beginning 「一日乃贾朝中大祭」. Is this the same day as 「清明之日」? This passage 「一日 … 豆說 … 可巧 … 」 is so clumsily written that it is quite impossible to say. As the chapter is so short, it seems possible that a whole episode is lost at the end of the 「一日…」 para (before 「外面說了…」 of course).

Friday 19th November 1976

58/740/3 「往鐵檻寺祭柩燒紙」
So also 庚辰本
有己 and 乾抄本 本 both have
T 往鐵檻寺上祭」
俞校字記 says '吾' '甲' ~~~~ also have 「祭柩…」
(甲辰)(程甲)

~~This looks as though one of the "correctins" in 乾己抄 are the result of collation done with this the draft of 程甲 had been prepared.~~

Here, at any rate, 高's 'alteration' must be the result of collation

Tuesday 7th December 1976
59/748 GJ's four principal maids given as
鴛鴦, 琥珀, 翡翠, 玻璃
In 29/343 they are given as
鴛鴦, 琥珀, 鸚鵡, 珍珠

鸚鵡 and 珍珠 in chp. 3 = 紫鵑 and 襲人.

翡翠 and 玻璃 look like an avoidance of these.

MS of chap. 58 completed.
~~Thursday 9th~~ Wednesday 8th December 1976
Rough T/S of chap. 58 completed.

Wednesday 19 January 1977

59 高本 begins「话说宝玉闲听贾母等回来，随多添了一件衣裳…」
　　俞校本．「话说宝玉多添了一件衣服…
　　　　　　This is a very short chapter.
~~庚辰 戚序等~~ If ends
高本：「袭人等听了咤异，不知何了，下回分解」
俞校本：「不知袭人问他果係何了，且听下回分解」

Evidently this was a continuous narration
The end (不知 etc. should come before, not after.
「袭人因问芳官」in ch. 60) was 脂砚斋's.
雪芹 must have indicated where he wanted the
chap. division.

乾拙原文 was diff.:
「你这裏些极小的，算不起数叨来，还有
大的可气可笑之事，不知何了且听下回
分解」　This looks like a text earlier than
庚辰 and 戚序.

Thursday 20 January 1977

59/746. 邢夫人 is not mentioned in the procession. [Corrected page proofs of vol 2 sent off 16 Feb]

Friday 18 Feb. 1977

59/751 「別人不知道,只說我媽和姨媽兩个…」 CC Wang must be right in taking 「別人不知道」 as if it were 「別人我不知道」

~~Tuesday~~ Monday 28 Feb. 1977

Rough TS of chap. 59 completed.

Tuesday 1st March 1977

60/758 「好哥哥,給我一半兒,寶玉只叫要給他,芳官心中因是薔官之贈不肯給別人,連忙攔住,笑說道,別動這个,我另拿些來,寶玉會意,也笑道,且包上拿去」

戚序本 as: 「好哥哥,給我一半兒,寶玉只叫要給他,芳官心中因是薔官相贈不肯与別人,連忙攔住笑說,別動

这个，我另拿出些来。宝玉会意，忙笑道上，说这快取来」

乾抄原文「好了给我些、芳官心中因是蕊官之赠说、别动这个，我另拿些来宝玉会意，芳官接了」

Wednesday 2nd March 1977

Letter dated 24 Feb. from Frances Balfour with proof-reader's queries on prop of vol 2. Letter not in reply.

Thursday 10 March 1977

60/764「咕嚷有去了」
  俞校业「咕嘟有去了」
But 有正 and 乾抄 have「咕哪有去了」
  「咕嘟有 is the 庚辰 read」（see 校字记 447: 663頁七行) 庚辰「嘴」has been noted afterwards.

Wednesday 16 March 1977
60/761「可巧宝玉往代玉那裏去了」

俞校 text is obviously better here:「可巧宝玉所见 代玉往那裏便往那裏去了」
乾抄 shows this misconnection.

Wednesday 30th March 1977

Letter from B. Radice re presentation copies
John & Rachel fly to Australia from Heathrow Airport.

Tuesday 19th April 1977

60/763「夏妈素日和芳官不对」

俞校:「夏妈和我们素日不对」
 Correction in 乾抄.
This looks like a misconnection. 夏妈 wasn't hostile to 芳官 in particular.
 But 高鹗 probably purposely「前頼藕官 烧纸」which wasn't 夏妈 (acc. ch. 59). 曹 himself probably confused about this. wasn't it?

Thursday 28 April 1977

60/765「前言切述…」something inaudibly

many with this piece. 「因使他到厨房说话去」 appears to be Gao E's attempt to improve matters; but it doesn't really cure the trouble. The fact is that, he said 前言为近, Cao wrote proceeds to another passage of 前言 as 「这裏宝玉 ... 到厨房说话去」

Previous 俞本, 「宝玉飞在 ... 今见他回来」 was an insertion. 「回罢了宝玉、又说还要些碗 现霁」 reads naturally & presents no problems.

Monday 2nd May 1977

60/768 「今日之同人来看望柳氏的话之 乾厚「今之来同人瞧望柳经」 One of (the) Gao E's improvements. 柳氏's elder brother's boy couldn't be 姓柳.

Sunday 8th May 1977

Rough T/S of ch. 60 completed

Tuesday 17th May 1977

61/772 「给颦献家送鸡米 ... 凑了二 千个〈鸡蛋〉」 CC Wong p. 396 'birth present' For eggs as traditional 'birth present' cf. 梦梁錄 p. 307. Noth exp. 「洗三蓐外婆、親朋争送了用来 炭醋」

Tuesday 28th June 1977

MS draft of Ch. 61 completed

Monday 18th June 1977

「可别和你哥哥说」Presumably has to mean 薛蟠 (as Itō says). His absence has already been referred to in this chap., so the author hasn't forgotten it. 'Don't ever tell ...' presumably.

Tuesday 2 Aug. 1977

芍藥欄中紅香圃

Because of 射覆 ~~maybe~~ this has to be translated 'the big screen-house in the peony garden' and the inscription「紅香圃」has to be translated 'Peony Garden'.

Monday 12th September 1977

62/788 the seating arrangement appears to be as follows

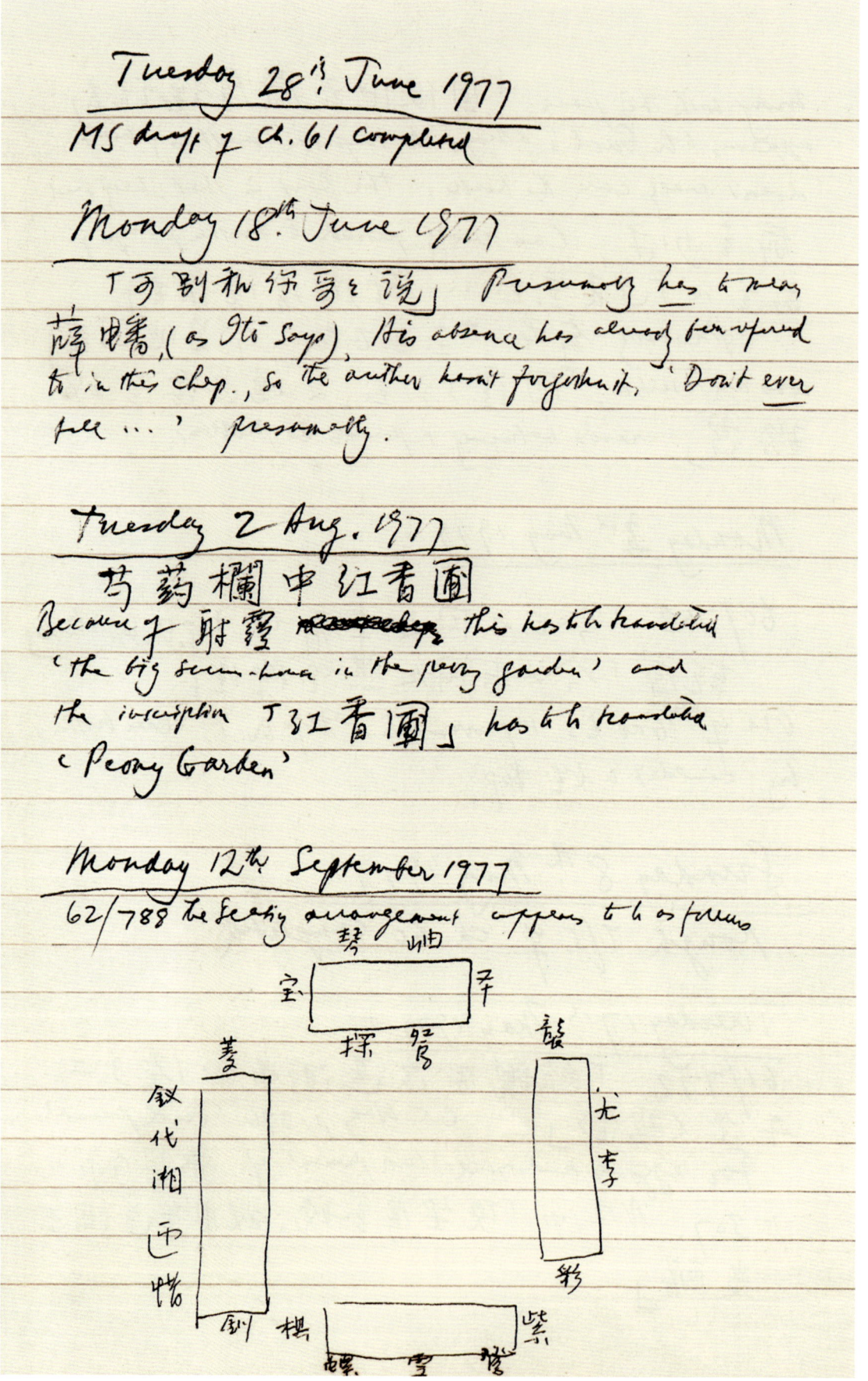

No, 「湘雲拾畫菱」 etc. not possible with that arrangement. The following seems likelier:

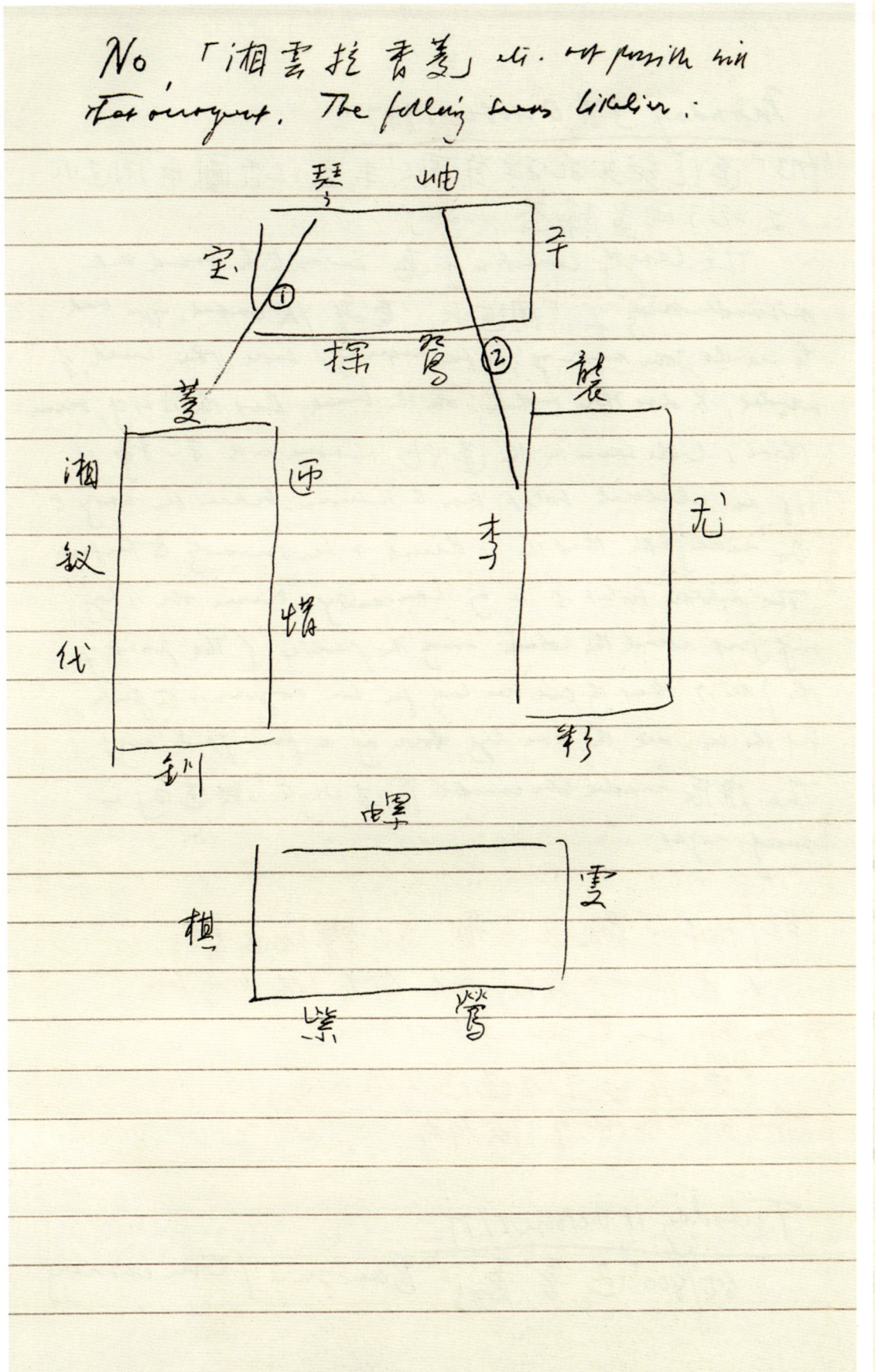

Monday 3rd October 1977

64/793 「連忙起身扎掙有同人來至紅香圃中用過小又吃了兩盞釅茶…etc」

The lengthy correction by 馮 seems to be based on a misunderstanding of 「用過水」, i.e. If you vomited, you had to re-do your make-up; & for propriety's sake, this could, if needed, be done there rather on the bench. But this is silly, because there's little sense in the 連忙 or even in the 扎掙 if if an elaborate toilet has to intervene between her wanting to be and realizable that she is drunk & her succumbing to her fear. The outdoor toilet is in my commentary, because she is lying only just round the corner among the peonies. (The point of the joke is that they had been hunting for her everywhere in the garden, but she has all the time been lying down only a few yards away). The 庚辰 reader who emended 「用過水」 to 「漱過口」 is surely right.

62/794 「既這么着、就攆他出去」
人民 (same as 庚辰) had 俞本 both wrong here.
※ 馮扬 has the correct text here
「探春忽然了頭道這么有…」
This is also the text of 戚序本

Tuesday 11 October 1977

62/800 「這菱蕙」 Bao-yu's flower is it rose

a 'purple skullcap' (並頭花) but a 並蒂菱 — whatever that is. It must be some sort of 菱; but to call it 'Caltrop' seems to obvious.

MS of chap. 62 completed.

Monday 17 October 1977

The two passages about 芳官 → 耶律雄奴 in 63 coming before and after 「圓飯後」 and 「── 的遊玩」 are not in 乾抄本 but are in 戚序本 and 庚辰. (see 乾抄. 7/63/fb-5a)
But 乾抄 原文 did have 雄奴 for 芳官 in ch.77:
8/77/3a 圖 原 「又問誰是什麼耶律雄奴. 老嬷們便將芳官指出」 改文 has:
~~又問誰是耶律雄奴~~ 「又問那芳官呢, 芳官此時过来」

Tuesday 18 October 1977 (ch. ctd.)

In 77 MS version 五兒 is referred to as dead and 芳官 accused of wishing to get her into 怡紅 heights.
乾 8/77/3a 原 「我且問你前年我們往皇陵上去是誰調唆寶玉要柳家的丫頭五兒来的, 幸而那丫頭短命死了. 不然進來你們又是連群聚黨遭害這園子呢」 改 simply erases the whole of the ¶. (see also 庚 1873)

Later in ch. 77 五兒 and her mother put in an appearance:

(人民)
77/1004 「……不是別人都是柳五兒和他母親兩个」
「那柳家的領着五兒剛進門來…」etc.
Almost a whole page inserted at this point (乙高?)
See 乾 8/77/5 and 人 77/1004.

Wednesday 19 October 1977

柳五兒 reappears in 109 (see 人民 4/109/1377 seq.

為 77. MS version makes 晴雯's 姑舅哥哥 a wife
多渾蟲 and '燈' 姑娘? The '舅' version
has 吳貴, with an anonymous wife.

Hard to believe that the flatnesses of 庚 77/704
are not interpolated.
Advantages of keeping these passages: (1) mention
of 芳官, etc. (2) mention of foreigners in 寶 household.
(3) possibility that 寶玉 was involved here in a counter-
political outline.
Disadvantages (1) evenness out of unshoulderable
business with names. (墜子驢子, etc.) (2) loss
of time sequence, esp. 「近」section ob. 湘雲 etc
(3) Are they in the 榆蔭堂 or aren't 巧? (一時到了
怡紅院) Looks as though this whole 抹奴 section
may have got displaced, if it wasn't actually interpolated.

Better leave them out. & make an abridgement.
Another problem is that 芳 was a 西旦 (23/11/72)

Thursday 20 Oct 1977

In chap. 62/792/11 「玩了一回大家方起席散了，却好妣……」
Since the poem goes on for hours after this, there's obviously something wrong. In fact Kao was incorrect about the MS text.
「顽了一回大家方起席散了一散」

Cf. 63/814/7 「这裏眾人且出去,再散了一散」
used in almost identical circs. with the same wording, where Kao hasn't altered it. (!)

Re 耶律雄奴 section. Perhaps too interesting to Western reader to miss.

Saturday 22 Oct. 1977
周 760 quots " 哄我 詩讚 " in
胡子晉 萬松山房叢書 本　飲水詩詞集
「某筆記載其刪削源委，謂，某時高廟幸臨滿人某家，適某外出，檢書籍，得此頭記，攜其一冊而去，某歸大惶，急就原本刪改進呈，高廟乃付武英殿刊印，書僅印百部，故了不多見，今本即當時武英殿刪削本也」

Sunday 23rd October (57) (cld)

「二人自好至貼喜宴」(Y706/1) seems to follow from 「都是太咸兒好些」

「況且这兩樣」(Y705/11) — 「芳官听了有理」(Y706/1) should be treated as interpolation

Better treat 「究竟 …… 薔薇」 as a "Stone's Note to Reader". All the rest (JY) can be retained. The 「一時的」is not opposing, out of place because in the section before it is not made clear that 尤氏's ordeal with the girls is well in advance of the party.

~~[struck out line]~~

Friday 28 Oct. 1977

Things are
~~(1) 806/10~~ ⑥ 5

(1) 806/10 晴雯 ⑥ 5 寶釵
(2) 807/14 寶釵 16 探春
(3) 807/12 探春 19 李紈
(4) 808/1 代玉 18 湘雲
(5) 808/10 湘雲 9 麝月
(6) 808/15 麝月 ⑩ 19 香菱
(7) 809/1 香菱 6 代玉
(8) 809/6 代玉 20 龍人

```
            李纨      宝钗      探春
         ┌─────────────────────┐ 探春
    黛玉 │                     │
    湘云 │                     │ 宝琴
    宝玉 │                     │ 香菱
         └─────────────────────┘
     袭 芳 碧 〇 春 秋 麝 晴
     人 官 痕 之 燕 纹 月 雯
```

(1) 五 and (6) 十九 in 戚本

In preceding graph, 乾抄 had got「十九」in (6) but 五 has been changed to「六」in (1)

Letter to DC Lau about the dice here.

Friday 4 November 1977

63/806/2「众人」is「探春 in MSS. (con. in 乾抄)

(「再来着探春」occur in all texts but 乾度, but unfortunately 乾度 is illegible)

Texting is a bit confused in this page. What seems to happen is

(1) 春燕 + 〇之 go to see 宝 + 代
(2) 袭人 and 晴雯 "   "   "   "   "   ✕
(3) "   "   "   "   " 探春
(4) 探春 sends 翠墨 to see 李纨 + 宝琴 ✳

Note「宝林二位」crossed out 乾段.

✳ PTO

The outstanding problem, of course, is: what happens to 燕 1 2 ※. Perhaps you are meant to think that 晴雯 went to Daiyu's 襲人 went to 寶釵's. (Hua 拉了香菱)

Wednesday 23 November 1977
63/815/7 「三日後便破孝開門」
乾抄：「三日後便開[門]破孝」
戚序本：「三日後開喪破孝」
庚辰：「三日後便開喪破孝」

Monday 28 November 1977
63/816/16 「那小家子的跟子上」;
乾抄 (63/6A) has 「瓢子」 deleted here;
庚辰 has 「瓢坎」;
戚序 has 「刨坎」.
No one appears to have any idea what this means.

Thursday 1 Dec. 1977
63/817/5 「咱們饒他們兩個」
人民本 校記 says 「'饒' 原作 '燙'、 照諸本改.
※ 藤本 (i.e. 嘉慶間刻本) 作 '饒'
俞本 has 「饒」 but 校字記 says 「己巳、庚、晉；原「饒那兩个丫頭」
This is in fact the text of 乾抄. Hand & Suey

this cannot thought of as the better text.

Friday 9 December 1977

64/825-6 「我今早晚給人看來…」 Say. Wholly inconsistent with ch. 48 in which he says that the poems have actually been published. This passage makes BY a liar and DY a conspirator.

Tuesday 3 January 1978

64/833-4 俞禄's movements don't seem to be meaningfully accounted for. 833/8 「拿過那邊去」 If 「那邊」 isn't 榮國府, then where is he now? Yet 「帶了俞禄過來」 (833/16) seems to imply that he's all the time been in the 中廳, a view apparently confirmed by 834/2: 「俞禄跟了賈璉去」. One can fudge over this in translation, but it looks like OFA again.

834/9 ~~received~~ 「他(尤氏)和二姐又並非一母」. According to what is said in 830/9 「二姐三姐都不是我老爺養的」, not 「一父」, either. OFA again? Probably.

Wednesday 4 Jan 1978

64/835/14 「尤老娘給了二十兩銀子」 俞「本銀十兩」 The 原 (?only) 「和銀十數兩」 (No 庚辰)

Friday 6 January 1978

Rough T/S of ch. 64 completed.

Tuesday 10th January 1978

書童: There are two 寿兒s:

(1) 宝玉's page: 28/332 'Oldie' (ii.52)

(2) 贾珍's page: 65/840 'Lively'

There are also two 喜兒:

(1) 贾珍's page: 53/659 'Merry' (ii.557)

(2) 贾璉's page: 65/846 ~~[illegible]~~ 'Joker'

Wednesday 25 January 1978

Ch. 65. Of the two versions, ~~about~~ of the passage about 贾珍 + 三姐 following 二姐's departure, the uncorrected one makes much more sense. In particular, the departure of the two maids seems wholly unaccountable in the 程高 version. It is actually explained in the orig. version.

Monday 30 January 1978

65: 842/12 — 843/2 ('只見那三姐索性卸了妝飾...') 程高本 here is a much better text than 'MS'. The 'MS' text is v. hard to make sense of.

On the other hand would 三姐 have performed a strip-tease at this point in the argument? Yet if she has already in this state, why is 二姐 earlier on in 大衣服?

Sunday 5 February 1978
65/844「賈璉來了…」seq. reads more like a synopsis of a discussion than finished narrative.

(1) 賈璉來了,只在二姐房内,心中又後悔來
    He began to regret having moved her

(2) 無奈二姐倒是個多情的人,以為賈璉是終身之主了,凡了倒還知疼相慣的
    But felt he couldn't leave her because she loved up to him and was so sympathetic.

(3) 雖然如今改過,但已經失了腳,有了一個淫字,憑有甚好處也不算了
    She felt she had ruined herself and could never make up for it

(4) 你这賈璉又說「誰人無錯…」
    But he said it didn't matter

(5) 二姐在枕邊衾内也常勸賈璉說…
    She thought he ought to do something about 三姐.

Monday 6th February 1978
65/845/2「剛剝上酒」: 乾扬 still has MS「酒过三巡」uncorrected.

Friday 10th February 1978

65/848/11 「或出門上車、或在園子裏遇見」

俞 has 「每常出門、或上車或一時院子裏瞥見一眼」

乾抄原文作「每常出門或上車或一時瞥見一眼」改文作「園」
But the pages never go inside the Garden.

Saturday 11th February 1978

~~Draft~~ MS of chap. 65 completed.

Wednesday 15th February 1978

TS of chap. 65 completed

The MS version of 尤三姐's ghost's encounter with 湘蓮 is much better (in which the horse turns into a kuyple?)
Forcow 俞校本 from 66/857/10 「自悔不及」 onwards.

Monday 20 Feb. 1978

66/852 「姐夫、你只放心…」 reinforces whether either has said. The earlier version is not an improvement.

Thursday 23 February 1978

66/854 The passage about 贾珍's abortive visits while 贾琏 was away (改文 in the 乾抄.) seems confusion. The section which follows 「贾琏进门看见"…这般景况」 has to refer to what immediately precedes it, + 贾琏 couldn't know all these things about 贾珍 by simply coming home + looking in.

Tuesday 28th February 1978

MS of chapter 66 completed.

Thursday 2nd March 1978

Rough T/S of chap. 66 completed.

67/859/12 「回来几个月了」 So 乾抄. But 俞本 「来回几个月了」 is obviously correct.

Tuesday 7th March 1978

Ch. 67. This and 64 were not in 庚辰 (1760). The text of 己卯 (1759) used instead. 文学古籍刊行社 edition (1955 p.5) say 「这两回 我们用乾隆间程伟元活字本对校过，误为其第六十回大约接近辛亥(1791)印本(甲本)，第六十七回则接近於壬子(1792)印本(乙本)。可见这两回写否是原著面目 尚属疑问。这是须要说明的」
According to 赵冈 (新编 83) these two

甲戌　　己卯　　庚辰
1754　　1759　　1760

chaps (64, 67) were obviously missing from 己卯 as well

「己卯本六十七回後面已註明:『石頭記六十七回終,按乾隆年間抄本,武裕菴補抄。』…

趙 85:「有己本的底本 ~~○○○○○○○~~ 看來緣是一位曹家人把己卯年經脂硯手中的定本過錄而已…」

<u>Wednesday 8 March 1978</u>
67/870 (2)「一会子你再各人打你的嘴巴子还不迟呢」
乾抄:「一会子你再打你自己的(…)还不迟呢」
俞 754 (甲)「一会子你再各人打你那嘴巴子还不迟呢」

<u>Monday 13 March 1978</u>

68/875「只待賈璉前脚走了回來」
Looks as if it might mean: 'When Jia Lian's messenger had returned' (so that JL should not get to know of where she was up to); but so far can find no authority for taking 前脚 in this sense.
The other possible meaning is that 凤姐's discov...

(in some earlier version) was made while 贾琏 was at home. She waited until he had gone.

Perhaps the best solution would be to follow 有正 in omitting ref. to 贾琏与薛蟠 & his guests. Later to 赵刚.

Tuesday 14 March 1978

The only way to deal with the 平安州 problem is (1) to alter 66/854 ~~so that it~~ using 68/875「偏偏平安節度巡邊在外约一个月方回」to justify 贾琏's return and second journey shortly later.

(2) 67/864 can be kept, perhaps with some slight modifne.

(3) 68/875 will need rewording a bit.「凤姐…只得贾琏前脚走了」can be taken to mean that she waited to make sure that he had left 二姐's place. (This can be made explicit somehow).

Friday 17 March 1978

有正 2569/2「扇套儿」 2570 6「扇子香墜」

Tuesday 21 March 1978

67/864/1「請了四位夥計,俱已那有…」
有正本 2577/9「三四个夥計俱个那有…」
Can't possibly be enough. Probably should be
「十三四个夥計…」. Note 853/4「主僕十幾雙」
Xue Pan's party 「次日」is a day later than

the paragraphs both preceding & following it, which should in any case be continuous. — Unless 寶釵到了自己房中.... 862/1 is supposed to take place a day after what precedes it.

Tuesday 11 April 1978
Letter to 趙岡 in reply to his of Mar 19 and 22.

Wednesday 12 April 1978
Rough TS of chap. 67 completed.

68/876/7「頭十天頭裏」有正原文
(2626/6)「前於十月之先」altered to
「前十天頭裏」

823 初七月

835/7 presumably 尤二's wedding to JL is 八月初三

838 眼見他已見兩月 光景

851「老爺要送二爺經塋安州去, 不過三五日就起身」

854「薔等弟探過姑母不過一月内」
855「十月前後」would be about a month's time.
855「八月内」is an impossibility. It should be 「九月内」

Monday 24 April 1978

Letter from 趙岡 of 15th April Replying to mine of Apr. 11th. Re 眼吃 etc.

Saturday 29 April 1978
Letter from 趙岡 (22/4/78)
Reconstruction from 62 as follows:

62/793   Bao-yu's birthday. Peonies in flower.   四月下旬
63/811-4 平兒還席、Jia Jing's death announced " "
63/815   入殮、賈璉入鄉、尤老娘看家 四月底.
.....
65/837   娶二姐   六月初三
          (cf. 66/856「我在那裏和她們混了一個月」)
65/838   「眼見回已是兩月光景」   七月中旬
65/846   賈珍賈璉在家廟裏鬧著做百日   " "
                                             (百日＝七月底)
66/851   賈敬命賈璉去平安州. Chases up 七月下旬
66/853   走了三日. 薛蟠's return   七月底
66/854   湘蓮 '不過一月內'
66/854   賈璉回來.   八月六,七日
66/855   「誰知八月內湘蓮才進了京」   八月中旬

66/855   次日 三姐自刎

⋮

68   賈璉兄平安節度etc.   十月初動身.

69/891 賈璉回京: 程高 suppres date
        but 庚辰 1651 says   十二月十二日.

69/894 「我來了半年、腹中已有身孕」(6月—12月)
        The doctor is told 「三月庚信不行」Chao
        says this proves that 賈璉 was still around in 九月.

70/899 二姐吞金。鳳姐一意不管「年近歲逼」十二月底

Re chs. 64, 67   KC mentions「考文討論」
与 周汝昌、馮其庸、+ 台湾的 徐高阮.

Sunday 7 May 1978

08/881 王信 Perhaps best treated as the
        王兴 who appears in vol. 1 (14: Ti 277 & 539)
        This avoids confusion & further multiplication of chars.
        Ch. 14 shows that 王兴 must be one of 'Xi-feng's
        people'.

Monday 5 June 1978

68/886-7 The passages indicating XP's & JK's special relationship are all late additions (see 全抄.) Post CXQ?

 MS of chap. 68 finished

Thursday 8 June 1978

68/881/1-4. Very hard to make any sense of this. It looks as if 察院 and 都察院 are thought of as two separate offices (!)

Sunday 11 June 1978

Better follow Itō (467 n. 2) in assuming that 尤老娘's death has somehow dropped out of the text.

Monday 12 June 1978

 Complete rough T/S of ch. 68

Thursday 22 June 1978

Why are 「嫌後门去灵不便…梨香院… 直街現開了一个大门」 excised from 全抄 & 程本. Because this gate is supposed to have disappeared in the alterations described in ch. 16? (16/158/14: cf. also 4/44/1「梨香院另有一门通街」 and 17/174/3) presumably 并leave the 一小善 of 贾 Y) 17/158 could all Y's figures.

which ran bd to the street on the south side — only then
south end would have had to be closed + incorporated in
大观园. This makes good sense here.
    But 「北界墙根下往外听」(897/6)
is very hard to make sense of, unless it means the N. wall
of the 梨香院 compound.

Friday 23 June 1978
69/897/14 「自己提自来烧」is utterly
baffling. After he's got the money 程 has「贾琏
收了银子」. 戚 and 乾原 had「贾琏拿了银子
和衣服」己、庚「拿了银子和裳」(庚 adds
a 「人」after the「裳」). Perhaps 烧 stands for
素.
    Finished MS of 69 today.

Saturday 24 June 1978
Rough T/S of 69 finished

Sunday 25 June 1978
70/899 「族中人与王姓夫妇尤氏婆媳
而已」
    俞校 has「族中人与王信夫妇尤氏婆媳而已」

This, & the 王信 of ch. 68 (TS 14) must surely be a
mistake for 王仁, xF's brother. Or her cousin?
    Perhaps 庶子 of 王子腾.

70/899

時覺：戲序幸 has 地主. Under the circs.
(50 乾屋) seems less awkward to follow that read'g.

70/899 「怪系……」 Looks very much as if the novel was taken up again here after having laid aside for a very long time.

70/900 寶妹姐出去了一个書蓉 Presumably when 薛蟠 came back in ch. 66, but not mentioned there.

71/909 Ch. 1-5 and ll. 6-10 seem incompatible.

Better go from 「老爺回來了」 to 「怪系」

Tuesday 27 June 1978
Much confusions about names in 71.
71/909 嘉蔭堂 must be 榆蔭堂 (63/814/1)
71/910 榮慶堂 " " 榮禧堂 (3/31)
71/910 臨昌伯 " " 臨安伯 (7/85)

Sunday 9 July 1978
Chaps 70-71 times very uncertain.
70/899/11 「仲春」 (i.e. 二月)
70/901/2 「初春」 (i.e. 正月)
70/901/8 「三月」
70/903/1 「〈賈政〉六月進入京」
—— /2 「六七月回京」
70/904/9 「七月底方回」 (俞本「冬底」)

In fact 71/909 and 俞子 71/791 both show him back for 寶釵's birthday (8/3) & the preparation for it begin on 7/28. Looks as if the better read 六月 & the Imperial rescript read 冬底 & 六七月 (903) 七月底 (904) are attempts at reconciling ch. 70 with ch. 71 (which weren't continuous)

Saturday 15 July 1978

70/907. How many maids get out how many kites, etc.? 程乙 makes a hopeless mess of this passage.
俞校 make it clear that in the first instance only DY's kite (美人) is fetched. Perhaps 907/5 was misunderstood. Actually 寶琴's remark is addressed to DY, though it is boy BC who answers it. This may have caused the confusion (有沙纸之语 to supply a kite for BC under the mistaken impression that BQ was asking for one).
70/908 The passage on receiving kites has been totally ruined 中乙程高.

Sunday 16 July 1978

The 俞校 text of the Kite-flying has to be preferred in principle; but it has been flown, which is the reason why it was altered. The 喜 Kite 挂 is^(bit upsetting) so crudely obvious that it seems almost incredible that XQ should have perpetrated it. It seems best to grow an editorial liberty to leave it out.

grave flaws

Monday 17 July 1978
MS of chap. 70 completed.

Tuesday 1 August 1978
71/917 「邢夫人直至晚间散时……」
71/919 「鸳鸯……晚间人散时……」

Wednesday 2 August 1978
Fair M/S copy of ch. 71 completed.

Thursday 3 August 1978
72/930 「若好了时，我也是一场痴心白使了」 These words of 旺兒媳婦 are given to 风姐 in 俞C. (810)

Wednesday 16 August 1978
Finish fair-copying of ch. 72 & begin 73.

Thursday 17 August 1978
73/936 「算起来连年闰近来艰诘、常把五连累些……别的就不记得……」
俞校 has 「算起来连年闰近来作诘，常把讨连读些……别的就不记得……」
程本 tests allows that covers 「别的」 to become meaningless.

Wednesday 13 Sept. 1978

73/941/13 「迎春的乳母之媳王柱兒媳婦」 乾抄. has 「玉柱兒」、 庚辰 & 俞校 have 「王柱兒」. The letter sent sent by the court from her husband would be called 「柱兒」

Tuesday 19 Sept. 1978

175 ј chap. ~~72~~ 73 completed

Thursday 21 Sept. 1978

74/947 「因此鳳姐要治柳家的罪」 So all texts. But unless 「要」 has the unusual sense of 'ought to', this seems unlikely. As soon as XF mentions the matter herself (74/948) she gives the lie to the idea that it is she who wants to 「治柳家的罪」. Probably read sbd. as 「因此要 …… 治柳家的罪」

Sunday 14 Oct 1978

74/955 「一副束帶上的帔帶、兩个荷包并扇套, 套内有扇子」
Suspect that 「帔帶」 is for 「佩帶」 and used in the same sense as 「佩物」 in ch. 17.
「A set of pei-dai for hanging on the belt, viz:」
(a set consists of 2 pouches & a fan-case)
(There is no such thing as a 「帔帶」)

74/956 「自己賠自好乞之奶抄家」 This is 乾抄, 改文: 原文 is 「家衰」. Probably 高 misunderstood this nature.

Tuesday 17 Oct 1978
74/958 「故順號先鈔这两處」「两」 doesn't seem to make sense.

Wednesday 18 Oct 1978
74/959 「誰知那老強…」— 74/960「不用仔説」
This invention (v. 乾抄) is a great improvement. Not functional — purely creative, unlike most inventions.

Thursday 19 Oct 1978
74/959 「打東西交与周瑞家的, 暫且拿着, 等明日对明再議」
74/962 「又命人將入畫的東西一概要来 书 先氏过目」   要来: from 周瑞家的.

Sunday 22 Oct 1978
74/963 「惜春分中」 庚辰 (1828)
Corr. from 怡 to 「分上」

Thursday 26 Oct. 1978
Complete MS 74.

Sunday 29 October 1978
Rough T/S of 73 finished.

Wednesday 8 November 1978
75/966「尤氏辞了李纨」
戚序本「尤氏等逐辞了李纨」
75/967「恰好見他姊妹来了」
Presumably 尤氏 and 探春. 宝琴 is there already.

Friday 17 November 1978

75/974 櫳翠庵 here and in ch.
71/909 probably not the same as 檻蘚堂
(63). In 71, 75 it is ostensibly part of
the Garden's main building. — when 元春 received
the family in state in ch. 18, 71 marks it in
the same part as 顧錦閣, whereas 檻蘚堂
in 63 is the scene of 寶玉's
party. A word would have to be used to get a
point for the juniors in the hall where GJ
entertained Dowager Princess & made solemn steps
at festival time. Probably its best to keep
櫳翠庵 a the main, downstairs part
of 大觀樓

Saturday 18 November 1978

75/974 主山. Outcrops of this invade the courtyard of the 蘅蕪院 (17/193). It also (presumably) lies b th near the 大觀樓. Probably it is behind the 大觀樓, just as 景山 is behind 故宮, & for the same reason. 凸碧山莊 must be on top of it, & 凹晶館 not too far fm 櫳翠庵.

In (ch. 40) the order is (1) 蘅蕪院 (2) 大觀樓 (綴錦樓) (3) 櫳翠庵. (4) 省親別墅 的牌坊

In (ch. 75-6) the order is (1) 大觀樓 (嘉蔭堂) (2) 凸碧山莊 (3) 凹晶館 (4) 櫳翠庵 (5) 瀟湘館.

Monday 20 Nov. 1978

75/974 It isn't entirely clear how an additional 3 persons can fill up a table only half-filled by 9. And where do the girls sit when they come? Assume the following order: but if this is correct, the text can hardly be said to make it clear.

[Diagram: two circles labeled 前 and 後 with Chinese characters arranged around them]

p.976「吉下賈蘭 … 後行起金來」
庚辰 has「…又做一首連本賈政，看時字道是…」 This bears all the marks of an interpolation. — Or perhaps more likely something 曹雪芹 put in to please the family. Why should 賈蘭 produce like this without anyone asking him?

Tuesday 21 November 1978
p.977「帶侄子姪們去吧」
The next chap. begins「賈赦賈政帶領賈珍等散去」

「等」Must include 賈璉 (子姪)
 but can't " 寶玉 (p.981:
「寶玉 … 王夫人再叫遣他去睡」).
The question is, does it or does it not include 賈環 + 賈蘭? Ans. probably no. 王夫人 could say could he presumed to have got them out of the way by chap. 76.
(子 could include 環, but then what about 蘭? CXQ is fairly particular about this sort of thing).

Saturday 25 November 1978
Rough T/S of 75 completed

Tuesday 28 November 1978
76/982 「我們擬定去尋......」 Hard to make sense of this abridgement. The 抄本 had:
「因他（寶玉）擬了几處，也有存的，也有刪去的，也有另擬的，這会須要我們大家把這沒有擬過的都擬出來了，注了去處，寫了這房屋的坐落，一併帶進去呈大妃之覽了。他又帶出來命給寶玉瞧過，說知寶玉喜歡起來，又說「早知這樣，那日該就叫他姊妹一併擬了，豈不有趣。所以凡我擬好一字不改，都用了」

For 匾 to 藕香榭 from 凹晶館, see 18 Nov. 78.

Thursday 30 Nov. 1978
76/978 「今年又添了兩个」
If 薛蚪科 and 宝琴 intended, this seems to be an inaccuracy (they had been there more than 2 y/s: see 910). But perhaps 薛蝌蟠 & 香菱 are intended.

Friday 1 Dec. 1978

53 正月15
54 元宵
55 春 ::
56 ::
57 清明
58 ::
59 春 ::
60 ::
61 ::
62 8/15 中秋的时候 early part ::
63 H.H. d. 6/3
64 Baoyu
65 2 mos. later
66 八月又半 xmas
67 Jo gnawn
68 十月
69 D. 中元
70 春 (Bedinner
71 ::
72 ::
73 ::
74 9/10 ::
75 ::中秋
? 去年了吃

Sunday 10 December 1978

Rough T/S of ch. 76 completed

Monday 11 Dec. 1978

77/1002「又说：这一病好了」
乾抄改为「又说可惜这两个指甲好容易
 长了二寸长，等这病好了，又损了好些」
「破了」remains「破了」in 乾抄。

77/1006 水月庵的智通
The picture given of 水月庵 in chs. 7
& 15 is of a small establishment with one 师父
(静虚) — who sometimes visits the 荣国府 —
with a couple of 徒弟 (both 智 —)
It seems highly probable that 智通 represents
a lapse of memory & that Energesia is the
person intended here.

Tuesday 12 Dec, 1978

77/999「冷笑道」is meaningless now that the
section before & after it has been removed.
Removed because it makes 龙人 too thoughtful?

Thursday 12 Dec. 1978

高本:「不但草木，凡天下有情有理的東西，
    又和人一樣，好了知己便覚験的」
有乙:「不但草木，凡天下之物皆是有情有理的，
    又和人一樣，好了知己，便極有覚験的」

Thursday 4 Jan. 1979

77/998/3 「曹旦說了，却又如今且說宝玉」
俞校亦「如今且說宝玉」
乾抄原文 3A/11 has 「曹旦⋯」

Sunday 7 Jan 1979

(See 12 Dec. above)
  乾抄原:「凡天下之物皆自有
情有理的」   cont. to:—
        「凡天下有情有理的東西」
This looks like a mis-correction. The intention is
to substitute 「好東西」 for 「之物」 but the
correction was made in the wrong place.

Monday 8 Jan. 1979   AND (PTO)
77/1000/15 「晚間果遣宋媽送去」
  1004/4 24's 柳五兒's mother, who
buys the things,
  Curiously enough 乾抄 also has worked this out.

「宝玉對一切人穩定」「對」加「待」？

* 1000/13 「情?的叫宋嗎」
乾抄改 has ㊀柳嬤

Tuesday 9 January 1979

77/1001 「又晴雯期…」etc
The 乾抄原文 version has the equivalent of
1 whole column (51字) missing between 「就者死了」
and 「的收買進來」 in the context of 77/4A.
The rather inept corrections of 程本 are designed
(1) to substitute 吳貴 for 多渾蟲
(2) to turn him into something other than a cook
(3) to imply that he was bought at the same time as
晴雯. NO*
It's probably best (i.e. novelistically) to keep him
anonymous. Don't think he occurs later in the novel.
The bit about 晴雯又忘了, which is part of the
程本 correction is followed, was kept (perhaps enough
(不脂硯) to annotate & showed therefore be kept.
* Note that 乾抄改文 is different from 程
「過了幾年賴大又把貴兒也收買進來
給他娶了一房媳婦」
程本 has
「過了幾年.賴大又給他娶母買了一房
媳婦」

Note that there is nothing about 吴贵's drunkenness in the corrected 程乙 version, though whoever was responsible for that version forgot to alter Baoyu's ref. in 999/11 (醉泥鳅哥哥)

Wednesday 10 January 1979

77/1002 29. The 程乙 version presents her as too weak to sit up unaided. Was it this that prompted the scissors alteration?

Thursday 11 January 1979

77/1004 Why do 柳五儿 and her mother come back into the Garden? There is nothing about 柳五儿 being Baoyu's maid yet, & her mother lives outside.

And why all this stuff about Moon-one having the gate kept open if BY (1005/1) is later believed to have been home his usual?

Better reread the bit about the 柳's coming to the Garden.

Saturday 13 January 1979

● MS of Chapter 77 completed

Monday 15 Jan. 1979
Rough T/S of chap. 77 completed.

Wednesday 17 Jan. 1979
78/10 13 未正三刻 2.45 p.m. Cf. 10 12/2 「老爺還未散，恐天黑了，所以先叫我們回來了」(!)
How to say was afraid that it might go on till late & didn't want us to ...

Thursday 18 Jan. 1979

程) 15/166/14 「原來這饅頭菴和水月寺一樣因他廟裏做的饅頭好就起了這個渾號離鐵檻寺不遠」

俞) 15/145/12 「原來這饅頭菴就是水月寺，因他廟裏做的饅頭好就起了這個渾號離鐵檻寺不遠」 This is text of 乾隆抄本
(15/3/6-7)

芙蓉誄: Translates by (Lotus), but the season (中秋後) & 掛在枝上 seems make it certain that hibiscus is intended. 池上 might suggest lotus, but the fact 代玉. always from the midst of this grove makes it unlikely

Monday 22 January 1979

78/1010/7「賈母歇晌後，王夫人便喚了鳳姐」 according to the text they are both still in 賈母's apartment, but from 1012/6「令人拿肖同寶玉、環、蘭前來見寶玉」it is evident that they must have gone to 王夫人's apart⁼

Wednesday 24 January 1979

78/1012/8「驚馬顛了…」
木板 reads「じつは落馬いたしたため…」But his grandmother would hardly have taken that information so calmly. She would have had all the grooms flogged at the very least. Prob. 顛了 is the 真了, 顛此了 of 北京話語滙 (S. 壹) This is in fact the 趙宁 43/528/2「跨上馬，一弯腰，順省街就趙下去了」(see Note on p.529「晚帯跳蹬的走」)

芙蓉神：78/1014「園中池上芙蓉花開」
In 乾抄 this「池上」has been added above the beginning of the column — obviously later.
The 戚序本 (3071/1) omits it altogether:「恰好这是八月節，園中芙蓉花開」

All texts have 「因至園中猛見池上芙蓉…」(1020/9).

1023/11 「却見个人影兒從芙蓉花裏走出来」
戚序本 & 舒本 w end 于誅文.
乾抄 is same as 程本.

79/1027/1 「只听花陰中有个人声」
乾抄：「只听花影中有个人声」
戚序：「只聽影中有人声」

1020 「將那誅文即掛於芙蓉枝上」
All texts have this.
王安石's 木芙蓉 poem has 「水邊無數木芙蓉, 露染臙脂色未濃」

木芙蓉 本草：「八九月始開, 故名拒霜」

Friday 26 January 1979

78/1014/16 「及回至房中」
庚辰 etc. 「待回至房中」 is obviously better & 乾抄's correction is for the worse.

78/1015/7. 「尋書之勝」
Prev. this is 程乙. 乾抄 and 程甲 both have 秋. 尋秋 is obviously correct. It means, in effect, "his visit. Hence「臨散時」continues the subject & does not repeat on

about cheng y sargent （臨散尋秋會散時）
(y. 77/1005/165 因今之有人請老爺賞秋菊」)
俞校本 77/882/6 actually has 「因今之有人
請老爺尋秋賞桂花」)
乾抄 had 「尋秋賞桂花」This is counted to
「賞菊花」

1015/11 「、極神奇，竟以蛾嬛下加
將軍二字反更覺嫵媚風流真絕世奇幻」
Must be at least in part 译文。

Saturday 27 January 1979
78/1017/14 「此必是長苓歌行方合傳式、
或擬溫八叉擊甌歌 或擬李長吉
會稽歌 或擬白樂天長恨歌 或擬詠古詞
半敘半詠、流利飄逸 始能盡妙」
~~庚辰~~ 乾抄原：
「此必是長苓歌行方合傳勢 或擬白樂天
長恨歌 或擬古詞半敘半詠流利飄逸…」
庚辰本：(乙)
「此必是苓歌行方合傳的，或擬白樂天長恨歌
或擬[李]古詞半敘半詠…」
戚序：「必要長苓歌行方合傳勢，或擬溫八叉
擊甌歌、或擬古詞 或擬白樂天長恨歌
半敘半吟…」

P10

Suggested emendation:

「必是蕃歌引方合作勢.或長篇似
白樂天長恨歌或擬古詞似溫八叉
擊甌歌或李長吉會稽歌……」
No. See Wed. 31 ???

Sunday 28 January 1979

78/1015/3「不如还是私蓑人厮混……」
The MS reads one much better. This text makes
蓑人 + 代玉 seem of equal importance in BY's eyes.
(抄改之 thus).

Wednesday 31 Jan 1979

(1017) —— 方合作勢 —— 始能盡妙.
乾抄原 is syntactically ts most coherent.
???

78/1020「眾人皆另別論……」
l.9「回至園中」contradicts l.8「各自回房」
The whole 芙蓉 姐姐 passage must be very early
because of (2) 廳月, 檀雲. Perhaps this
explains the 芙蓉 confusion.
Even the 眾人皆另別論 is very awkward
after 「三人……」

The romanization this passage is wholly inadequate
「因用…楷字篆戎…」 where? In its form?

程「備了晴雯素喜的了檳吃食」
俞「備了檳晴雯所喜之物」
「夜用下」(in 俞本). What is 代王 doing there?
And bending over to read?

Sunday 4 February 1979
Rough TS of ch. 78 completed.

Monday 5 Feb. 1979
79/1026/12 「廠之芳燼」
人民校記 says 程乙本 had 燼.
But 甲本 (y 始 is to be trusted) had 焰

Wednesday 7 Feb. 1979

79/1026/10 「你花這裏怕有還可以」
俞校本:「你居此則可」
Is this all 脂硯齋?

Sunday 11 Feb. 1979

Chap.	Time
53	四月初
69	X Peking 七月瓜
70	春-初水 初瓜
71	八月三 (初三 bday)
75	八月十二
78	A few days 中秋 (shu) (八月)

Friday 16 February 1979
79/1032/9「一家鳳凰似的」
MSS「鳳凰蛋似的」 乾挹 deletes: but obvious error.

Sunday 18 February 1979
Complete MS of ch. 79.

Wednesday 14 March 1979
80/1042/12「君逭之際…」MSS「君逭之配以」乾挹, as you in this chap., but MS text — uncovered.

Saturday 24 March 1979
MS of chap 80 complete.

Monday 26 March 1979
Rough T/S of ch. 80 completed.

Monday 2 Apr. 1979
Copy 3 of 3/64–9 to Dorothy Site.

Friday 1 June 1979

Mem Con. on Copy 1 79/5, /7, /8, /10

PART IV

紅樓夢

The Burial of the Flowers

The blossoms fade and falling fill the air,
Of fragrance and bright hues bereft and bare.
Floss drifts and flutters round the Maiden's bower,
Or softly strikes against her curtained door.

The Maid, grieved by these signs of spring's decease,
Seeking some means her sorrow to express,
Has rake in hand into the garden gone,
Before the fallen flowers are trampled on.

Elm-pods and willow-floss are fragrant too;
Why care, Maid, where the fallen flowers blew?
Next year, when peach and plum-tree bloom again,
Which of your sweet companions will remain?

This spring the heartless swallow built his nest
Beneath the eaves of mud with flowers compressed.
Next year the flowers will blossom as before,
But swallow, nest, and Maid will be no more.

Three hundred and three-score the year's full tale:
From swords of frost and from the slaughtering gale
How can the lovely flowers long stay intact,
Or, once loosed, from their drifting fate draw back?

323

Blooming so steadfast, fallen so hard to find!
Beside the flowers' grave, with sorrowing mind,
The solitary Maid sheds many a tear,
Which on the boughs as bloody drops appear.   Cf. 歐陽修(再和
                                                    明妃曲)「明妃去時淚
                                                    灑向枝上花」

At twilight, when the cuckoo sings no more,
The Maiden with her rake goes in at door
And lays her down between the lamplit walls,
While a chill rain against the window falls.

'I know not why my heart's so strangely sad,
'Half grieving for the spring and yet half glad:
'Glad that it came, grieved it so soon was spent,
'So soft it came, so silently it went!

'Last night, outside, a mournful sound was heard:
'The spirits of the flowers and of the bird.
'But neither bird nor flowers would long delay,
'Bird lacking speech, and flowers too shy to stay.

'And then I wished that I had wings to fly
'After the drifting flowers across the sky:
'Across the sky to the world's farthest end,
'The flowers' last fragrant resting-place to find.

323.
'But better their remains in silk to lay
'And bury underneath the wholesome clay,
'Pure substances the pure earth to enrich,
'Than leave to soak and stink in some foul ditch.

'Can I, that these flowers' obsequies attend,
'Divine how soon or late *my* life will end?
'Let others laugh flower-burial to see:
'Another year who will be burying me?

'As petals drop and spring begins to fail,
'The bloom of youth, too, sickens and turns pale.
'One day when spring has gone and youth has fled,
'The maiden and the flowers will both be dead.'

333
       Two lovely ~~boys~~
   Are both in love with me
And I can't get either from my mind.
    Both are ~~so beautiful~~
        so wonderful
        so marvellous
        so debonair
To give up either one would be unkind.
    Last night I promised I would go

333   ~~Then I heard you~~
              To meet one of them in the arbour)
           (Where the roses grow
              The other came to see what she could find.
              And now that we three are all
              Here in this tribunal
              There are no words that come into my mind.

333   [Bao-yu]
        The girl's upset:
            The years pass by, but no-one's claimed her yet.
        The girl looks glum:
            Her true-love's gone off to follow ambition's drum.
        The girl feels blest:
            The mirror shows her looks are at their best.
        The girl's content:
            Long summer days in pleasant pastimes spent.

334   Still weeping tears of blood about our separation:
       Little red love-beans of my desolation.
       Still blooming flowers I see outside my window growing,
       Still awake in the dark I hear the wind a-blowing.
       Still oh still I can't forget those old hopes and fears.
       Still can't swallow food and drink, 'cos I'm choked with tears.
       Mirror, mirror on the wall, tell me it's not true:

334.   Do I look so thin and pale, do I look so blue?
        Mimi, mimi, this long night how shall I get through?
           Oh — oh — oh!
        Blue as the mist upon the distant mountains,
        Blue as the water in the ever-flowing fountains.

        Rain whips the pear-tree, shut fast the door!

334   [Feng Zi-jing]
      The girl's upset:
         Her husband's ill and she's in debt.
      The girl looks glum:
         The gale has turned her room into a slum.
      The girl feels blest:
         She's got twin babies at the breast.
      The girl's content:
         Awaiting a certain pleasureth event.

              You're so exciting
              And so inviting
              You're my Mary contrary
              You're a crazy, mad thing.
      You're my goddess, but oh, you're deaf to my praying:
         Why won't you listen to what I am saying?
      If you don't believe me, make a small investigation;

334.   You will soon find out the true depth of my adoration.

        From moonlit cot the cry of chanticleer.

334.   [Yun-er]
          The girl's upset:
            Not knowing how the future's to be met.
          The girl looks glum:
            Nothing but blows and hard words from her mum.
          The girl feels blest:
            Her young man's rich and beautifully dressed.
          The girl's content:
            She's been preparing for a big event.

                A flower began to open in the month of May
                Along came a honey-bee to sport and play
                He pushed and he squeezed to get inside
                But he couldn't get in however hard he tried
                So on the flower's lip he just hung around
                A-playing the see-saw up and down
                    Oh my honey-sweet
                    Oh my sweets of sin
                    If I won't open up
                    How will you get in?

335   So bonny blooms the peach-tree-o

335   [Xue Pan]
         The girl's upset:
              She's married to a marmoset.
         The girl looks glum:
              His dad's a baboon with a big red bum.
         The girl feels blest:
              In bridal bower she takes her rest.
         The girl's content:
              She's got a big prick up her queynt.

              (The Hum-bum Song)
                  One little gnat went hum hum hum
                  Two little flies went bum bum bum
                  Three little ...

335   [Jiang Yu-han]
         The girl's upset:
              Her man's away, she fears he will forget.
         The girl looks glum:
              So short of cash she can't afford a crumb.
         The girl feels blest:
              Her lampwick's got a lucky crest.
         The girl's content:
              She's married to a perfect gent.

336.   A mischievous bundle of charm and love
        Or an angel come down from the skies above?
            Sweet sixteen
            And so very green
       Yet eager to see all there is to be seen.
          Aie aie aie
         The galaxy's high
        In the roof of the sky
      And the drum from the tower
      Sounds the midnight hour
So trim the lamp, love, and come with me
Inside the bed-curtains and you shall see

The flowers' aroma breathes of hotter days.

409 ⎫ after 441.
414 ⎭

441 Dear Brother,

Some nights ago, when the moon came out in a sky freshly clear after the rain, the garden seemed veritably awash with moonlight, and sleep, in the face of so rare a spectacle, was unthinkable. Thrice the clepsydra had been turned and still I lingered beneath the tall paulownias, unwilling to go in; but in the end the treacherous night air betrayed me, and by morning I was lamentably indisposed. How kind ~~how exquisitely thoughtful~~ of you to ~~have~~ visited me in my sickroom, and to have sent your maidservant shortly afterwards with solicitous inquiries and with those delicious lychees and the calligraphy by Yan Zhen-qing!

While I have been lying here quietly on my own, I have been thinking how in the olden days even men whose lives were spent amidst the hurly-burly of public ~~life~~ affairs would keep some quiet retreat for themselves, with its tiny corner of mountain and trickle of running water; ~~and~~ how they could ~~x~~ ~~by using every art and~~ blandishments ~~at their command, they would~~ ~~seek to~~ a little group of kindred spirits ~~who might~~ to share in their enjoyment of it on the basis; and how, of such leisure-time associations, rhymers' guilds and poetry clubs were then founded, ~~and~~ so that the fleeting inspirations of an idle hour ~~might sometimes~~ ought often be ~~perpetuated~~ in imperishable masterpieces of verse.

Now, although I am no poet myself, I am privileged to live 'midst rocks and streams' and in the company of such

441 gifted practitioners of the poetic art as Xue and Lin; and it seems to me a great pity that the romantic courts and pavilions of our Garden should not echo with the jocund carousal of assembled bards, and its flowering groves and blossoming banksides not become of wine and song. Why should the founding of poetry clubs be the sole prerogative of the whiskered male and female versificators, allowed a voice in the tuneable concert of the muses only when some enlightened patriarch sees fit to invite them?

Will you come, then, and rhyme with us? The pathway to my door is swept to receive you and your arrival is eagerly awaited by

      Your affectionate Sister,
      Tan-chun.

441 Dear Father,

I have the Honour to present my Humble Duty and hope this finds you as it leaves me in the Best of health, ever since you did me the great Kindness to recognize me as your Son and ~~ever since~~ I have been looking for some means of showing my appreciation of your great Kindness but so far ~~there was~~ no opportunity has presented itself, to date. However, thanks to your esteemed Advice ~~now~~ I have got to know several Nurserymen also a number of famous gardens and now ~~however~~ through this contacts I have come across a very rare Variety of ~~that apple~~ autumn begonia (Pure White) only very little to be had, but using every means possible I have got two pots of it I hope you will think of me as a real Son and not refuse to keep them ~~same~~ for your enjoyment. However, owing to the present Hot Weather I did not like to call in Person as the Young Ladies are outside in the Garden a lot owing to the heat, and not wishing to give Inconvenience.

I remain,
Honoured Father,
Your Dutiful and Affect. Son,
Jia Yun

414.   A place remote, where footsteps seldom pass,
       And dew still glistens on the untrodden moss.

457.   Lotus reflections shelter at the dip of a lazy
                          oar-blade;
       Lotus fragrances float up from the sand round a
                          bamboo bridge-pile

409.

(1)

Seeing my idle tears, you ask me why
These foolish drops fall from my teeming eye:
Then know, your gift, being by the mer-folk made,
In merman's currency must be repaid.

(2)

Jewelled drops by day in secret sorrow shed
Or, in the night-time, in my wakeful bed,
Lest sleeve or pillow they should spot and stain,
Shall on these gifts shower down their salty rain.

(3)

Yet silk preserves but ill the naiad's tears;
Each salty trace of them fast disappears.
Only the speckled bamboo stems that grow
Outside the window still her tear-marks show. ①

① See Appendix ... p. ... NAIAD'S TEARS

446.   (1) Tan-chai

A wintry sunset gilds the vine-wreathed door
Where stands, mossed by old rains, the flower-pot.
Its snowy blooms, as snow impermanent,
Are pure as pure white jade that alters not,
O fragrant frailty, that so fear the wind!
Most radiant whiteness! Full moon without spot!
White flower-sprite, shake your silken wings! Away!
And join with me to hymn the dying day!

               (2) Bao-chai

Conceal the sweet scent behind closed courtyard door,
And with prompt waterings dew the mossy pot!
The carmine hue their summer sisters wore
These snowy autumn blossoms envy not.
For beauty in plain whiteness best appears,
And only in white jade is found no spot.
Chaste lovely flowers! Silent, they seem to pray
To autumn's White God at the close of day.

446.

(3) Bao-yu

White Autumn's sister stands beside the door;
Like summer snow her blossoms fill the pot —
A Yang-fei rising naked from the bath,
With a cool, chaste allure that she had not.
The dawn wind could not dry those pearly tears
With which night's rain each floweret's eye did spot.
Pensive and grave, her blossoms gently sway,
While a sad flute laments the dying day.

(4) Dai-yu

Beside the half-raised blind, the half-closed door,
Crushed ice for earth and white jade for the pot,
Three parts of whiteness from the pear-tree stolen,
One part from plum for scent (which pear has not) —
Moon-maidens stitched them with white silken thread,
And virgins' tears the new-made flowers did spot,
Which now, like bashful maids that no word say,
Lean languid on the breeze at close of day.

452 Shi Xiang-yun (1)
  Of late a goddess came down to my door
  And planted seeds of white jade in a pot,
  From which a wondrous White Frost Maiden grew,
  Who, loving cold, all other things loves not.
  Last night a cloud passed by, whose autumn shower
  Her cold, unweeping eyes with tears did spot.
  Since when, the poet here takes up his stay,
  To praise her loveliness by night and day.

     (2)
  Where flower-fringed steps approach the ivied door,
  At the wall's foot or in a graceful pot —
  What flowers do more sad autumn-thoughts inspire
  Than these, whose sweetness others rival not?
  Wax tears their petals seem, by wind congealed,
  Or filtered moonlight, flecked with many a spot.
  Weep they because the shadows stole away
  Their goddess-queen, who now makes dark night day?

462   ① <u>Remembering the Chrysanthemums</u>
            by Lady Allspice
     The autumn wind that through the knotgrass blows
     Blurs the sad gazer's eye with unshed tears;
     But autumn's guest, who last year graced this plot,
     Only, as yet, in dreams of night appears.
     The wild geese from the North are now returning;
     The dhobi's thump at evening fills my ears.
     Those golden flowers for which you see me pine
     I'll meet once more at this year's Double Nine.

463   ② <u>Seeking the Chrysanthemums</u>
            by Green Boy
     The crisp day bids us go on an excursion —
     Resistant to the wineshop door's temptation —
     Some garden, where, before the frosts, was planted
     The glory of autumn, being our destination:
     Which, after weary walk, having found, we'll sing
     An autumn song in unsubdued elation.
     And you, gold flowers, if what the poet told
     You understood, would not refuse his gold!

463 ③ Planting the Chrysanthemums
        by Green Boy
Brought from their nursery and, with loving hands,
Planted along the fence and by the door —
A shower last night their wilting leaves revived,
Opening the morning-buds all silver-hoar.
Sweet flowers! a thousand autumn songs I'll sing
To praise your beauty, and libations pour,
And water you, and ridge with earth around.
No dust on *my* wet well-path shall be found!

463 ④ Admiring the Chrysanthemums
        by Cloud Maiden
Transplanted treasures, dear to me as gold —
Both the pale clumps and those of darker hue!
Bare-headed by your wintry bed I sit
And, musing, hug my knees and sing to you.
None more than you the villain would disdain;
None understands your proud heart as I do.
The precious hours of autumn I'll not waste
But with you bide and savour their full taste.

463. ⑤ Arranging the Chrysanthemums
           by Cloud Maiden

What greater pleasure than the lute to strum
Or sip wine by your delicate display?
To hold the garden's fragrance in one vase,
And see all autumn in a single spray?
On frosty ~~winter~~ nights I'll ~~think of you~~ *me you my dear*,
And in the garden bare, at close of day.
Since with your shy disdain I sympathize,
'Tis you, not summer's gaudy blooms, I prize.

463. ⑥ Celebrating
       ~~Receiving~~ the Chrysanthemums
           by River Queen

Down garden walks, in search of inspiration,
A restless demon drives me all the time;
Then brush blooms into praises, and the mouth
Grows acid-sweet, hymning those scents sublime:
Yet easier 'twere a world of grief to tell
Than to lock autumn's secret in one rhyme.
That miracle old Tao did once attain;
Since when a thousand bards have tried in vain.

463. (7) Painting the Chrysanthemums
              by Lady Allspice
The brush that praised them, eager for more tasks,
Would paint them now — for painting, is no great cost
When curving block-ink blots the flowers' leaves make,
And white the petals, silvered o'er with frost.
Fresh scents of autumn from the paper rise,
And shapes unmoving by the wind are tossed.
No need at Double Ninth live flowers to pluck:
These living seem, upon a fine screen stuck!

464. (8) Questioning the Chrysanthemums
              by River Queen
Since none else autumn's mystery can explain,
I come with murmured questions to your gate:
Who, world-disdainer, shares your hiding-place?
Of all the flowers, why do yours bloom so late?
The garden silent lies in frosty dew,
The geese return, the cricket mourns his fate.
Let not speech from your silent world be banned:
Converse with me, since me you understand!

464. ⑨ Wearing the Chrysanthemums
             by Plantain Lover
   Just to admire, and not for our adornment,
   Were these reared and arranged with so much care;
   Yet young Sir Fop, with whom flowers are a passion,
   And drunk old Tao both dote on flowers to wear.
   One's head-cloth reeks of autumn's acrid perfume;
   Chill dew of autumn pearls the other's hair.
   The vulgar crowd, which nothing understands,
   Stops in the street and, jeering, claps its hands.

464. ⑩ The Shadow of the Chrysanthemums
             by Cloud Maiden
   The autumn moonlight through the garden steals,
   Filtered in patches variously bright.
   Flowers by the house as silhouettes appear;
   Flowers by the fence are flecked with coins of light.
   In the flowers' wintry scent their souls reside,
   Not in those frost-forms, than a dream more slight.
   Even the gross vandal, squinting through drunken eyes,
   Can, by their scents, the crushed flowers recognise.

464. ⑪ The Dream of the Chrysanthemums
　　　　　　by River Queen
　　　　　　　　　　　　in my autumn bed
Light-headed ~~amidst autumn flowers~~ I lie
And seem to chase the moon across the sky.
Well, if immortal, I'll go seek old Tao,
Not imitate Zhuang's flittering butterfly!
　Following the wild goose, into sleep I slid;
From which now, startled by the cricket's cry,
'Midst cold and fog and dying leaves I wake,
With no-one by to tell of my heart's ache.

464. ⑫ The Death of the Chrysanthemums
　　　　　　by Plantain Lover
The feasting over and the first snow fallen,
The flowers frost-shrunken lie or sideways lean,
Their perfume lingering, but their gold hue dimmed,
　　　　　poor,
And ~~two~~ few ~~tattered~~ leaves bereft of green.
Now under moonlit bench the cricket shrills,
　　　　　　　　flies
And weary goose-~~~~ in the cold sky are seen.
　　　of you
Yet ~~~~ partly let me not complain:
Next ~~autumn~~ equinox we'll meet again!

466.   (1) Bao-yu
How delightful to sit and a crab's claw to chew
In the cassia shade — with some ginger-sauce, too!
Old Grim-chops wants wine, though he's got no inside,
And he walks never forwards, but all to one side.
The 'yolks' are so tasty, who cares if we're ill!
Though our fingers we've washed, they are crab-scented still.
'O crabs,' Dong-po said (and his words I repeat)
'You have not lived in vain if you're so good to eat!'

(2) Dai-yu
In arms and in armour they met their sad fate.
How tempting they look now, piled up on a plate!
The white flesh is tasty, the pink flesh as well —
Both the white in the claws and the pink in the shell;
And we're glad he's an eight- not a four-legged beast
When there's plenty of wine to enliven the feast.
So with crab let us honour the Double Ninth Day,
While chrysanthemums bloom 'neath the cassia's spray.

466.   (3)   Bao-chai
                With winecups in hand, as the autumn day ends,
                And with watering mouths, we await our small friends.
                A straightforward breed you are certainly not,
                And the goodness inside you has all gone to pot.
                For your cold humours, ginger; to cut out your smell,
                We've got wine and chrysanthemum petals as well.
                As you hiss in your pot, crabs, d'ye look back with pain
                On that calm moonlit cove and the fields of fat grain?

485   My name it is Jia
       I'm a treacherman true
       I can eat a whole sow
       With her little pigs too

488   My heart has discovered true ease amidst the clouds and
                              good   mists of the mountains
       My life has ~~learned~~ a fierce freedom from the rocks and
                              torrents of the fells.

                        dead lotus leaves for the rain to play on.
489   Leaves but ~~the sound of rain on dying lotus leaves.~~
                                          — Li Shang-yin

492   Grandmother Jia
       6/   On my left the bright blue sky
       /6   — The Lord looks down from heaven on high

       5/   Five and six together meet
       /6   — By Six Bay Bridge the flowers smell sweet

       6/   Leaves six and ace upon my right
       /1   — The red sun in the sky so bright.

       6/6 : 5/6 : 6/1   Altogether that makes 'a shock-headed
                         devil with hair like tow.'
                         — The devil shouts 'Zhong Kui, let me go!'

493   Aunt Xue

5/5   On my left all the fives I find
      — Plum-blossoms dancing in the wind.

5/5   On my right all the fives again
      — Plum-blossoms in the tenth month's rain

2/5   Between them, two and five make seven
      — On Seventh Night the lovers meet in heaven

5/5 : 2/5 : 5/5   Together that gives 'the Second Prince plays
                   in the Five Holy Hills'
                   — The Immortals dwell far off from mortal ills.

Xiang-yun

1/1   All the aces, one and one
      — Two lamps for earth, the moon and sun

1/1   On my right once more aces all
      — And flowers to earth in silence fall

1/4   Between them ace again with four
      — Red sun reclining on a red-petalled floor.

1/1 : 1/4 : 1/1   Together that makes nine ripe cherries
                   — Winged thieves have stripped the Emperor's
                     trees of berries.

493   Bao-chai

3/   A pair on the left then, three and three
/3   — Swallows in pairs round the old roof-tree

3/   A pair of threes upon the right
/3   — Green duckweed-trails on the water bright.

3/   A three and six between them lie
/6   — Three peaks upon the rim of sky.

3/3 : 3/6 : 3/3   Together that gives 'the lone boat tied with
                  an iron chain'
                     — On every hand the waves and the heart's pain.

           Dai-yu

6/   Sky on the left, the good fresh air
/6   ~~And the bright air feeds my despair~~
          — Bright air and brilliant moon feed my despair.

4/   A four and a six, the Painted Screen
/6   — Na Hong-niang at the window seen.

2/   A two and a six, four twos make eight
/6   — In twos walk backwards from the Hall of State

6/6 : 4/6 : 2/6   Together makes 'a basket for the flowers you pick'
                     — A basket of peonies slung from his stick,

493   Ying-chun
  4/   Four and five, the Flowery Nine
  /5   — The flowering peach-tree drenched with rain.

494   Grannie Liu
  4/   A pair of fours on the left; the man
  /4   — Is it a farmer?

  3/   Green three, red four, contrasting colours
  /4   — The fire burns up the caterpillars

  1/   Red four on the right and the ace is red
  /4   — A turnip and a garlic-head.

  4/4 : 3/4 : 1/4   'The Flower' these three together show
                   — That flower will to a pumpkin grow.

529   Fluttering like the wing-beats of a startled swan
       Swaying with the ~~limber~~ curves of ~~the~~ water-dragon
                        ~~swung to & listen~~
       Like: 'a lotus-flower emerging from the green ~~sea~~' (water)
          or 'the morning sun ~~shining over~~
                          ~~shining~~ above the mist-bank'
                          rising

Autumn Window: A Night of Wind and Rain
(Spring River: A Night of Flowers and Moonlight)

555

The autumn flowers are dead, and the leaves sere;
Lamp-light comes soon; the nights grow long again.
Outside my window autumn's signs appear,
More dismal in the wind and rustling rain.

The rustling rain came in such swift downpour
It startled me from autumn-dream-filled sleep.
Now, in a muse, unable to sleep more,
I watch the candle at my bedside weep.

The candle weeps down to its socket low,
And my heart weeps and desolation feels.
Yet the same wind in other courts must blow;
The sound of rain through other windows steals.

The wind's chill strikes through quilt and counterpane,
The rain drums like a mad clock in my ears;
All night it falls, and each night comes again,
Companion to my own swift-coursing tears.

The courtyard now with mist begins to fill,
The bamboo's drip persists without a pause.
When will the wind cease and the rain be still,
That soaked the window's gauze?

591 Behind snug curtained doors the incense lingers on
In old familiar grave the ground ink settles

LU YOU (1125-1210)

592 A campfire's smoke perpendicular
And the round sun in the Great River sets.

WANG WEI (701-761)

Where the sun sets, the water whitens
When the tide rises, all the world is green.

WANG WEI

Down by the ford the setting sun lingers,
A thread of smoke above the hamlet climbs

WANG WEI

573 Half-lost in haze the distant haunts of men;
smoke the hamlet marks,

TAO YUAN-MING (365-427)

594   (1)

A chilly radiance bright, a fair round shape,
The cold white moon hangs in the middle sky.
The poet for inspiration seeks her oft;
The homesick traveller from her turns his eye.
Like a jade mirror hanging on azure wall,
Or disc of ice suspended from on high.
No need for lamps on such a glorious night,
When every beam and post is bathed in light.

595   (2)

Silver on water on the casement cold?
See its round source in yon clear midnight sky!
Blanched ghostly white, plum-blossoms spread their scent,
And dew on willow-strings begins to dry.
Is it white powder on the paving spilled?
Or grains of frost that on the railings lie?
I wake to find no other soul in sight,
But that still face which through the blind sheds light.

598

(3)

Ethereal splendour no cloud can blot out!
Chaste lovely presence of the cold night sky!
From a white world the washer's dull beat sounds,
Till in the last watch cocks begin to cry;
While by a fisherman's sad flute enhanced,
A lady leans out from her casement high;
And you, White Goddess, lulled in sweet delight,
Wish every night could be a fifteenth night.

611

(1) [Xi-feng] Last night the north wind blew the whole night through —

[Li Wan] Today outside my door the snow still flies.
(2) On mud and dirt its pure white flakes fall down —

612 [Caltrop] And powdered jade the whole earth beautifies.
(3) Flakes on the dead plants wear a winter dress —

[Tan-chun] And on dry grasses gemlike crystallise.
(4) Now will the farmer's brew a good price fetch —

[Li Qi] His full barn to ~~the year's richness~~ a good year testifies.
(5) The ash-filled ~~gauge~~ au shows winter's solstice near —

[Li Wen] And the Wain turns as yang revivifies.
(6) Snow robs the cold hills of their emerald hue —

[Xiu-yan] And frost the river's motion petrifies.
(7) Snow settles thickly on sparse willow boughs —

[Xiang-yun] But on dead plantain-leaves less easy lies.
(8) Now perfumed coals in precious braziers burn —

[Bao-qin] And heavy furs the girls' slim shapes disguise.
(9) Firelight the mirror by the window catches —

612		[Dai-yu]	And turning hard the chamber purifies.
	(10)		Still sobbing through the night the mournful wind —
613		[Bao-yu]	Each sleeper's dreams with sadness sanctifies.
	(11)		Somewhere a melancholy flute is playing —
		[Bao-chai]	Whose sad notes with the wind's plaint harmonise.
	(12)		With groans the Earth Turtle sideways shifts his load —
		[Xiang-yun]	As dragons brawl, the cloud-wrack liquefies.
	(13)		A lone boat from the lonely shore puts out —
		[Bao-qin]	While from the bridge a horseman waves goodbyes,
	(14)		Now warm ~~furs~~ clothes to the frontier are despatched —
		[Xiang-yun]	And wives to distant dear ones send supplies.
	(15)		On still untrodden ways masked pitfalls threaten —
		[Bao-chai]	In snowbound woods a bough's creak terrifies.
	(16)		The wind-blown snow around the traveller whirls —
		[Dai-yu]	And clouds of powdery snow at each step rise.
	(17)		~~Roast sweet yams~~ Steamed taros make a good snow-party fare —
			cf.618下蒸的大芋頭 cf.618 [red annotations]
614		[Bao-yu]	The guests on 'scattered salt' themes improvise,
	(18)		Now is the woodman's axe no longer heard —

614   [Bao-qin] Yet still his rod the straw-clad fisher plies,
(19)   Mountains like sleeping elephants appear —

      [Xiang-yun] A snake-like path the climber's skill defies,
(20)   After long cold the trees strange frost-fruits bear —

      [Tan-chun] ~~And~~ Which, bold in beauty, winter's blasts despise.
(21)   The hushed yard startles to a cold chough's chatter.

      [Xiu-yan] An old owl wakes the vale with mournful cries,
(22)   The driving flakes make angles disappear —

      [Xiang-yun] But dimples on the water's face incise.
(23)   In the clear morn how radiant gleams the snow! —

      [Dai-yu] How ghostly, as the too short daylight dies!
(24)   Its cold the Chengs' disciples could withstand —

      [Xiang-yun] Its promise can a King's cares exorcise.
(25)   Who'd lie abed all stiff with cold indoors —

615   [Bao-qin] When friends invite to red-cheeked exercise?
(26)   Who o'er the land the merfolk's silk unrolls? —

    B [Xiang-yun] Who the white weft from Heaven's loom unties?

615 (27) A [Dai-yu] The tall pavilions cold ~~bare~~ and empty stand —

B [Xiang-yun] Rude thatch the poor man better satisfies.

(28) A [Bao-qin] Ice lumps we thaw and boil to make our tea —

B [Xiang-yun] The fuel being damp, they greatly tantalise.

(29) A [Dai-yu] The Zen recluse with worn-broom sweeps the ground —

B [Bao-qin] His stringless lute-play still more mystifies.

616 (30) A [Xiang-yun] On the stone tower a stork unwatchful sleeps —

B [Dai-yu] On the warm mat a cat contented sighs.

(31) A [Bao-qin] In moonlit caves the silvery water laps —

B [Xiang-yun] And red flags flutter against sunset skies.

(32) A [Dai-yu] Soaked winter plums the breath make fresh and sweet —

B [Bao-chai] And melted snow the wine-fumes neutralise.

(33) A [Bao-qin] The stiffened aigrette gradually thaws —

617   B [Xiang-yun] The snow-soaked silken ~~sash~~ girdle ~~but~~ slowly dries.

(34) A [Dai-yu] The wind has dropped, but snow still ~~mtly~~ falls —

     B [Bao-qin] And frequent drips the passers-by baptize.

(35) A [Li Wan] Our verses ~~shall this happy day record~~ —

     B [Li Qi] And a wise Emperor loyally eulogise.

619   Xing Xiu-yan (RED)

So brave, so gay they bloom in winter's cold,
Before the fragrant peach and almond red,
~~Like~~ rosy clouds that clothe the springtime slopes
Of Yu-ling, where my dream-soul oft has sped.
Each little lamp in its green calyx lies,
Like drunken snow-sprites on a rainbow bed.
Yet do these flowers, of hue so rich and rare,
Reckless, in ice and snow their charms outspread.

Li Wen (PLUM)

What richness blooms before my drunken eyes?
'Tis not the white I sing, but the red plum.
See, its pale cheeks are streaked with blood-red tears,
Even though its bitter heart with cold is numb.
No flower this, but a fairy maid transformed,
And here transplanted ~~hither~~ from Elysium!
In the frozen North ~~both north and south~~ it makes such brave display,
I'll tell the bees that spring's already come.

619   Xue Bao-qin (FLOWER)

  Like spendthrift youths in spring's new fashions dressed,
  Its bare thin branches burst in glorious flower.
  Snow no more falls, but a bright rosy cloud
  Tints hills and streams in one long sunset hour.
  Through this red flood my dream-boat makes its way,
  While flutes sound chill from many a maiden's bower.
  Sure from no earthly stock this beauty came
  But trees immortal round the Fairy Tower.

620   On Visiting Adamantina with a Request for Red Plum-Flower
                                          by Bao-yu

  A) Wine not yet broached nor verses yet composed,
  B) In quest of spring I sped to Elysium,
  C) ['Twas not the balm from Guanyin's vase I craved
     [Across that threshold, but her flowering plum.
  D) [frozen wordling, for red snow
     [The saint cut fragrant clouds and gave some.
     [Pity my verse, languous and thin,
     [For convent snow has soaked to the skin!

624   Li Wan:
    (1) Guan-yin lacks a biography.
        — Though good, yet having no memorial
                            (中庸)

625   (2) What is the green yet that grows in the water?
        — It is a fast-growing rush. (中庸)

    Li Wen:
        Beside the rocks the water runs cold.
        — Shan Tao.

    Li Qi:
        Firefly. (The answer is a single word)
        — Flower: Corrupt grass by transmutation breedeth fireflies.
                            (礼记 月令)

626   Bao-chai
        Tier upon compact tier of fragrant wood:
        No craftsman's hand could carve one half so well.
        A gale blows all about the temple's eaves,
        Yet, though it shakes, no sound comes from my bell.

626   Xiang-yun
         Far away
         From the high fell
         Where I used to dwell
         Amidst men I play.
         But for what gain?
My labour's vain.
         My ~~tale~~ tale

    Bao-yu
        'Twixt heaven and earth amidst the clouds so high
        Bamboo gives warning to the passer-by.
        Eyes strain some feathered traveller to descry,
     To ~~behold~~ bear my ~~answering message~~ back into the sky.

    Dai-yu
        See my little prancing steed!
        Of silken rein he has no need.
        Round the city wall he goes,
        Wreaking havoc on his foes.
        At his master's touch he moves
        With thunder of advancing hooves.
        In isles by tortoises supported
        His deeds are honourably reported.

629 Bao-qin. People and Places: Ten Poems on Historical Sites

(1) Red Cliff
The river at Red Cliff was choked with the dead,
And the ships without crew carried naught but their names.
A clamour and shouting, a wind took the blaze,
And a host of brave souls rode aloft in the flames.

(2) Hanoi
His column of brass bade the nations obey;
The noise of him spread through barbarian parts.
Brave Ma Yuan to conquest and empire was born:
He needed no "Iron Flute" to teach him those arts.

(3) Mt. Zhong-shan
Though ambition had never been part of your nature
And the call from retirement was none of your choosing,
You danced in the end at another's direction;
So you can't be surprised if we find it amusing.

(4) Huai-yin
The brave must beware of the vicious dog's bite:
The gift of a throne on your fate set the seal.
Let us learn from your story the humble to prize,
And due gratitude show for the gift of a meal.

629   (5) <u>Gouang-Ling</u>
           Your crows and cicadas no more you shall hear
           By the old Sui embankment back home in the South.
           The scandalous story of those wanton times
           ~~Provides~~ Wags in many
           ~~Gives much work~~ for an idle, unsavoury mouth.

630   (6) <u>Peach Leaf Ford</u>
           In the water a scene of decay is reflected;
           Long since from its boughs the last peach-leaf (did fall) ~~has fallen~~.
           Your old Southern mansion has tumbled in ruins,
           And only your likeness looks down from the wall.

       (7) <u>Green Mound</u>
           The Amur's black flood for pure grief is arrested;
           The frozen string twangs with a heartbroken sound;
  fixed, ~~Replacing the harsh rule that ordered~~ this exile,
           A few crooked trees bow in shame to the ground.

       (8) <u>Ma-wei</u>
           The sad, ravaged face seemed to shine in its sweat;
           Then soon that sweet softness all vanished away.
           Yet something remained, for the well-known perfume
           In the clothing she wore lingers on to this day.

630 (9) The Temple at Pu-dong

 Young Reddie was ever a light, empty creature,
 Always to-ing and fro-ing in all kinds of weather.
 Though her Mistress in ire hung her up from the ceiling,
 These two had already been walking together.

 (10) The Plum-tree Shrine

 'I will be by the willow and not by the plum.'
 But who is it there will her likeness discover?
 Let not her full moon make you think that Spring's coming;
 For the cold parts her now till next year from her lover.

648 The Land of Eternal Spring
 Last night in ~~earthly~~ halls I ~~dreaming lay~~;
 Tonight beside the watery waste I sing.
 The island's cloud-cap drifts above the sea,
 And mists about its mountain forests cling.
 Our pasts and presents to the moon are one;
 Our lives and loves ~~beyond~~ our reckoning.
 Yet still my heart yearns for that distant South,
 Where time is lost in one eternal Spring.

665

ANCESTRAL TEMPLE
OF THE
JIA FAMILY

With loyal blood willingly shed upon the ground
    a myriad subjects pay tribute to their beneficent rulers.
For famous deeds resoundingly lauded to the skies
    a hundred generations offer sacrifices to their heroic ancestors.

HIS MINISTERS ARE AS SHINING STARS

Their achievements outshone the celestial luminaries
Their fame is reflected upon the generations that come after them

HONOUR THE DEAD AND KEEP THEIR MEMORIAL

Sons and grandsons enjoy the fruits of their blessedness
Common people recall Ning and Rong with kindness.

陸游

村居書喜　(1KKai p.120)

1202
ae. 78

紅橋梅市曉山橫
白塔樊江春水生
花氣襲人知驟暖
鵲聲穿樹喜新晴
坊場酒賤貧猶醉
原野泥深老亦耕
最喜先期官賦足
經年無吏叩柴荊

The flowers' own warmth of late days
~~And hush~~
Trees loud with ~~magpie~~ cries, clear skies

Frodsham: p. 38

李紳　　憫農詩
(古風二首：一作憫農)

春種一粒粟　　　鋤禾日當午
秋成萬顆子　　　汗滴禾下土
四海無閒田　　　誰知盤中餐
農夫猶餓死　　　粒粒皆辛苦

~~Each~~ ~~Un~~ ~~a grain of rice in ate ate~~
~~Has cost the farmer~~ ~~did~~ ~~~~

Each grain of rice we eat ate
Cost someone else a drop of sweat

猴子身輕站樹梢 —— 打一果名

荔枝

The monkey's tail reaches frr tee-hop to ground.

(Long'an)　LONGAN

266.　　寶釵　　　蘅蕪院　　　　蘅蕪君
　　　　黛玉　　　瀟湘館　　　　瀟湘妃
蕉下客（　迎春　The Parental Chamber　綴錦樓 —— 菱洲 Amaryllis
　　　　探春　　　秋掩書齋　Chap 37 (v.2) 秋爽齋. 秋爽居士
　　　　惜春　　　蓼風軒　　　藕榭 Lotus Pavilion
　　　　李紈　　　稻香村　　　稻香老農
　　　　寶玉　　　怡紅院　　　怡紅公子　　Green Boy

↳ p.443 寶釵道「他住的是紫菱洲...」

↳ 443 「丫頭住在藕香榭，就叫他藕榭」

　　　　　蕉下客

　　　　　　　　　　　　　西廂記
306　(1) 每日家情思睡昏昏　　聽琴第一折「油葫蘆」
　　 (2) 若共你多情小姐同鴛帳　鬧簡第二折「小梁州么篇」
　　　　怎捨得叠被鋪床

寧府花園賦

p. ×30

黃花滿地　　　　　Golden chrysanthemums covered the ∧over grass∧ lot
行柳橫坡　　　　　Stray willows bordered the walk's edge
小橋通荒耶之溪　　A little bridge ~~spans~~ ∧arches over∧ a (sky-lark?) ~~slim~~ ∧fairytale∧ stream ~~optimistic~~
曲徑接天台之路　　A winding path
石東清流滴滴　　　A rock ∧east∧ leaks a crystal brook
籬落飄香　　　　　A ~~sprawling hedge~~ ∧quietent hedge∧ ~~shed~~ ∧perceiving∧ fumes
樹頭紅葉翩翩　　　Upon the boughs the crimson leaves
疏林如畫　　　　　A lean [?] and a ~~fine~~ ∧wintry∧ copse suggested allegories ∧leaves∧

西風乍緊
獨聽鶯啼喧語
暖日又添蛩語　　　　　　　　　　　giống
遙望東南　　　　　　　　　　　　　nhất
建几處依山之榭
近觀西北
結三間臨水之軒
笙簧盈座
別有幽情
羅綺穿林
信添韻致

Note:「只見」— This is supposed to be a description of the garden as it was — in winter. 黃花 and 紅葉 just possible — but what about 花飄香, 鶯啼, 蛩語?

p.132 　双官誥

戯曲の名、明 陳二白の作、馮仁の妻 碧蓮貞節を守り、子を撫育し栄を受けたことを記す

See 曲海総目提要 1385 cq

So. 子 faithful 碧蓮。 th 道房婦 々 浮琳如

Coleeu 双官誥 bream

「父子官誥, 皆由碧蓮」

(曲海総 ⓒ清 陳二白). C Faithful Pi-Cien

榆 elanced 菜 jiè Rebs, seeds.

還魂 punning 牡丹亭 と 湯顕祖

彈詞 Gou't fradee being fly a sea.

長生殿 第三十八齣

洪昇 1645-1704

Lei Kuei-nien plays his guitar

252

A crude gloss to try & break oxide the meaning of a monkish home who turned in my bound feet less than. & [...]

漫揾英雄淚
相離處士家 [...]   [乞士家] [且住，我從今日打起了
謝慈悲剃度在蓮台下 [恁個] 鄭屠，怎那師父相抱。
沒緣法   幸有今日，師父呀]
轉眼分離乍   There was no time to say why
赤條條~~輕裝~~來去無牽掛   And now king I only other
那裏討   Naked & empty & regret must
烟蓑雨笠卷單行。   I ask no love a charm to bear again.
一任俺   [敲碎缽]   by other smiles or a direct love
芒鞋破鉢隨緣化。   To try for a place to place a
                    bed I try

卷單，捲單，捲堂：謂寺院中僧人全散。
乞士：僧之別稱
漫：胡亂，隨便。
乍：猝乍，衝動，緊張。（心慌乍，etc）
牽去：牽絆，
缽盂
蓮台：佛座   p. 38 詩人：陸游 村居書喜
緣法：緣分   (一海 120) 1202 ae. 78
                    poem
                    with the pleasure of village life.
                    ll. 3、 花氣襲人知驟暖
                       4   鵲聲穿樹喜新晴

NOTES.

p.209 「謝家池塘」
南史 謝惠連傳

惠連十歲能屬文，族兄靈運嘉賞之，云每有篇章
對惠連輒得佳句，嘗於永嘉西堂思詩，
竟日不就，忽夢見惠連，便得「池塘生春草」之
句，大以為工。

蘅蕪：香名。拾遺記「〈武〉帝息于延涼室、臥夢李夫人
授帝蘅蕪之香、帝驚起、而香氣尤著衣枕、歷
月不歇」

蘅薛 Kazura just means 'vines' 'creepers'

p.207 金谷酒 石崇 金谷園詩序：「余以元康六年從太僕卿
出為持節、監青徐諸軍事、征虜將軍有別廬在河陽
縣界金谷澗中，有清泉茂林、眾果竹柏、藥草之屬，莫不
畢備、又有水碓魚池土窟、其為娛目歡心之物備矣。時征西大將軍祭酒王詡當還長
安、余與眾賢共送、往澗中、晝夜遊宴、屢遷其坐，或登
高臨下、或列坐水濱。時琴笙筑合載車中、道路並
作、及住令鼓吹遞奏。遂各賦詩以敘中懷，或不能者
罰酒三斗」

蘅芷：
芷芸+若芷

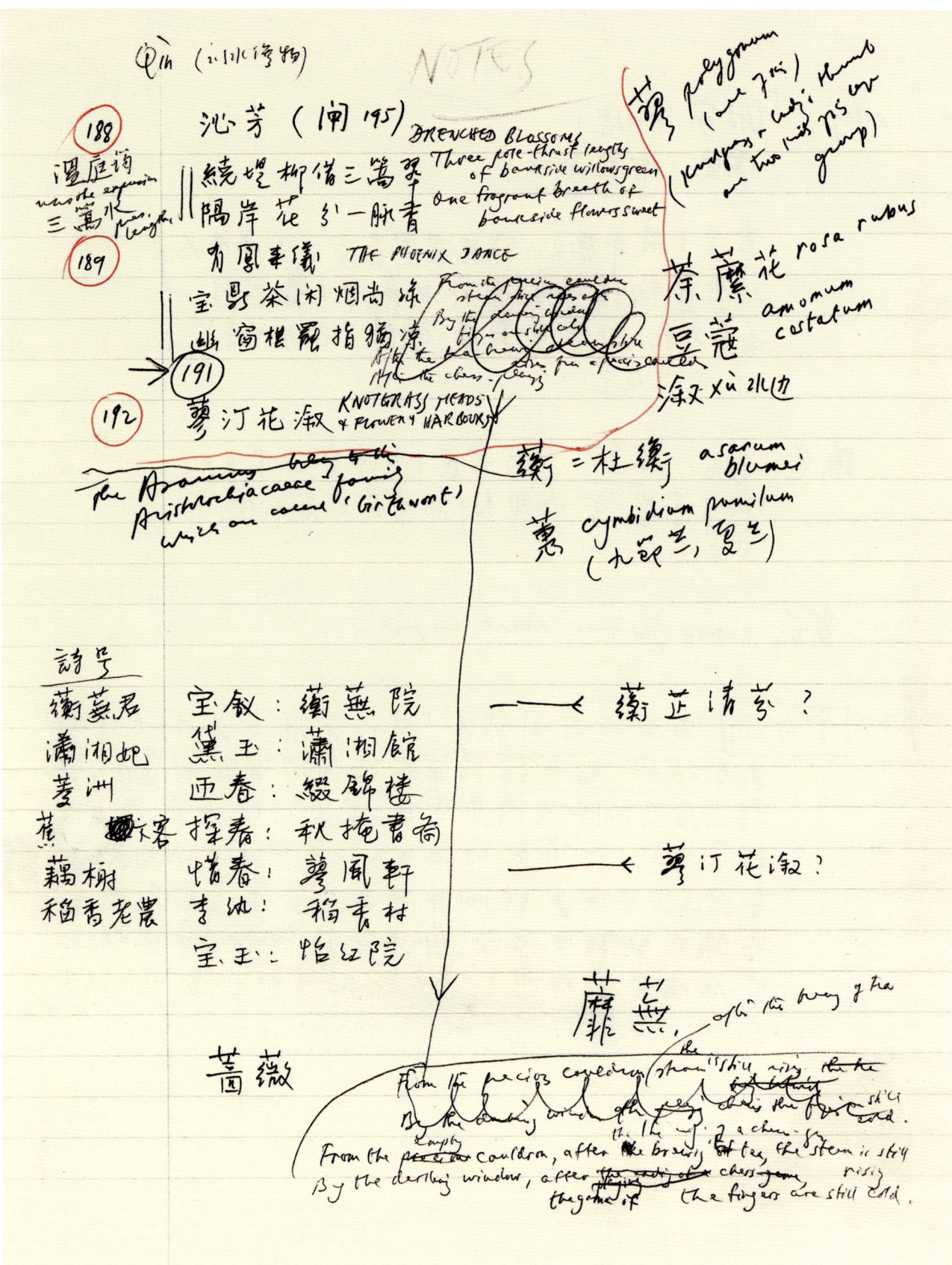

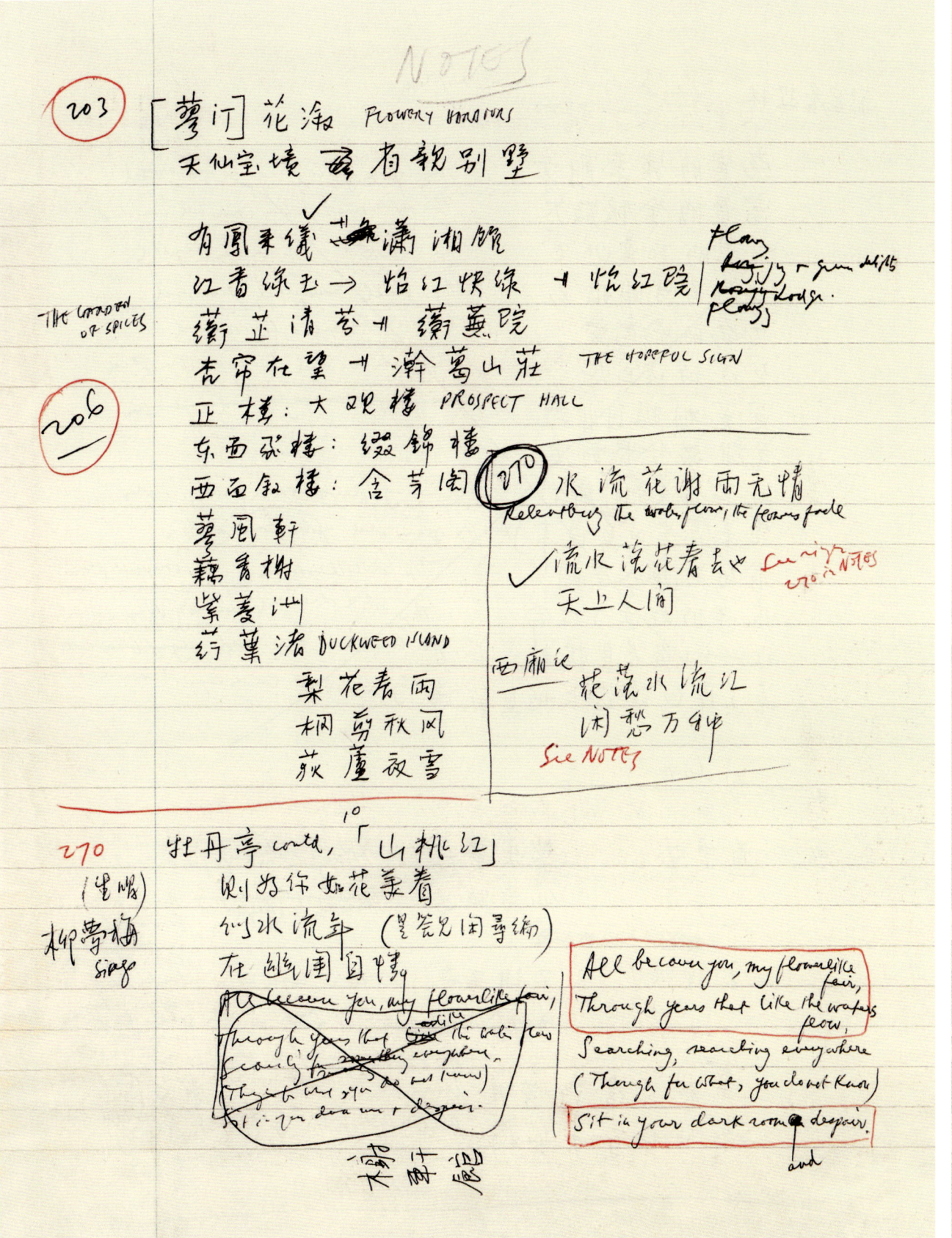

飛鳥各投林   The birds into the wood have flown

為官的家業雕零　　The office jack's come [is shifted]
富貴的金銀散盡　　The rich man's fortune now all vanished
有恩的死裏逃生　　The kind soul's life has been requited
無情的分明報應　　The cruel exemplarily punished
欠命的命已還　　　The one who owed a life is dead
欠淚的淚已盡　　　The tears we owed have all been shed
冤冤相報自非輕　　~~Wrong begets wrong is hard enough to bear~~
分離聚合皆前定
欲知命短問前生　　Unking death sin in past life rights
老來富貴也真僥倖　　And prospers old youths painless lies
看破的遁入空門　　The disillusioned to the convent flies
癡迷的枉送了性命　　The still deluded miserably dies
好一似食盡鳥投林　　As birds who, having fed, to the wood upon
落了片白茫茫大地真乾淨　　The cruel landscape desolate & bare.

untimely death

96. 通靈寶玉：　莫失莫忘 } Mislay me not forget me not
　　正面：　　仙壽恆昌 } ~~And length of days~~ I shall be your life
　　　　　●●●●●●●●●
　　金鎖正面　不離不棄 } Ne'er leave me or abandon me
　　　　反面　芳齡永繼 } Long years & heart ~~give you to thee~~
　　　　　　　　　　　　　While in youth.

144.　三春去後諸芳盡　　When the three springs' have gone the flowers
　　　各自須尋各自門　　And each for living must find as best she
　　　　　　　　　　　　　　may.

(1) 鵬賦:「達人大觀兮物無不可」, 范仲淹〈岳陽樓記〉「予觀夫巴陵勝狀在洞庭一湖，銜遠山，吞長江，浩浩湯湯，橫無際涯，朝暉夕陰，氣象万千，此則岳陽樓之大觀也」(3) 晉書·李意經「吉凶時成，融暉大觀」

192　新綠漲添浣葛處　Fresh ripples widen where the ~~green buds swell~~ ~~kerchief washer~~ ~~emergent~~ strongly soaked ~~too close~~
　　好雲香護採芹人　A fresh tang rises where the cress-gatherer ~~smokes~~ his incense ~~cloth~~

浣 huan³ = 浣

194　麝蘭芳靄斜陽院　A musky perfume of orchids hangs in the ~~forest~~ courtyard (sunset)
　　杜若香飄明月洲　A sweet aroma of galingale floats over the moonlit island

SEE 杜詩 蘼蕪

　　三徑香風飄玉蕙　Down garden walks a fragrant breeze caresses the banks of melilot ~~Throughout~~ ~~the garden~~ Fills the courtyard bright moonlight glitters on
　　一庭明月照金蘭　garden orchids

　　吟成豆蔻詩猶艷　~~Composing~~ ~~amidst~~ ownonous ~~verses~~ Sweet on verses like flowers your
書成好葉　睡足荼蘼夢亦香　Sleeping amidst the roses ~~sweet dream fragrant~~
　　(your verses are like flowers, your dreams are fragrant)

204　金門玉戶神仙府　The dwelling of the ~~immortals~~ has golden doors and jewelled windows
　　桂殿蘭宮妃子家　The abode of the princess has cassia halls and orchid chambers

　　顧恩思義
　　~~gratitude~~ ~~touch~~ ~~loyalty~~　FAVOUR RECEIVED KINDNESS LOYALTY ~~BLESS~~ OWED

(大觀園對聯)

206　天地啟宏慈　For all ~~on~~ earth to share a great compassion has been
　　赤子蒼生同感戴　extended that children and humble folk may gratefully enjoy
　　古今垂曠典　For all ages to admire a noble institution has been
　　九州万国被恩榮　provided that ~~all ~~~~~~ people of every land and clime may exult in.

(元春題匾句)

　　銜山抱水建來精　Embracing hills & streams, with skill they wrought;
　　多少工夫築始成　At last their work is to perfection brought.
　　天上人间諸景備　Earth's fancied prospects all are here installed,
　　芳園應錫「大觀」名　~~The best~~ So 'Prospect Garden' let its name be called!

Prospect Garden

NOTES

270　再词中又有「流水……」

　　from 浪淘沙 号 南唐後主李煜 (937–978: he lost his Kingdom ae. 40 in 976 and was poisoned on his birthday. t.t)

簾外雨潺潺
春意闌珊
羅衾不耐五更寒
夢裏不知身是客
一晌貪歡
* * * *
獨自莫憑闌
無限江山
別時容易見時難
流水落花春去也
天上人間

I must not from the window gaze alone
At that great wealth of lands and lake
So soon but so irrevocably gone.
The blossoms fall, the water flows,
The glory of the spring is done
In ~~our~~ nature's world as in the human one.

270　忽又想起前日見古人詩中，有「水流花謝……」

　　from 春夕 号 崔塗 (江南人，光啓四年 [888] 進士)

See 全唐詩 10/7783

水流花謝兩無情
送盡東風過楚城
胡蝶夢中家萬里
子規枝上月三更
故園書動經年絕
華髮春催滿鏡生
自是不歸歸便得
五湖煙景有誰爭

Relentlessly the water flows, the flowers fade

NOTES

270　　又兼方才所見西廂記中「花落⋯⋯」
　　　From 西廂記 第一本 楔子 賞花時么篇 (旦扮鶯鶯唱)

可正是人值殘春蒲郡東,
門掩重關蕭寺中*
花落水流紅　　　　　*This line is from 李紳's
閒愁萬種　　　　　　鶯鶯歌 (hence 可正是)
無語怨東風

~~Here, east of P'u-chou, as the springtime ends,
Behind cloud doors within the monastery walls confined
As flows fall and the flowing stream runs red
~~and chide~~ sickly fancies crowd the mind
A thousand ~~tantalizing~~ thoughts arise
And chide the heartless wind with words unsaid.~~

Here, east of P'u-chou, at the springtime's ends,
Within these monastery walls confined
As flows fall and the flowing stream runs red
A thousand sickly fancies crowd the mind
And chide the heartless wind with words unsaid.

191　舊詩云:「紅杏梢頭掛酒旗」?
　　　~~hitherto~~ Midst apricots a hopeful inn-sign hangs

太和6 殿中　　唐人詩裏還有「柴門臨水稻花香」(丁卯集上8a)
　監察御史　　　　　　　　　　　　　　　　　SPTK
大中3
　　　元稹 隱春郊園、　許渾 晚至章隱居郊園
全唐詩 8/6090　晚自朝臺津至韋隱居郊園
秋來鳧雁下方塘,繫馬朝臺步夕陽。村徑繞山松葉暗,野門
臨水稻花香。雲生海氣琴書潤,風帶潮聲枕簟涼。西下
磻溪猶萬里,可能垂白待文王。

NOTES

269　　我就一个「多愁多病的身.....」
　　　　　西廂記　第一本第四折　雁兒落 (生唱)
　　我則道這玉天仙離了碧霄
　　元來是可意種來清醮......　How can I, full of sickness and of woe,
　　小子多愁多病身　　　　　　withstand that face which Kingdoms
　　怎當他傾國傾城貌　　　　　could o'erthrow?

270　　原來也是个「銀樣....」
　　　　　西廂記　第四本　第二折　小桃紅 (紅娘唱)
　　既然泄漏怎干休
　　是我相投首
　　俺家裏陪酒陪茶到擂就
　　你休愁　　　　　　　　　...You are a sham spear with
　　何須約定通媒媾　　　　　　soft leaden head.
　　我豈了部署不收
　　你元來苗而不秀
　　呸、你是个銀樣鑞鎗頭

---

(194)　　那人引古詩「蘼蕪滿院泣斜陽」
　　　The garden's gilly- The garden's violets at sunset weep.
　　　　　flower

194.　　這兒套的「書成蕉葉文猶綠」
　　　　written in plantain-leaves, and cool [?] upon
　　　　I shall give verse made

254 巧者勞而智者憂，無能者無所求，蔬食而遨遊，泛若不系之舟
　　　莊子 列禦寇 (Giles 305)

山木自寇　The timber tree
　　莊子．人間世 (Giles 62)

源泉自盜
　　doesn't appear to come in Chuang Tzu

巧者勞而智者憂　　The cunning waste their powers
無能者無所求　　　The wise are vex their brains
飽 蔬食而遨遊　　　But the simpleton, he wants no gains.
泛若不系之舟　　　He's belly full, he wanders free
　　　　　　　　　　Like drifting boat upon the sea.
　　　　　　　　　　No boat

256 身是菩提樹　　　Our
　　　心如明鏡台　　The The body's like the Bo-tree is,
　　　時時勤拂拭　　Our
　　　莫使有塵埃　　The mind's a mirror bright.
　　　　　　　　　　Then
　　　　　　　　　　So keep it clean & free from dust
　　　　　　　　　　And just so reflect the light

　　　菩提本非樹　　No real Bo-tree the body is,
　　　明鏡亦非台　　The mirror not mirror bright.
　　　本來無一物　　Since of the pair none's really there
　　　何處染塵埃　　On what could dust alight?

南宗六祖惠能[慧能]　　上座 神秀　senior monk
五祖宏忍　　　　　　　　　　Bo-tree

207

〈迎春：曠性怡情〉　　　　HEART'S EASE
園成景物特精奇　　The garden finished, all its prospect please.
奉命羞題額曠怡　　Bidden to write, I name this spot 'Heart's Ease'.
誰識世間有此境　　Who would have thought on earth such scene to find
游來寧不暢神思　　To here refresh the heart & ease the mind?
　　　　　　　　　PRECIOUSNESS (BRILLIANCE AND GRACE)

〈探春：文采風流〉　　　BRIGHTNESS AND BEAUTY
秀水明山抱復回　　Water on hills and hills on waters smile,
風流文采勝蓬萊　　More bright and beauteous than the Immortal Isle.
綠裁歌扇迷芳草　　Midst odorous herbs the singer's green fan hides;
紅襯湘裙舞落梅　　~~And bird flies~~ 'Mid crimson skirts through falling petals glides.
珠玉自應傳盛世　　A radiant jewel to the world is shown;
神仙何幸下瑤台　　A fairy princess from her tower comes down.
名園一自邀遊賞　　And since her steps the garden's walks have trod,
未許凡人到此來　　No mortal foot must desecrate its sod.

〈惜春：文章造化〉　　　BEAUTY'S HANDMAID ART THE CREATOR
山水橫拖千里外　　The garden's landscape far outside extends
樓台高起五雲中　　High as the clouds its buildings raise their heads;
園修明月光輝靄　　Serene is moonlight, radiant is the sun —
景奪文章造化功　　Great Nature's handiwork has been outdone.

〈李紈：萬象爭輝〉　　　ALL THINGS BRIGHT AND BEAUTIFUL
名園築就勢巍巍　　The finished garden is a wondrous sight.
奉命多慚學淺微　　Unlettered and unskilled, I blush to write.
精妙一時言不盡　　Its marvels are not in one phrase expressed,
果然萬物有光輝　　Yet 'Bright & Beautiful' I judge it best.

⟨薛宝釵：凝暉鍾瑞⟩ AUSPICIOUS SKIES

207　芳園築向帝城西　West of imperial walls the garden lies;
　　華日祥雲籠罩奇　The sun beams on it from auspicious skies.

瞻仰：　高柳喜遷鶯出谷　Its willows orioles from the vale invite;
觀看他人事物　修篁時待鳳來儀　Tall bamboos tempt the phoenix to alight.
之敬辭　　文風已著宸遊夕　Poetic arts this night must celebrate

ruì zǎo:　孝化應隆歸省時　Filial affection dressed in robes of state.
天子所製之　睿藻仙才瞻仰處　Dare I, who here those jewelled phrases read,
文章　　　自慚何敢再為辭　Add more to what they have already said?

⟨林黛玉：世外仙源⟩ THE FAIRY STREAM

chén yóu　宸遊增悅豫　To fairy haunts far from the world's away
　　　　　仙境別紅塵　A royal visit brings a double joy.
敷 one can　借得山川秀　A thousand borrowed beauties here combined
（如：界下　添來氣象新　In this new setting a new magic find.
敷之城）　　香融金谷酒　Its odours scent a poet's wine enrich;
玉堂：妃嬪　花媚玉堂人　Its flowers a queenly visitor bewitch.
所居之處　何幸邀恩寵　May she wed in this favour hope to join:
　　　　　宮車過往頻　oft times

⟨宝玉：有鳳來儀⟩ THE PHOENIX DANCE

208　秀玉初成實　Perfected now at last, this place is fit
　　堪宜待鳳凰　For Bird of Paradise to visit.
　　竿竿青欲滴　Each graceful wand lets fall a dewy tear;
　　个个綠生涼　Each glossy leaf breathes coolness on the air.
　　迸砌防階水　Through narrow parted rocks the pent stream leaps;
　　穿簾礙鼎香　Through chinks of blind the incense thinly seeps.
　　莫搖分碎影　Let none the checkered shade with violence rude
　　好夢正初長　and disrupting on the slumberer's dreams intrude.

THE GARDEN OF SPICES

〈宝玉：蘅芷清芬〉

蘅芜满静苑　Fragrance of flower-drifts in these quiet confines
萝薜助芬芳　Mixes with the headier scents of eglantines,
软衬三春草　And summer's herbs in a soft, spicy bed
柔拖一缕香　Their aromatic perfumes subtly spread.
轻烟迷曲径　Light mist half screens the winding walks from view:
冷翠湿衣裳　Where chilly verdure rocks the cloak with dew.
谁谓「池塘」曲　Here slumbering quietly at the fountain's side,
谢家幽梦长　The dreaming poet all day long may bide.

THE PLACE OF GREEN DELIGHTS

〈宝玉：怡红快绿〉 Resistibly lords rank in rout appear:

深庭长日静　In this quiet plot when peace reigns high the year
两两出婵娟　A thousand long ———— appear:
绿蜡春犹卷　Some in the spring wear waxy sheaths curled tight,
红妆夜未眠　Some, scarlet caps, that are not doffed at night
凭栏垂绛袖　Some from the trellis trail their purple sleeves,
倚石护青烟　Some lean on rocks, where thin mists cool their leaves
对立东风里　Their master, standing in the soft summer breeze,
主人应解怜　Finds quiet content in everything he sees.

〈宝玉：杏帘在望〉 THE HOPEFUL SIGN

杏帘招客饮　Though the orchard half-screened
在望有山庄　An inn-sign, + a drink well-earned.
菱荇鹅儿水　Promises ———— shelter
桑榆燕子梁　Through water-weeds the pond's green surface showing
一畦春韭熟　Midst elms and mulberry-trees the swallows play
十里稻花香　The garden's chives are ready to prepare;
盛世无饥馁　The scent of young rice perfumes all the air
何须耕织忙　When want is banished, as in times like these,
　　　　　　The spinner & the ploughman take their ease.

菱荇
榆 elm

⟨代玉：絕句⟩

243
無端弄筆是何人
剿襲南華莊子文
不悔自家無見識
卻將醜語詆他人

What wretch would dare, with scurrile pen,
The text of Chuang-tzu plagiarize,
And, heedless of his own great fault,
Fright others with his horrid lies?

254) 你證我證
心證意證
是無有證
斯可云證
無可云證
是立足境

252 ⟨寄生草⟩ 集成.金集卷7.6a

255
無我原非你
從他不解伊
肆行無礙憑來去
茫茫著甚悲愁喜
紛紛說甚親疏密
從前碌碌卻因何
到如今，回頭試想真無趣

You were at fault, if not I;
But why should I care if they disagree?
Free come, free go, no need to...
No more I'll grieve or rejoice...
Or endlessly debate the depth of our relation
When I look back it seems scarce worth the bother

I swear, you swear,
with heart & mind declare
But our protest
is no true test
It would be best
without [words] to understand
And on to find
To have no ground
on which to stand
were yet more sound

258
賈政
Inkstone
身自端方
體自堅硬
雖不能言
有言必應

My body's square
Iron-hard am I
I speak no word
But words supply.

259
元妃
Firework
能使妖魔膽盡摧
身如束帛氣如雷
一聲震得人方恐
回首相看已化灰

At my coming the devils turn pallid with wonder
My body's all folds & my voice is like thunder
When, alarmed by the sound of my thunder crack
You look round, you have already turned to ash.

迎春：
Abacus
天運人功理不窮
有功無運也難逢
因何鎮日紛紛亂
只為陰陽數不通

Man's works & heaven's laws I execute.
Without heaven's blessing, man's works bear no fruit.
Why must I hustle-bustle all day long?
Because I fear my numbers may be wrong.

My strength is gone when once its bed is past
And on it and I drift of breath-bereaved.

"ride so proudly in"

259 探春: Kite
階下兒童仰面時
清明妝點最堪宜
游絲一斷渾無力
莫向東風怨別離

In spring the little boys look up & stare
To see me ~~spread of beauty~~ proudly in the air.
~~...~~
wherein the

代玉: Incense clock
朝罷誰攜兩袖烟
琴邊衾裡兩無緣
曉籌不用雞人報
五夜無煩侍女添
焦首朝朝還暮暮
煎心日日復年年
光陰荏苒須當惜
風雨陰晴任變遷

At court levée my smoke is in your sleeve
Music and beds to others ~~for~~ sort I leave.
At dawn ~~with me~~ you need no watchman's cry
At night no maid need trig a fresh supply.
My head burns through the night & thye'll day
And yearly year my heart consumes away.
The precious moments I would have you spare,
But come fair, foul or fine, I don't care.

宝玉: Mirror
南面而坐
北面而朝
象憂亦憂
象喜亦喜

~~Face~~ Southward you stare,
He'll northward glare.
~~You~~ Grieve, and he is sad.
~~You~~ Laugh, and he is glad.

---

260 宝釵: Bamboo wife
有眼無珠腹內空
荷花出水喜相逢
梧桐葉落分離別
恩愛夫妻不到冬

My 'eyes' cannot see & I'm hollow inside,
When the lotuses surface, I'll be your bride.
When the autumn leaves fall I ~~shall~~ bid you adieu
~~For~~ For our marriage must end once the summer is through.

春 / SPRING

266

春霧綃雲幄任鋪陳 Behind silk hangings, in warm quilts cocooned,
隔巷蛙聲聽未真 His ears half doubt the first frogs' muffled sound.
枕上輕寒窗外雨 Rain at his window strikes, the pillow's cold;
眼前春色夢中人 Yet to the sleeper's eyes spring dreams unfold.
盈盈燭淚因誰泣 Why does the candle shed its waxen tears?
宊宊花愁為我嗔 Why on each flower do angry drops appear?
侍兒小鬟嬌懶慢 By uncouth din from giggling maids
梳鬟不耐笑言頻 She burrows deeper in his silken nest.

夏 / SUMMER

267

倦繡佳人幽夢長 A tired maid sleeps at her embroidery.
金籠鸚鵡喚茶湯 A parrot in its gilt cage calls for tea.
窗明麝月閒宮鏡 Full moonbeams on an opened mirror fall
室霭檀雲品御香 And burning sandal marks a fragrant pall.
琥珀杯傾荷露滑 From amber cups thirst-quenching nectar flows
玻璃檻納柳風涼 A willow-breeze through crystal curtains flows
小亭廊廊閒次動 on poolside kiosk light dews flit
簾卷朱樓罷晚妝 Or, by open casements sit.

麝月：古女子妝號，釵鈿之類。But Mor. says 二月.
有此二朝 examples, of 此 use of 產品.

秋 / AUTUMN

絳芸軒 ruta graveolens, common rue, herb of grace
麝月：茶名

絳芸軒裏絕喧嘩 In book-lined study, far from worldly din,
桂魄流光浸茜紗 Through rosy gauze moonlight comes flooding in.
苔鎖石紋容睡鶴 Outside, a stork sleeps on moss-wrinkled rocks,
井飄桐露濕棲鴉 And dew from well-side trees the crow's wings soaks.
抱衾婢至舒金鳳 A maid the quilt's gold phoenix unspread
倚檻人歸落翠花 Her languid master drops his raven hood
靜夜不眠因酒渴 Wine-parched & sleepless, in the still night he cries
沉烟重撥索烹茶 For tea, & soon thick smoke & steam arise.

WINTER

267
梅魂竹夢已三更　Midnight and winter: plum with bamboo sleep,
錦罽鵷衾睡未成　[crossed out] one midst Indian rugs his vigil keeps.
松影一庭惟見鶴　Only a stran[crossed out] [crossed out] found:
梨花滿地不聞鶯　No sides, though white petals mark the ground.
女奴翠袖詩懷冷　Chill strikes the maid's bones though her garments fine;
公子金貂酒力輕　Her fur-clad master's somewhat worn for wine.
卻喜侍兒知試茗　But [crossed out], in the [crossed out] mystic's dry skill,
掃將新雪及時烹　[crossed out] with fresh [crossed out] the kettle [crossed out] fired.
　　　　　　　　　　/new-swept

297
鼻如懸膽兩眉蒼　A bottle-nose he had and shaggy brows
目似明星有寶光　Through which peered eyes that twinkled like bright stars.
破衲芒鞋等閒過　[crossed out]
朣朧更有一頭瘡　(His undern[crossed out] [crossed out] [crossed out] noted with unsightly scars
　　　　　　　　　(His robe all patched & tattered)

298
一足高來一足低　Up, down he tipped on his unequal legs
渾身帶水又拖泥　From mud & puddle not a stitch left dry.
相逢若問家何處　If you observed [crossed out] his where his home might be,
卻在蓬萊弱水西　'Westward of Paradise', he would reply.

天不拘兮地不羈　Time nor you bind in perfect liberty,
心頭等喜亦等悲　Your heart alike from joy & sorrow free,
只因鍛煉通靈後　[crossed out]
便向人間惹是非　[crossed out]

Till by the smith's alchemy transformed,
Late the world you come to stir up misery.

剔小毛蛋
地蛋數
鵚 (a.鵡)
= 鷫鷞
sù-shuāng
jungueise
Kingfisher

áng-zāng

298 云二淳泿 wǔ	粉渍脂痕污宝光 房栊日夜困鸳鸯 沈酣一梦终须醒 冤债偿清好散场	The jewel with ~~paint & powder~~ is besmirched; pulpy is jade's hue The pair bird sleeps, in its close prison perched. From drunken dream one day you'll ~~recover~~ ~~the day from this drugged dream you~~ then, When all debts are paid, the play will soon be over.
312	花魂点点无情绪 鸟梦痴痴何處惊	Tears filled each flower & grief these hearts pulsed And silly birds were on from their dreams disturbed
	孽冤才貌世应稀 独抱幽芳出绣闺 呜咽一声犹未了 落花满地鸟惊飞	Few in this world surpassed Frowner's looks ~~in most beauty~~ she was unmatched both ~~virtues~~ The first sob scarcely from her lips had passed When flowers fell & birds flew off distressed
257	大哥有角只八个 二哥有角只两根 木哥只在床上坐 二哥爱在房上蹲	Elder brother ~~has~~ with eight ~~cats~~ sits all day on the bed Younger broth' with two sprouts on its roof's head.
姹 chà 270 嫣治 嫣yān (诸艳蔻蔻花)	原来是姹紫嫣红开遍 们这般 都付与断井颓垣	Here multiflorate splendour Flowers forlorn 'Midst broken fountains, mouldery ways,
270	良辰美景奈何天 赏心乐事谁家院…	And the bright air, the brilliant morn or Feed my dejection Joy & gladness have withdrawn To other gardens, other halls.

牡丹亭·10 惊梦 (或·游园)「皁罗袍」

Chen-chu	(珍珠)	Pearl	
Ch'ien-hsüeh	(茜雪) p.86	Snowpink	
Chin-ch'uan	(金釧)	Golden	(Jewel's sister)
Ch'ing-wen	(晴雯)	Skybright	
Ch'iu-t'ung	(秋桐)	Autumn	
Ch'iu-wen	(秋紋)	Ripple	
Chui-erh	(墜兒)	~~Gem~~ ? Trinket — Felicity	
Feng-erh → Hsi-jen	(襲人)(説)	~~Fragr~~ Aroma	Cathy
Hsiang-ling	(香菱)	~~Golding Lily~~ ~~? Cotton~~ Lotus	
Hsiao-hung	(小紅)	~~Reddie~~ Crimson ? ~~tiny~~ ~~Ruby~~	
Hsüeh-yen	(雪雁)	Snowgoose	
Ju-hua	(入画)	Picture	
Jui-chu	(瑞珠)	Gem	
Lin Wu-erh	(柳五兒)	Five / Liu Five Little Fin	
Mei-jen	(媚人)	Winsome	
~~ Pao-chu	(宝珠)	~~Pearl~~ Jewel	
Pi-hen	(碧痕)	Emerald	
P'ing-erh	(平兒)	Patience	
Sha-ta-chieh	(傻大姐)	~~Dafnee~~ ? Simple	
→ Shih-shu	(侍書)	~~Booksy~~ Bookgirl	
She-yüeh	(麝月)	Musk	
(Ssu-erh	(四兒)	Little Four ~~Chessie~~ ? Chessie ~~Gamesy~~ ~~Chess~~	
(Ssu-ch'i	(司棋)	~~Chess~~ Sunset Chessgirl	
Ts'ai-hsia Ts'ai-ming	(彩霞) (彩明)	Sunset Sunshine	
Ts'ai-yun	(彩雲)	~~Cloud~~ Suncloud	
Ts'ui-lü	(翠縷)	Kingfisher	Yuan-yang
Ying-ko → Tzu-chüan	(紫鵑)	Nightingale Parrot ← 鸚哥	(鴛鴦) ~~Duckie~~ ? Faithful
Ying-erh	(鶯兒)	Oriole Silver Jewel	
Yü-ch'uan	(玉釧)	~~Bracelet~~ Jewel	(Gold's sister)

58　文官　蕊官　莒官　官
　　　芳官　藕官　艾官　官
　　　齡官　葵官　茄官　官
　　　　　　　　　　　葯官

Lady Wong
Lady Hsing
Lady Chia (Grandame Chia)　葯

Aunt Hsieh
Prince Pei-ching

Sir Cheng, Chia Cheng
Sir She, Chia She
Sir Ching, Chia Ching

Auntie Chao, Mrs. Chao

Nannie Li

賴大　Old Lai　　Big Lai?
焦大　Old Chiao　Big Chiao

Grannie Liu　　　——姑娘 Miss...
　(劉老老)　　　——奶奶 Mrs...

　　　　　　　　賈璉　Mr Lien
　　　　　　　　鳳奶奶 Mrs Lien

——家的 Chou's wife
　　Wong's wife

二錢 : 2 drams	人參	Panax ginseng (ginseng)
二錢 : 2 drams	白朮	Atractylis ovata
三錢 : 3 drams	雲苓 = 茯苓	Pachyma Cocos. (angl. Lycoperdon) ('Indian Bread')
四錢 : 4 drams	✗ 熟地 (熟地黃) 地黃 = 沙參	Adenophora verticillata (processed by being soaked, powdered and dried. (Blue bell) ✗
二錢 : 2 drams	歸身 (當歸)	Aralia edulis (處方用名:「白歸身」)
二 : 2 drams	白芍 = 白芍藥	Paeonia albiflora (white peony root)
一錢五分 : 1½ drams	川芎	conioselinum univittatum (hemlock parsley)
三錢 : 3 drams	黃芪	Astragalus hoangtchy (root) (Yellow vetch)
二錢 : 2 drams	香附米	(root of) cyperus rotundus (束 pre? ground) nutgrass
八分 : ⅘ dram	醋柴胡	Bupleurum falcatum (?醋) (sickle-leaved hare's ear)
二錢 : 2 drams	懷山藥	山藥: 薯蕷之別名 Dioscorea japonica. (薯蕷生懷慶山中者 白細堅實, 入藥用之) (Chinese yam)
二錢 : 2 drams.	真阿膠	asses' glue. (原產出山東省東阿縣, 以阿井之水煮驢皮熬膠而成之)
一錢五分 : 1½ drams	延胡索	Corydalis bulbosa (Mod.Sys C. ambigua)
八分 : ⅘ drams	炙甘草	Glycyrrhiza glabra (炙××: 即甘草焙炒成者之處方用名) (Liquorice)
	肉桂	cortex cinnamomi Cassiae
	附子	aconitum autumnale 'autumn root' (a kind of aconite)
	麥冬 (= 麥門冬)	liriope spicata 'black leek'.
	玉竹	polygonatum officinale 'Solomon's seal'.
	鱉甲	
	独參湯	

中國藥學大辭典

[水陸儀軌]　（法界聖凡水陸勝會修齋儀軌）　宋志磐撰
　　　　　　　　　　　　　　　　　　　　　明袾宏重訂
續藏經 第二編乙（129）p.1860 sq.

法師觀地獄因緣業障根塵榮召請,未能脫離,有異方便可使畢至表白振鈴,破閉地獄:

「……我今奉宣華嚴會中覺林菩薩所說破地獄偈及為持誦破地獄真言……」

法師想十方地獄鐵門戶一振兩開,其中一切苦具悉皆隱沒,一切因緣蒙聞咒音咸識本心苦相告報,來赴法會,念求解脫,表白振鈴持開道經

「……久處三塗,祗今自便於此時,猶或未通於前路,既至於嶮峨之地,應身於幽闇之鄉,若此多艱,何能善達,載憑初寶功,示現光明之幢,將激照於昏衢……」

(1884) 法單,表白振鈴施主道衣服於法堂前變化冥衣,無則已,白云:

———

前二日　詢內壇外壇。
前一日　法師親視牌軸扁安之
　　　　午後內壇鳴擂鼓諷誦金光懺文一卷
第一日　三更外壇灑淨
　　　　四更內壇結界
　　　　五更遣使捎擔
第二日　四更請上堂
　　　　五更奉浴
第三日　四更供上堂
　　　　五更請赦
　　　　是日午刻通壇內外僧皆以錢代飯
第四日　三更請下堂
　　　　四更奉浴
　　　　五更說戒

第五日　四更　誦信心銘
　　　　五更　供下堂
　　　　是日午刻齋僧並上供

第六日　四更　主法親視上下堂　洞宣情懇
　　　　巳時　行放生
　　　　未時　結勝幡

第七日　五更　普供上下堂
　　　　巳時　結願
　　　　午時　齋僧並上供
　　　　未時　迎至外壇
　　　　申時　送聖
　　　　戌時　大衆行瑜珈焰食
　　　　　　　刻明畢

終一日　主法接見外壇人天，示以法器無始終義宣。

破地獄　魏國水陸通論　324頁 has a list.

澤田瑞穗　地獄變　cap. 1984 emphasizes importance of 五七日
(接五七) It was the day of H 35th of the 15 spins. 7it and called the
塔鄧名 + listed with boutique duration. Sun pears loves
the deceased clan n its cage.

　　　　佛說閻羅王受記經

（閻羅王 is "Yes" そに5"7.）

　　玉曆勸得（玉帝慈恩警戒……）

女兒悲   The girl's upset
- 宝 青春已大守空閨   The years pass by & he has been claimed kept yet
- 馮 兒夫染病在垂危   Her husband's ill, she fears there is a knot
- 雲 將來終身倚靠誰   What ~~~~ ready
- 薛 嫁了个男人是烏龜   She's married to a ~~~~
- 圖 丈夫一去不回歸   Her husband's gone & she prays he won't forget

女兒愁   The girl ~~~~ fies all glum
- 宝 悔教夫婿覓封侯   She let her true love flew out of his dream
- 馮 大風吹倒梳妝樓   The gale has turned her room into a glum
- 雲 綉房鉆出个大馬猴   John Thomas has slopped ~~~~ dig-a-da-dum
- 薛 媽媽打罵何時休   Nosy her cross ~~~~ ends for ~~~~
- 圖 無錢去打桂花油   So short of cash she can't afford a comb

女兒喜   The girl ~~~~ beached
- 宝 對鏡晨妝顏色美   The mirror shows her just at their best
- 馮 頭多養了雙生子   She's got twin babies at the breast
- 雲 情郎不舍還家裏   Her young man ~~~~
- 薛 洞房花燭朝慵起   In bridal bower she takes her rest
- 圖 燈花并頭結雙蕊   Her lamp wick's got a lucky crest

女兒樂   The girl's content
- 宝 秋千架上春衫薄   Long summer days in pleasant pastimes spent
- 馮 私向花園掘蟋蟀   ~~~~ a certain pleasurable event
- 雲 住了簫管弄弦索   She's used her talents to the full extent
- 薛 一根琵琶往裏戳   She's got a big prick up her vent
- 圖 夫唱婦隨真和合   She's married to a perfect gent

Two lovely boys
Are both in love with me
And I can't get either off my mind
Both are so beautiful
    So wonderful
    So marvellous
To give up either one would be unkind
Last night I promised I would go
To meet one of them where the roses grow
The other came to see what he could find.
    And now that on three are all
    Here in this tribunal
There are no words that come into my mind.

334 「鷄鳴茅店月」
　　　温庭筠　~~盛也東詩~~　商山早行　（全唐詩 9/6741）
　　　　晨起動征鐸　　　　　　（伊藤 say '高山早行'）
　　　　客行悲故郷
　　　　雞聲茅店月
　　　　人迹板橋霜
　　　　槲葉落山路
　　　　枳花明驛牆
　　　　因思杜陵夢
　　　　鳧雁滿回塘

335 「桃之夭夭」
　　　詩經・周南　桃夭　(6)
　　桃之夭夭、灼灼其華、之子于歸、宜其室家。
　　桃之夭夭、有蕡其實、之子于歸、宜其家室。
　　桃之夭夭、其葉蓁蓁、之子于歸、宜其家人。

336 「花氣襲人知晝暖」
　　　陸游　杜康書喜　（Ikkai 120）

414　西廂記 第二本（崔鶯鶯夜聽琴），第三折：
　　「脫布衫」
　　幽僻處可有人行
　　點蒼苔白露泠泠

　　　　(N.B. cf. p.311 (ch.26)「蒼苔露冷
　　　　　　　　　　　　　　花徑風寒」)

　　How silent when footsteps seldom pass
　　And dew still glistens on the untrodden moss

436　牡丹亭（還魂記）第十齣「驚夢」
　　「步步嬌」　　　　　　(旦唱)
　　裊晴絲吹來閒庭院　In these quiet courts the floating gossamer…
　　搖漾春如線
　　停半晌，整花鈿
　　沒揣菱花，偷人半面
　　迤逗的彩雲偏
　　步香閨怎便把全身現

457　芙蓉影破歸蘭槳
　　菱藕香深瀉竹橋

　　Lotus images shatter at the dip of a lazy oar-blade, &
　　Lotus fragrance float up from the stream round a bamboo
　　　　　　　　　　　　　　　　bridge-pile.

409　　　　　(1)
　　　眼空蓄淚淚空垂
(y.卻為)　暗灑閑拋更向誰　　庚辰「卻為」乾抄 corr. 更向
　　　尺幅鮫綃勞惠贈　　　　jiao-xiao 博物志：「鮫人水居,
　　　為君那得不傷悲　　　　出寓人家，賣綃，臨去，從主人索器，泣而去
(鮫人)　　　　　　　　　　　珠滿盤以卒主人.」

　　　　　　(2)
　　　拋珠滾玉只偷潸　　　真卿墨迹 At first 鮮荔 it's
　　　鎮日無心鎮日閒　　　tempting to understand this as 'picture
　　　枕上袖邊難拂拭　　　of Yang Kuei-fei (Tai-chen)' but
　　　任他點點與斑斑　　　clearly 墨迹 can be used in this
　　　　　　　　　　　　　way, probably just a pompous way of
　　　　　　　　　　　　　saying 'your calligraphy'. Tan-ch'un
　　　　　　　　　　　　　elsewhere pretends that this is about the
　　　　　　　　　　　　　only kind of present he is able to give.

　　　　　　(3)
　　　彩線難收面上珠　　　　Yü's explanation of 桐檻 is
　　　湘江舊迹已模糊　　　　not very convincing. How can you
　　　窗前亦有千竿竹　　　　(wade) the pillars?
　　　不識香痕漬也無　　　　庚辰 has 「桐檻」乾抄 has
　　　　　　　　　　　　　「梧桐」威 G. has
　　　　　　　　　　　　　「桐槐」.
　　　　　　　　　　　Wonder whether this is the「桐檻」of ch. 18 (桐剪秋
　　　　　　　　　　　　　　　　　　　　　　　　　　　　　　風)

440.　　妹探謹啟
　　　二兄文几：前夕新霽，月色如洗，
　　　因惜清景難逢，未忍就臥，漏已三轉，
　　　漏已三轉，猶徘徊桐檻之下。
　　　竟為風露所欺，致獲采薪之患。
　　　昨親勞撫嘱，已複遣侍兒問切，
　　　又鐘兼以鮮荔并真卿墨迹見賜，
　　　抑何惠愛之深耶！

投轄：tóu-xiá 轄是「車軸之鍵」？="linch-pin". 投轄之則車不能去。
攀轅臥轍：挽留賢長官不使他去之意
些山：初清 杜荇 [?] 入 些山集

跨今固伏几處默，忽思歷來古人，處名改利釋之場，
猶置些山滴水之區，遠招近攬，投轄攀轅，
務結二三同志，盤桓其中，或醫詞壇，或問吟社；
雖因一時之偶興，每或千古之佳談。
※姊妹雖不才，幸叨陪泉石之間，兼慕薛林雅調。
風庭月榭，惜未宴集詩人；
簾杏溪桃，或可醉飛吟盞。
※孰謂雄才蓮社，獨許鬚眉，
不教雅會東山，讓余脂粉耶？
若蒙造[雪]而來，敢請掃花以俟。謹啟。

*庚辰：
下姊妹雖不才，竊
同叨棲處于
泉石之間而慕
慕薛林之technique

※原底「孰謂
連社之雄才
獨許……境
以東山之雅會
讓余脂粉

All these corrections are made in the 乾隆抄本.

441. 不肖男芸恭啟
父親大人萬福金安：男思自蒙

花兒匠
nurseryman

天恩，諂於膝下，日夜思一孝順，竟無可
孝順之處。前因買辦花草，上托
大人洪福，竟認得許多花兒匠，并認得許多
知園。前因見有白海棠一種，又多
得的，故要盡方法，只弄得兩盆。
大人若視男是親男一般，便留下賞玩。
因天氣暑熱，恐園中姑娘們妨礙不便，
故不敢面見；謹奉書恭啟，並叩
台安。 男芸跪書。

The 高鶚 text is long, because 蓮社 is most unsuitable in the sense of 「詩社」; 「連社之雄才」 is a better text. Also,
「些山東山之雅會……」 is much better than the 「不教……」, which merely echos 「孰謂……」 in other words.

446.　　咏白海棠

(1) 探春：

斜陽寒草帶重門　　A wintry sunset gilds the vine-wreathed door
苔翠盈鋪雨後盆　　Where stands, moss-mantled from the rain, the pot
玉是精神難比潔　　It blooms like snow, like snow's pageant.
雪為肌骨易銷魂　　Yet pure as purest jade its alabaster
芳心一點嬌無力　　O fragrant, tender heart that fears the wind,
倩影三更月有痕　　O visage ravished, full moon without spot, &
莫道縞仙能羽化　　White flower-sprite, shall you sicken away
多情伴我咏黃昏　　And come with me to sing at the dying day!

(2) 宝釵：

珍重芳姿晝掩門　　Guard well thy prize, thou keep'd door
自攜手甕灌苔盆　　Shall pour clear water in thy mossy pot.
胭脂洗出秋階影　　The carmined hue that summer's whisper stained
冰雪招來露砌魂　　Then autumn kisses of chaste snow hoar not
淡極始知花更艷　　True beauty then is purer
愁多焉得玉無痕　　Pure, passionless is what jade spot
欲償白帝宜清潔　　Chaste flower, your vigil honors true
不語婷婷日又昏　　To Autumn's White God at the close of day

got plot
west plot
best spot
slot shot

door]　assure, adore　　　　　　lore　　　　　　pot　bore
pot cot　before, bore　　　　　more　　　　　　four　sore
tor hot　core　　　　　　　　　　　　　　　　hole moi pour　wore
got hot　explore, evermore　　nor, nevermore　toll ror　core
put hot　for, four, floor, furthermore　poor, pore　　　gore
spot hot　gore　　　　　　　　　roar　　　　　　　　　　stole
sot　hoar, heebore　　　　Sure, shore, sore, store, score, spore
what dot　　　　　　　　　　tor, tore
　　　　implore, insane　　wore　　　　　　yore

446. (3) 宝玉: 秋容浅淡映霜门
七节攒成雪满盆　　Mr. soup 「七夕のこと」 and cites this verse.
出浴太真冰作影　　Tp hand. 時じくの雪をあつめし
捧心西子玉为魂　　'tokijikuno' 'unseasonable' (非時の)
晓风不散愁千点
宿雨还添泪一痕
独倚画栏如有意
清砧怨笛送黄昏

(4) 黛玉: 半卷湘帘半掩门
碾冰为土玉为盆
偷来梨蕊三分白　　Beside the half-rolled blind & half-closed door,
借得梅花一缕魂　　Crushed ice for earth and white jade for a pot.
月窟仙人缝缟袂　　Three part of whiteness from the pear-thistle
秋闺怨女拭啼痕　　(stolen) but the fragrance, which the pear has not
娇羞默默同谁诉　　Moon-maidens stitched up with white silken thread
倦倚西风夜已昏　　And weeping as from the new-well flows doth spot
　　　　　　　　　Which now, like bashful maids that no word
　　　　　　　　　say, dying in a breeze at dawn day. sigh.

452
(5) 湘云: 神仙昨日降都门　　A goddess yesterday came to this door
(i) 种得蓝田玉一盆　　And planted seeds of white jade in a pot,
自是霜娥偏爱冷　　From which a marvellous frost maiden grew
非关倩女欲离魂　　Who loves chaste ice, by other things loves not
秋阴捧出何方雪　　Whence last night came the cloud where autumn showers
雨渍添来隔宿痕　　Those cold morning eyes with tears did spot?
却喜诗人吟不倦　　The gentle poet, moved, with her true story
肯令寂寞度朝昏　　To praise her loveliness night & day.

452
(6) 湘雲 (ii)

蘅芷階通蘿薜門　Where freshly-fetched steps approach the ivied door,
也宜墻角也宜盆　At the wall's foot or in a graceful pot —
花因喜潔難尋偶　What flower sad autumn's blights do more inspire
人為悲秋易斷魂　Than these, when purer others toil not?
玉燭滴乾風裏淚　Wax tears their petals seem, by wind congealed
晶簾隔破月中痕　Or pickled moonlight, flecked with many a spot.
幽情欲向嫦娥訴　Weep they because the shadows slide away
無那盧廊月色昏　Their goddess-mom, who own made dark night day?

---

462 ⑧ 憶菊 （蘅蕪君 = Lady Allspice Bao-chai）

悵望西風抱悶思
蓼紅葦白斷腸時
空籬舊圃秋無迹 ✗
冷月清霜夢有知 ✗
念念心隨歸雁遠
寥寥坐聽晚砧遲
誰憐我為黃花瘦
慰語重陽會有期

探春：「到底要等蘅蕪君沈着：「秋無迹」，「夢有知」把个「憶」字竟烘染出來了」

歸雁 coming south to ~~greet and~~ winter with us.
Double Ninth

菊 花 葉：「秋日…出花穗…呈紅色」「栽培於庭園間」「供觀賞用」

463　　　訪菊　　怡紅公子（宝玉）

閑趁霜晴試一遊
酒杯藥盞莫淹留
霜前月下誰家種？×
檻外籬邊何處秋？×
蠟屐遠來情得得
冷吟不盡興悠悠
黃花若解憐詩客
休負今朝挂杖頭

白居易「重酬周判官」
白菊山詩 460

宝玉笑道：『...難道「誰家種」，「何處秋」，「蠟屐遠來」，「冷吟不盡」，那都不是詩不成？...』

蠟屐 一晉 阮孚. But y.
× 皮日休詩「悠然思夫君,
　　　忽憶蠟屐著」
白居易「秋愛冷吟春愛醉
　　　詩家眷屬酒家仙」

種菊　怡紅公子（宝玉）

携鋤秋圃自移來
籬畔庭前處處栽
昨夜不期經雨活 ×
今朝猶喜帶霜開 ×
冷吟秋色詩千首
醉酹寒香酒一杯
泉溉泥封勤護惜
好知井逕絕塵埃

（宝玉笑道...『難道...』「昨夜雨」，「今朝霜」，都不是種不成：...』

(an autumn song)

酹léi：灌酒祭地

對菊　枕霞舊友（Xiangyun 湘云）

別圃移來貴比金
一叢淺淡一叢深
蕭疏籬畔科頭坐 ×
清冷香中抱膝吟 ×
數去更無君傲世
看來惟有我知音
秋光荏苒休孤負
相對原宜惜寸陰

傲世：輕視世人

李紈笑道：『那么有，象「科頭坐」，「抱膝吟」竟一時也拿不出離了菊花、菊花有知，倒還要膩煩了！』說的大家都笑了

枕霞詩：「翻葉轉藕號」
范成大詩：
「烟草蕭疏不似秋」

科頭：不冠 hatless
王維詩：「科頭箕踞長松下」

463

⑥
供菊
枕霞旧友
(Xiang-yun)

弹琴酌酒喜堪俦
几案婷婷点缀幽
隔坐香分三(经)露
抛书人对一枝秋
霜清纸帐来新梦
圃冷斜阳忆旧游
傲世也因同气味
春风桃李未淹留

宝钗：味如橄榄

陶潜 归去来辞：「三径就荒，松菊犹存」

代玉道「据我看来，头一句好的是『圃冷斜阳忆旧游』这句背面傅粉；『抛书人对一枝秋』已经妙绝，将供菊说完，没处再说……」

①
咏菊
潇湘妃子
(Dai-yu)

无赖诗魔昏晓侵
绕篱欹石自沈音
毫端蕴秀临霜写
口角噙香对月吟 ×
满纸自怜题素怨
片言谁解诉秋心？
一从陶令评章後
千古高风说到今

代玉道「我那个也不好，到底伤于纤巧些」
宝钗道「巧的却好，不露堆砌生硬」

李纨笑道「固如此说，你的『口角噙香』一句敌的过」

⑦
画菊
蘅芜君
(Bao-chai)

诗馀戏笔不知狂
岂是丹青费较量
聚叶泼成千点墨
攒花染出几痕霜
淡浓神会风前影
跳脱秋生腕底香
莫认东篱闲采掇
粘屏聊以慰重阳

跳脱：腕钏也 ??

p.455
（既然画菊，若是默默无言，究竟不知菊有何妙处，不禁有所问。第八便是「问菊」；菊若能解语，使人狂喜不禁…）

464
问菊 ②
潇湘妃子
(Dai-yu)

欲讯秋情众莫知
喃喃负手扣东篱
孤标傲世偕谁隐 ✕
一样开花为底迟 ✕
圃露庭霜何寂寞
雁归蛩病可相思
莫言举世无谈者
解语何妨话片时

喃喃：多言也、细碎不绝

湘云笑道：「偕谁隐」，「为底迟」，真真把个菊花问的无言可对。

簪菊 ④
蕉下客
(Tan-chun)

瓶供篱栽日日忙
折来休认镜中妆
长安公子因花癖
彭泽先生是酒狂
短鬓冷沾三径露 ✕
葛巾香染九秋霜 ✕
高情不入时人眼
拍手凭他笑路旁

宝钗笑道：「你的『短鬓冷沾』、『葛巾香染』，已就把簪菊形容的一个缝儿也没有。」

菊影
枕霞旧友
(Xiang-yun)

秋光叠叠复重重
潜度偷移三径中
窗隔疏灯描远近
篱筛破月锁玲珑
寒芳留照魂应驻
霜印传神梦也空
珍重暗香踏碎处
凭谁醉眼认朦胧

传神「用图画或文字摹写人物，能得其神情曰传神」

464
菊夢 ③
瀟湘妃子
(Dai-yu)

籬畔秋酣一覺清
和雲伴月不分明
登仙非慕莊生蝶
憶舊還尋陶令盟
睡去依依隨雁斷
驚迴故故惱蛩鳴
醒時幽怨同誰訴
衰草寒煙無限情

李白月下獨酌：「暫伴月將影…」
尋盟：「國際間之重申舊約，復歸和好」
(／.陶飲酒之七：「秋菊有佳色，裛露掇其英」
……注：「採菊東籬下」)
故故：屢屢：薛能詩「青春背我堂堂去，
白髮欺人故故生」

殘菊
蕉下客
(Tan-chun)

露凝霜重漸傾欹
宴賞才過小雪時
蒂有餘香金淡泊
枝無全葉翠離披
半床落月蛩聲切
萬里寒雲雁陣遲
明歲秋分知再會
暫時分手莫相思

離披：散開貌。

×××××××××××××

466.
持螯更喜桂陰涼
潑醋擂薑興欲狂
饕餮王孫應有酒
橫行公子竟無腸
臍間積冷饞忘忌
指上沾腥洗尚香
原為世人羞口腹
坡仙曾笑一生忙

擂俗研物 (／.擂鉢 'mortar') ?pound
*註：「口腹」語意雙關，指因竟
美食口罪被謫，藉以下文「螯毒」「筍香」之
美食

蘇東坡集 卷十一 (3/111)
『初到黃州』：
「自笑平生為口忙
老來事業轉荒唐
長江遶郭知魚美
好竹連山覺筍香
逐客不妨員外置
詩人例作水曹郎
只慚無補絲毫事
尚費官家壓酒囊」

466
(代玉) 铁甲长戈死未忘
　　　 堆盘色相喜先尝　　　佛家语：一切有形质相状皆统谓之色相
　　　 螯封嫩玉双双满
　　　 壳凸红脂块块香
　　　 多肉更怜卿八足
　　　 助情谁劝我千觞
　　　 对兹佳品酬佳节
　　　 桂拂清风菊带霜

(宝钗) 桂霭桐阴坐举觞
　　　 长安涎口盼重阳　　　With a wine cup in hand as the autumn day ends
　　　 眼前道路无经纬　　　And with watering mouths we await our small friends
　　　 皮里春秋空黑黄　　　(xiàn) A straightforward breed they are certainly not
　　　 酒未涤腥还用菊　　　And the goodness inside them has all gone to pot
　　　 性防积冷定须姜　　　皮里春秋：外不臧否而内有褒贬
　　　 于今落釜成何益
　　　 月浦空馀禾黍香

485　老刘 老刘　My name is Liu
　　　 食量大如牛　I'm a henchwoman true
　　　 吃个老母猪不抬头　I can eat a whole sow with the little pigs too.

488　烟霞闲骨格
　　　 泉石野生涯

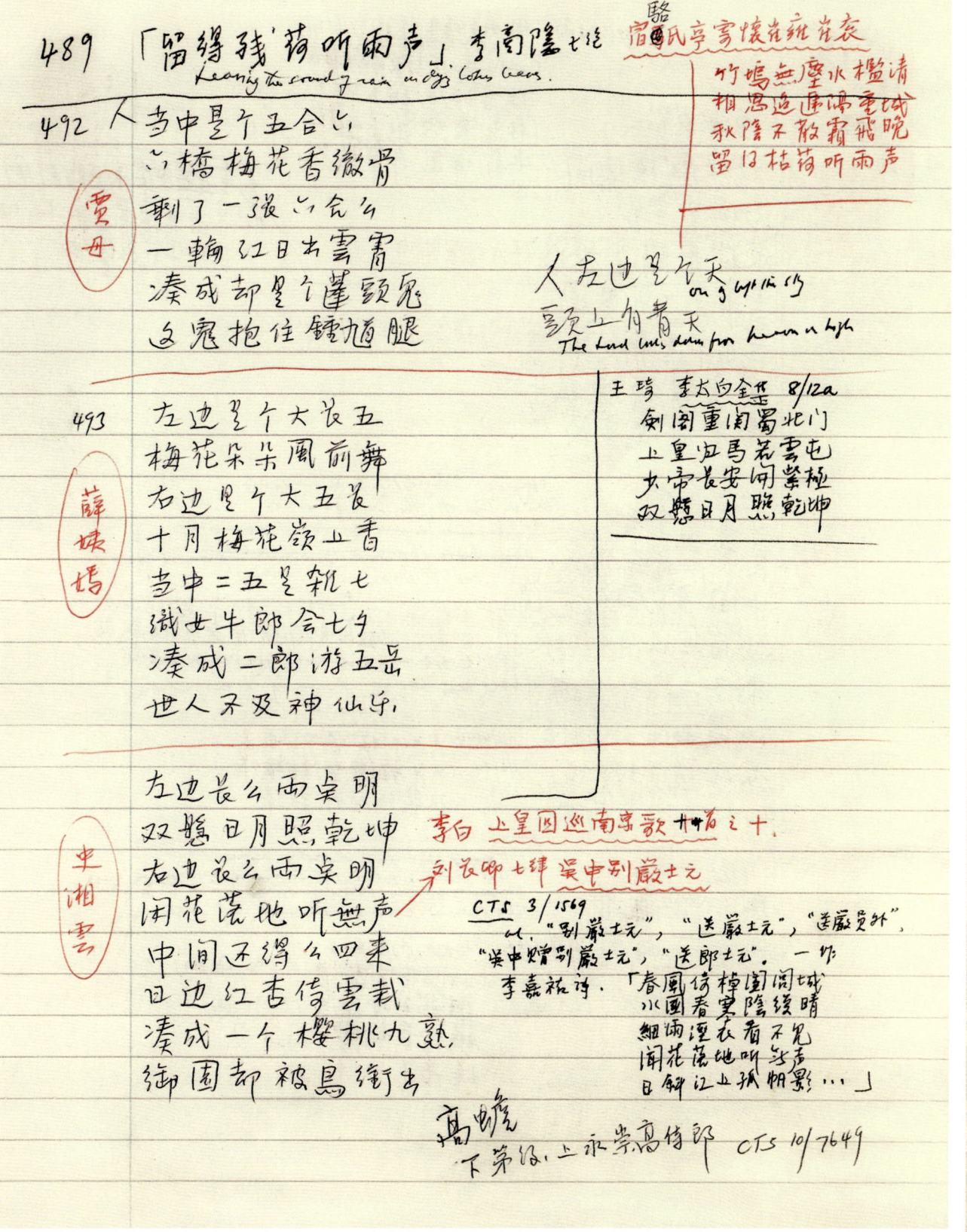

used again p.902

493

曲江对雨：仇 杜少陵集详注 1/6/113
「城上春雲覆苑牆
江亭晚色靜年芳
林花著雨燕支濕
水荇牽風翠帶長」

宝钗
左边望三丈
双双燕子语梁间
右边望三丈
(水荇牽風翠帶長) 杜甫 七律 曲江對雨
当中三六九寞在
三山半落青天外 李白 七律 登金陵鳳凰台
凑成铁锁练孤舟
处处风波处处愁

李太白全集 3/21/96
「…三山半落青天外
一水中分白鷺洲…」

代玉
左边一个天   Sky on the left, the four funds air
良辰美景奈何天 And the bright air the brilliant heaven (270)
中间锦屏颜色俏   牡丹亭
纱窗也没有红娘报 西厢记 1/4 「俺門不許老僧敲
剩了二六八寞斋   駐馬聽 紗窗外定有紅娘報」
                All keys has tie, Running a misquotation.
双瞻玉座引朝仪   杜甫 七律 紫宸殿退朝口号
凑成篮子好采花 1/6/94「户外昭容紫袖垂
仙杖香挑芍药花   双瞻御座引朝儀…」

迎春
          Four o five,
左边四五成花九 On my left the flowery nine
桃花带雨浓 李白 五律 訪戴天山道士不遇
  The flowing peach be drenched with showy rain
3/23/10a 「犬吠水聲中
          桃花帶露濃 (露一作雨)
          樹深時見鹿
          溪午不聞鐘…」

494　　左边大四是个人
　　　　是个庄家人罗
刘　　　中间三四线配红
老　　　大火烧了毛毛虫
老　　　右边么四真好看
　　　　一个萝蔔一头蒜
　　　　凑成便是一枝花
　　　　花儿落了结个大倭瓜

春江花月夜
① 北京大学中文系 中国文学史二, 41-42
② 王士菁 唐代诗歌 45-6
③ 唐诗合解笺注读本卷三 (卅二)
④ CTS 2. 1183-4

555　　秋窗风雨夕 (春江花月夜)　　　代玉
　　　　秋花惨淡秋草黄。　　　J. stanzas.
again　耿耿秋灯秋夜长。
　　　　已觉秋窗秋不尽　　　张若虚 (660-?720)　春江花月夜
rain　　那堪风雨助凄凉。
　　　　助秋风雨来何速×　　春江潮水连海平　　可怜楼上月徘徊
　　　　惊破秋窗秋梦绿×　　海上明月共潮生　　应照离人妆镜台
　　　　抱得秋情不忍眠　　　滟滟随波千万里　　玉户帘中卷不去
　　　　自向秋屏挑泪烛×　　何处春江无月明　　捣衣砧上拂还来
　　　　泪烛摇摇爇短檠　　　江流宛转绕芳甸　　此时相望不相闻
　　　　牵愁照恨动离情。　　月照花林皆似霰　　愿逐月华流照君
秋　　　谁家秋院无风入　　　空里流霜不觉飞　　鸿雁长飞光不度
闺　全　何处秋窗无雨声　　　汀上白沙看不见　　鱼龙潜跃水成文
怨　梁　罗衾不奈秋风力×　　江天一色无纤尘　　昨夜闲潭梦落花
1078 诗　残漏声催秋雨急×　　皎皎空中孤月轮　　可怜春半不还家
　　　　连宵脉脉复飕飕　　　江畔何人初见月　　江水流春去欲尽
　　　　灯前似伴离人泣×　　江月何年初照人　　江潭落月复西斜
　　　　　　　　　　　　　　人生代代无穷已　　斜月沈沈藏海雾
　　　　　　　　　　　　　　江月年年只相似　　碣石潇湘无限路
　　　　　　　　　　　　　　不知江月待何人　　不知乘月几人归
　　　　　　　　　　　　　　但见长江送流水　　落月摇情满江树
　　　　　　　　　　　　　　白云一片去悠悠
　　　　　　　　　　　　　　青枫浦上不胜愁
　　　　　　　　　　　　　　谁家今夜扁舟子
　　　　　　　　　　　　　　何处相思明月楼

555　寒烟小院轉蕭條
　　　疏竹虛窗時滴瀝
　　　不知風雨幾時休
　　　已教淚灑窗紗濕

秋 15 times
風雨 5 times (in each stanza)
窗 5 times (3 y then 秋窗)

591　陸游　書室明暖終日婆娑其間,倦則扶杖
　　1125-1210　至小園,戲作長句　(1194 ae 69/70 鄉居詩)
　　　美睡宜人勝按摩
　　　江南十月氣猶和
　　　重簾未捲留香久
　　　古硯微凹聚墨多
　　　月上忽看梅影出
　　　風高時送雁聲過
　　　一杯太淡君休笑
　　　牛背吾方扣角歌

Behind snug curtained doors the
incense lingers long
In an old familiar groove the groundink
settles thick.

592　王維　使至塞上　(150)　737 涼州の崔希逸の幕中
　　　單車欲問邊　　　　　　　　　節度判官
　　　屬國過居延
　　　征蓬出漢塞
　　　歸雁入胡天
　　　大漠孤煙直　A campfire's smoke blazes perpendicular
　　　長河落日圓　And the round sun in the great river set.
　　　蕭關逢候騎
　　　都護在燕然

Graham NV

592　王維　送邢桂州

　　鐃吹喧京口
　　風波下洞庭
zhě qí　赭圻將赤岸
　　擊汰復揚舲
　　日落江湖白　The water whitens in the setting sun
　　潮來天地青　when the tide rises, all the world is green
　　明王歸合浦
　　后逐使臣星

　　王維　輞川閒居贈裴秀才迪
　　寒山轉蒼翠
　　秋水日潺湲
　　倚杖柴門外
　　臨風聽暮蟬
　　渡頭餘落日　over by the ford the setting sun delays
　　墟里上孤煙　A small smoke above the hamlet climbs
　　復值接輿醉
　　狂歌五柳前

529　曹植　洛神賦：
　　余告之曰：其形也翩若驚鴻
　　　　　　　婉若　游龍

　　遠而望之　皎若太陽升朝霞
　　迫而察之　灼若芙蓉出淥波

593　　陶潜　归田园居　第一首
　　　少无适俗韵
　　　性本爱邱山
　　　误落尘网中
　　　一去十三年
　　　羁鸟恋旧林
　　　池鱼思故渊
　　　开荒南野际
　　　守拙归园田
　　　方宅十馀亩
　　　草屋八九间
　　　榆柳荫后檐
　　　桃李罗堂前
　　　暧暧远人村　　Half-lost in haze the distant hamlets gleam
　　　依依墟里烟　　Where straggling smoke the buried hamlet veils.
　　　狗吠深巷中
　　　鸡鸣桑树巅
　　　户庭无尘杂
　　　虚室有馀闲
　　　久在樊笼里
　　　复得返自然

594 月　香菱
　　月桂中天夜色寒
　　清光皎皎影團團
　　詩人助興常思玩
　　野客添愁不忍觀
　　翡翠樓邊懸玉鏡
　　珍珠簾外掛冰盤
　　良宵何用燒銀燭
　　晴彩輝煌映畫欄

595 非銀非水映窗寒
　　試看晴空護玉盤。
　　淡淡梅花香欲染
　　絲絲柳帶露初乾。
　　只疑殘粉塗金砌
　　恍若輕霜抹玉欄。
　　夢醒西樓人迹絶
　　餘容猶可隔簾看

598 精華欲掩料应難
　　影自娟娟魄自寒
　　一片砧敲千里白
　　半輪雞唱五更殘
　　綠蓑江上秋聞笛
　　紅袖樓頭夜倚欄
　　博得嫦娥应自問
　　何緣不使永團圓

35 韻 (下平二蕭)

611	1	一夜北風緊		(surprise) flies.
李紈	FLIES	開門雪尚飄 ✓		
	2	入泥憐潔白		
香菱	BEAUTIFIES	匝地惜瓊瑤 ✓		beautifies
	3	有意榮枯草		
探春	CRYSTALLISE	無心飾萎苗 ✓		crystallise
	4	價高村釀熟		
李綺	TESTIFIES	年稔府粱饒 ✓	稔 rěn: 穀熟, 如言豐稔	testifies
	5	葭動灰飛管	葭灰 jiāhuī 古時占氣候法之一, 以葭莩之灰置於律管以占, 故名至節稱葭管灰飛	KYTT
李紋	REVIVIFIES	陽回斗轉杓	biǎo 北斗之柄 cf. 王勃 寅月鬥遍賦:「斗柄潛移」 葭灰稍暢 cf. 杜甫 小至詩: 吹葭六琯動飛灰	revivifies
	6	寒山已失翠		
岫烟	PETRIFIES	凍浦不生潮 ✓		petrifies
	7	易挂疏枝柳	(i.e. the snow hangs — covers on the willow like on the peartree)	
湘雲	LIES	難堆破葉蕉 ✓		lies
	8	麝煤融寶鼎		
寶琴	DISGUISE	綺袖籠金貂 ✓		disguise
	9	光奪窗前鏡		
黛玉	PURIFIES	香黏壁上椒		purifies
	10	斜風仍故故		
寶玉	SANCTIFIES	清夢轉聊聊		with ?? sanctifies
	11	何處梅花笛		
寶釵	HARMONISE	誰家碧玉簫		harmonise
	12	鰲愁坤軸陷		
湘雲	LIQUEFIES	吟鞭指灞橋 龍鬥陣雲銷		liquefies
	13	賜裘憐撫戍 野岸迴孤棹		
寶琴	GOODBYES	加絮念徵徭 吟鞭指灞橋		goodbyes

※ 世说新语 笺疏:「谢太傅寒雪日内集,与儿女讲论文义。俄而雪骤,公欣然曰:白雪纷纷何所似。兄子胡儿曰:撒盐空中差可拟。兄女曰:未若柳絮因风起。公大笑乐。」

㊟ 袁安传 in 袁张韩周列传第三十五 後漢書 卷四十五 (中华书, 6/1518
注:「汝南先贤传曰:時大雪積地丈餘,洛陽令身出案行,見人家皆除雪出,有乞食者。至袁安門,無有行路,謂安已死,令人除雪入戶,見安僵臥。問何以不出,安曰:大雪人皆餓,不宜干人。令以為賢,舉為孝廉也。」

湘雲	613	14	賜裘憐撫戍	SUPPLIES / supplies
	SUPPLIES		加絮念紹繰	
寶釵		15	坳垤審夷險	ad-die / knifes
	TERRIFIES		枝柯怕動搖	
代玉		16	皚皚輕趁步	invert
	RISE		翦翦舞隨腰	
寶玉		17	苦茗成新賞	煮芋(庚辰)
	IMPROVISE		孤松訂久要	撒鹽是舊謠(庚辰)※ / improvise
		18	泥鴻從印迹	葦簇猶泊釣(庚辰) / invert
寶琴	PLIES		林斧或聞樵	不(庚辰) / plies
		19.	伏象千峯凸	
湘雲	DEFIES		盤蛇一徑遙	The climber defies
		20	花緣經冷結	Shape part finite bourgeoise.
探春	DESPISE		色豈畏霜凋	despite
		21	深院驚寒雀	invert
岫煙	CRIES		空山泣老鴞	cries
		22	階墀隨上下	
湘	INCISE		池水任浮漂	incise (the surface)
雲		23	照耀臨清曉	
代玉	DIES		繽紛入永宵	daylight dies / dies?
		24	誠忘三尺冷	
湘雲	EXORCISE		瑞釋九重焦	exorcise (cue)
		25	僵臥誰相問	汝南先賢傳「令人除雪,入戶見安僵臥」※
寶琴	EXERCISE		狂游客喜招	exercise, cries
		26	天機斷縞帶	invert
湘雲	UNTIES		海市失鮫綃	unties

615　　　　　　　　　庚辰本(對)

代玉 27	寂寞對台榭	封(高去)	
湘雲 SATISFIES	清貧懷簞瓢		satisfies
寶琴 28	烹茶水漸沸	冰(庚辰)	
湘雲 TANTALISE	煮酒葉難燒		tantalise
代玉 29	沒帚山增掃	shew	
寶琴 MYSTIFIES	埋琴稗子挑		mystifies
湘雲 30	石樓閒睡鶴		
代玉 SIGHS	錦罽暖親貓		sigh (anor satisfaction)
寶琴 31	月窟翻銀浪		
湘雲 SKIES	霞城隱赤標		skies
代玉 32	沁梅香可嚼		
寶釵 NEUTRALISE	淋竹醉堪調		neutralise
寶琴 33	或濕鴛鴦帶		
湘雲 DRIES	時凝翡翠翹 (head ornament)		dries
代玉 34	無風仍脈脈		
寶琴 BAPTIZE	不雨亦瀟瀟		~~oppose~~
李紈 35	欲誌今朝樂		
李綺 EULOGISE	憑詩祝舜堯		eulogise

翹 = 首飾 cf. 陸機「日出東南隅行」「金雀垂藻翹,瓊珮結瑤璠」and 梁簡文帝 詩;「寶吉珊瑚翹」? invent

Compare chap. 76 (pp. 983-9) 「三五中秋夕」
"中秋夜大觀園即景聯句三十五韻"
　　韻：十三元

619　　　賦得紅梅花

邢岫烟
桃未芳菲杏未紅
冲寒先喜笑東風
魂飛庾嶺春難辨
霞隔羅浮夢未通
綠萼添妝融寶炬
縞仙扶醉跨殘虹
看來豈是尋常色
濃淡由他冰雪中

李紋
白梅懶賦賦紅梅
逞艷先迎醉眼開
凍臉有痕皆是血
酸心無恨亦成灰
誤吞丹藥移真骨
偷下瑤池脫舊胎
江北江南春燦爛
寄言蜂蝶漫疑猜

薛寶琴
疏是枝條艷是花
春妝兒女競奢華
閑庭曲檻無餘雪
流水空山有落霞
幽夢冷隨紅袖笛
遊仙香泛絳河槎
前生定是瑤台種
無復相疑色相差

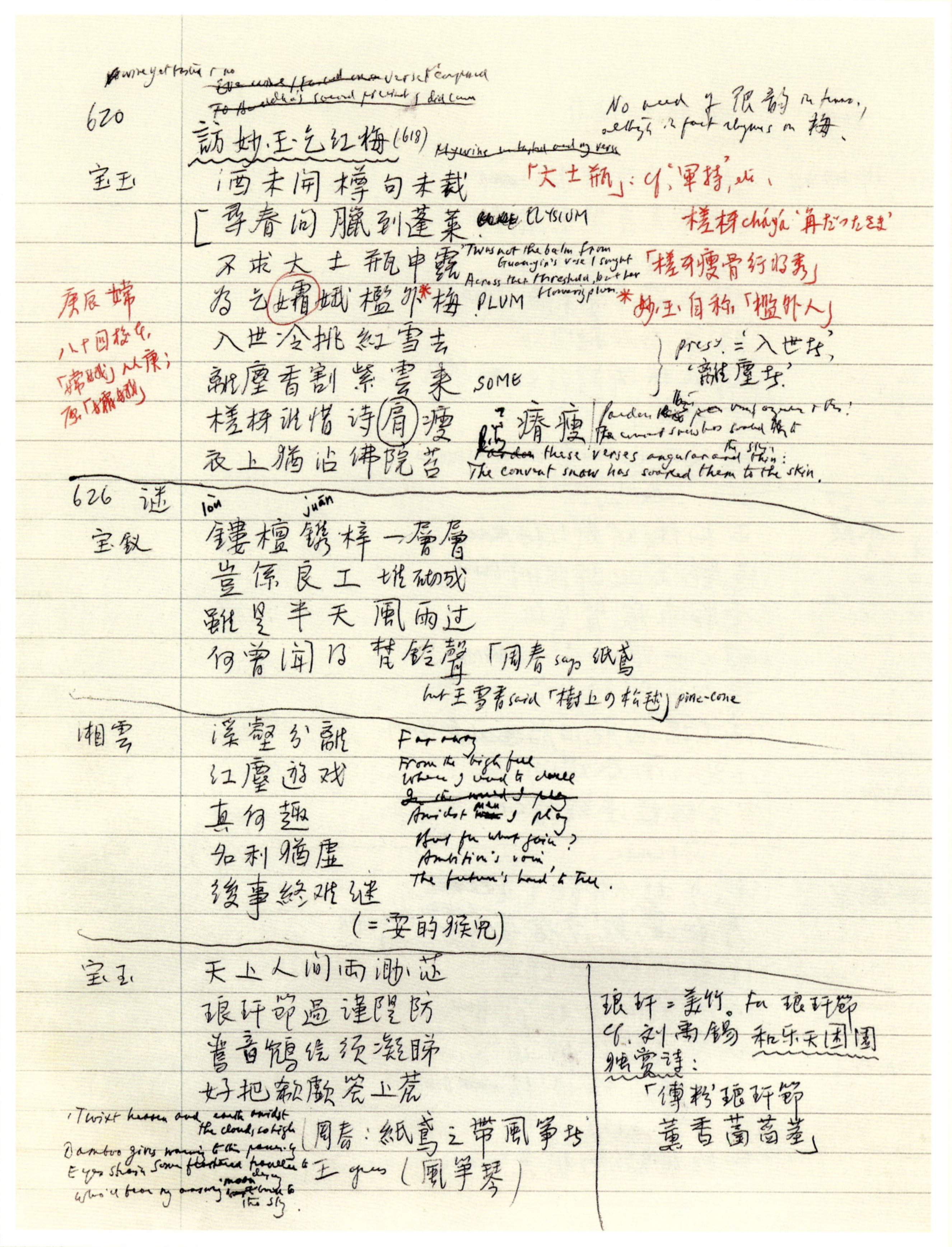

Handwritten notes page — annotations on Chinese poems (Dream of the Red Chamber / 紅樓夢) with English glosses and marginalia.

620 訪妙玉乞紅梅 (618)

宝玉
　酒未開樽句未裁
　[尋春問臘到蓬萊]　ELYSIUM
　不求大士瓶中露　'Twas not the balm from Guanyin's vase I sought
　為乞嫦娥檻外梅　PLUM　Across the threshold, but her flowering plum
　入世冷挑紅雪去
　離塵香割紫雲來　SOME
　槎枒誰惜詩肩瘦　Pardon these verses angular and thin:
　衣上猶沾佛院苔　The convent snow has soaked them to the skin.

Marginalia (right side):
- No need 乎 限韻 n times, although 2 part rhymes on 梅.
- 「大士瓶」cf.「軍持」etc.
- 槎枒 chá yá '角だった えだ'
- 「槎枒瘦骨行好秀」
- ＊妙玉自称「檻外人」
- press. =「入世去」「離塵去」

Left marginalia: 庚辰嫦 / 八十回校本「嫦娥」从庚; 原「嬌娥」

626 謎
　lóu   juān
宝釵
　鏤檀鍥梓一層層
　豈係良工堆砌成
　雖是半天風雨過
　何曾聞得梵鈴聲　「周春 says 紙鳶
　　　　　　　　　　but 王雪香 said「樹上の松毬」pine-cone

湘雲
　溪壑分離　Far away
　紅塵遊戲　From the high fell
　真何趣　Where I used to dwell
　名利猶虛　Amidst ___ I play
　後事終難繼　About for what gain?
　　　　　　　Ambition's vain
　　　　　　　The future's hard to tell.
　(=耍的猴兒)

宝玉
　天上人間兩渺茫
　琅玕節過謹隄防
　鸞音鶴信須凝睇
　好把唏噓答上蒼

Right marginalia:
琅玕 = 美竹. for 琅玕節 cf. 劉禹錫 和樂天閒園獨賞詩:「傅粉琅玕節 / 薰香菡萏莖」

Bottom left:
'Twixt heaven and earth amidst the clouds so high
Bamboo girts waving to the passing
Eyes shall scan flickering travel to the sky
Who'll bear my uneasy ___ to the sky

(周春：紙鳶之帶風箏 cf 王 opus (風箏琴))

624
燈謎 李紈：(四書)
     觀音未有世家傳
     雖善無徵 (中庸)

中庸29.「上焉者雖善無徵
無徵不信不信民弗從。
下焉者雖善不尊,不尊
不信,不信民弗從」
Hughes: "If the man at the head is good but
does not give such visible proof of his
goodness, then, being unattested, he does not
inspire confidence."
"left as memorial without"
"though good, yet being no memorial"

625
     湘雲：(四書)
     一池青草草何名
     蒲蘆也 (中庸)

中庸20/3:「夫政也者蒲蘆也」
Li Wa (naturally) follows Chu Hsi:
「蒲蘆,沈括以為蒲葦是也,以人之政
猶以地種樹,其成速矣,而蒲葦又易生之物,
其成尤速也,言人存政舉其易如此」
But 鄭注:「蒲蘆蜾蠃謂土蜂也...
蒲蘆取桑蟲之子去而變化之以成己子。
政之於百姓若蒲蘆之於桑蟲也」
See 夢溪筆談 p.153「蒲蘆說者以為螺蠃
疑不然。蒲蘆即蒲葦耳故曰敏速敏
政地速敏藝夫政猶蒲蘆也,人之為政
猶地之藝蒲葦,速而已,亦行之兩
豺了也」*

李綺(1) 水向石边流出冷
            (古人名)
         山濤

李綺(1)   螢
         二花 (礼記·月令 腐草爲螢)
         (季夏之月...腐草為螢)

「或作『腐草化為螢』」
呂氏春秋,淮南子,周書時訓解 皆有化字
in its corrupt
the corrupt grass by a transmutation
doth breedeth fireflies.   (十三經注疏 校勘記)

The corruption grass by a transmutation breedeth fireflies

* Hughes (119) "Man's right way is to be prompt in good govt. as the earth's
  way is to be prompt in making things grow. This good govt. is like
  the speed with which some reeds grow."

  Legge   ("this govt. might be called an easily-growing reed.")

鐵笛說子序

鐵笛 is pseudonym of 楊維楨 who called himself 鐵崖, 鐵笛道人, 鐵冠道人, 鐵心道人, 梅花道人, etc. etc. See 明史 285 (first of the biogs. in 文苑). Also 東維子文集 (collected works) and 鐵崖先生古乐府.

The problem is to find any connection 楊維楨 with 張良

Alternative possibility is that '鐵笛' is used vaguely of '仙人', in which case the second couplet could mean simply that Ma Yuan was a great strategist without having received the supernatural instruction given to

桃葉：

  樂府詩集、清商曲辭、吳聲曲辭 「桃葉歌」

  「古今樂錄曰：桃葉歌者晉王子敬(獻之)之所作也。
桃葉子敬妾名，緣於篤愛所以歌之。隋書五行志曰：
陳時江南盛歌王獻之桃葉詞云：

  桃葉復桃葉
  渡江不用楫
  但渡無所苦
  我自迎接汝

後隋晉王廣伐陳，置船桃葉山下，及韓擒虎渡江，大抵任
蠻奴至新亭，以導北軍之應」

See 乐府詩集 卷45 (p.86)

626

代玉　驍騄何勞縛紫繩
　　　馳城逐塹勢猙獰　qiàn 繞城之水
　　　主人指示風雷動
　　　鰲背三山獨立名
　　　（周春 say 走馬燈。　KYTT 謂以紙剪馬形, 黏於特製紙輪之下,
　　　　　　　　王氏同）　藉燭煙以轉動 用以慶祝元宵時玩之
　　　　　　　　　　　　　　revolving lantern

629　宝琴　懷古十首

(1)　赤壁懷古　　　　　　　（法舫 流詩沈溺）
　　　赤壁沈埋水不流　燕京歲時記「法舫」:「中元日各寺院製
　　　徒留名姓載空舟　　　造法舫, 至晚 焚之, 有長至數丈者」
　　　喧闐一炬悲風冷　xuān-tián
　　　無限英魂在內遊
　　　（周春：走馬燈之用戰艦水操也）
　　　（bt 偶得 give 盂蘭盆焚 法舫 + 寵愛的 敀子燈

(2)　交趾懷古
　　　銅柱金城振紀綱　廣州記 up, 後漢書 馬援傳:
　　　聲傳海外播戎羌　「援到交阯, 立銅柱, 為漢之
　　　馬援自是功勞大　　極界也」
　　　鐵笛無煩說子房　朱子鐵笛亭詩序「侍郎胡明仲嘗為武夷山隱者
　　　（周春：喇叭）　　　劉君蒼寫遠遊, 劉善吹鐵笛, 有穿雲裂石之聲. 故
　　　　　　　　　　　　胡公詩有『更煩橫鐵笛.
　　　　　　　　　　　　吹出紫仙聽之句…」

(3)　鍾山懷古 (Nanking) E. of.
　　　名利何曾伴汝身　宋書93　385-448, Recluse who declined
　　　無端被詔出凡塵　南史75　his invitation of serving but
　　　牽連大抵難休絕　「元嘉十五年 (438 a.e. 53) 徵次宗
　　　莫怨他人嘲笑頻　至京師 開館於雞籠山, 聚徒教授 置生
　　　　　　　　　　　　百餘人 (…)朱(一)廬 並以佛學醫經諸生…」
　　　　　　　　　　　　Later he refused to Lushan but was summoned back
　　　　　　　　　　　　the last year of his life & specially constructed
　　　（肉　俉僩, 耍猴兒）　　 (招隱館) under the W. wall
　　　　　　　　　　　　　 於鍾山 near the capital.
　　　Study 劉宋, 雷次宗 v. 人名大辭典 p.1345

359

629   「狡兔死，良狗烹」

(4) 淮陰懷古
　　壯士須防惡犬欺
　　三齊位定蓋棺時
　　寄言世俗休輕鄙
　　一飯之恩死必知
　　Guess: 兔、馬桶、納寶瓶、Story of 韓信

(5) 廣陵懷古
　　蟬噪鴉棲轉眼過   zào
　　隋堤風景近如何
　　只緣佔盡風流號
　　惹得紛紛口舌多
630.　Guess: 柳絮、簫、柳木牙籤、剔牙棒
　　　　(Story 7 煬帝's canal)

(6) NANKING 桃葉渡懷古
　　衰草閒花映淺池   ∵朝華注：「桃葉渡在縣南一里秦淮口、桃葉
　　桃枝桃葉總分離   乃王獻之愛妾名也、其妹曰桃根、獻之嘗
　　六朝梁棟多如許   臨此渡歌送之。」
　　小照空懸壁上題   ⊛ Turn back.
　　桃葉 was the name of 王獻之's 婢。
　　　　　　　　　　　　'如許' = 这樣 (強)
　　Guess: 團扇、門神紙。
　　　　　　　　　　　Besides the Tang generals 秦叔寳 and 胡敬
　　　　　　　　　　　德, 門神 (戶神) are sometimes identified as
　　　　　　　　　　　神荼鬱壘 who are the original 桃人
　　　　　　　　　　　of 風俗通義、etc.
　　　　　　　　　　　See '神荼鬱壘' in
　　　　　　　　　　　Mathews 8/ p.457

(7) 青塚懷古   樗櫟
　　黑水茫茫咽不流   yè   shū lì 皆不材之木
　　冰絃撥盡曲中愁   喻人之无用者，詳見莊。
　　漢家制度誠堪笑   樗: ailanthus glandulosa: 'stinking cedar'
　　樗櫟應慚萬古羞   櫟: quercus bungeana: Chinese oak.
　　Guess: 3 say 墨斗 (in mud story), me (周) say 枇杷!

630

(8) 馬嵬懷古
　　寂寞脂痕積汗光
　　溫柔一旦付東洋　　「付之流水」=事情落空。Presumably
　　只因遺得風流跡　　this is the sense of 付東洋。
　　此日衣裳尚有香
　　guess: 白芍藥, 肥皂

(9) 蒲東寺懷古　Pú-dōng-sì
　　小紅骨賤一身輕
　　私掖偷攜強撮成　　cuō (聚而取之 KYTT)
　　雖被夫人時吊起
　　已經勾引彼同行　　──王希廉評
　　guess: 紅天燈, 骰子, 竹窗　　(Sty: 西廂記)

(10) 梅花觀懷古　　　　　　　　紈扇:「團扇,團其用細絹製成、
　　不在梅邊在柳邊　　　　　故稱,如『紈扇如圓月,出自機中素』
　　个中誰拾畫嬋娟　　㑹個中(箇中)=此中 見江淹詩」(KYTT)
　　團圓莫憶春香到　　(also 箇裏, found in Wong Wei's poem)
　　一別西風又一年
12 (p.101)　　guess: 秋牡丹, 紈扇　　(Sty: 還魂記)
因小姐遺言就葬
後園梅樹下,又恐
不便,後官眷往已
付剗取,經園起建
梅花菴觀,安置小女　The quatrain on 杜麗娘's portrait was:　(26韻)
神位,就著这陈
最姑焚修看守　　近覩分明似儼然　　(14韻)
　　　　　　　　　　遠觀自在若飛仙
　　　　　　　　　　他年得傍蟾宮客
　　　　　　　　　　不在梅邊在柳邊

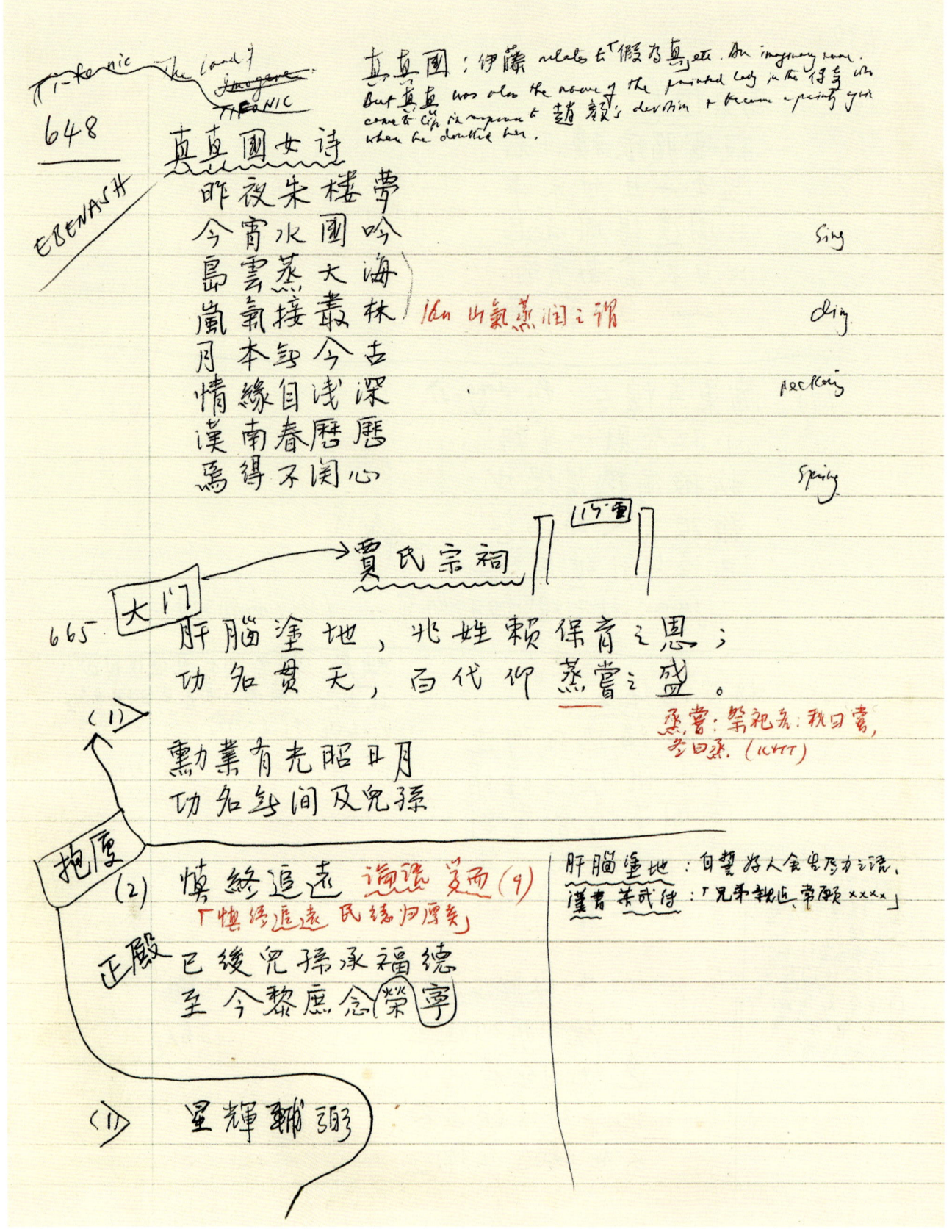

NOTES

p.375　古人云「千金難買一笑」
　　　　梁、王僧孺、詠寵姬
　　　　　及君高堂還
　　　　　値妾姸妝罷
　　　　　曲房襞錦帳
　　　　　迴廊笥珠履
　　　　　玉釵時可挂
　　　　　羅襦讵班解
　　　　　再願連城易
　　　　　一笑千金買

p.740　綠葉成陰子滿枝　from 杜牧 悵詩 (七絕)

杜甫　秋興八首之一　　　　（詳註和冊，卷十七、六十三）
　　　　玉露凋傷楓樹林
　　　　巫山巫峽氣蕭森
　　《江間波浪兼天湧》——(p.791)
　　　　塞上風雲接地陰
　　　　叢菊兩開他日淚
　　　　孤舟一繫故園心
　　　　寒衣處處催刀尺
　　　　白帝城高急暮砧
　　(Graham: "The waves between the river banks merge in the swelling sky")

羅隱　牡丹花　（全唐詩 10/7532）
　　　　似共東風別有因
　　　　絳羅高卷不勝春
　　　　若教解語應傾國
　　《任是無情亦動人》——(p.806)
　　　　芍藥與君為近侍
　　　　芙蓉何處避芳塵
　　　　可憐韓令功成後　　　　（韓壽，pumung)
　　　　辜負穠華過此身　　　　（宮至州尹）

歐陽修　秋聲賦「…聞有聲自西南來者，悚然而聽之，曰，異哉
　　　　初淅瀝而蕭颯，忽奔騰而砰湃，如波濤夜驚，
　　　　風雨驟至…」

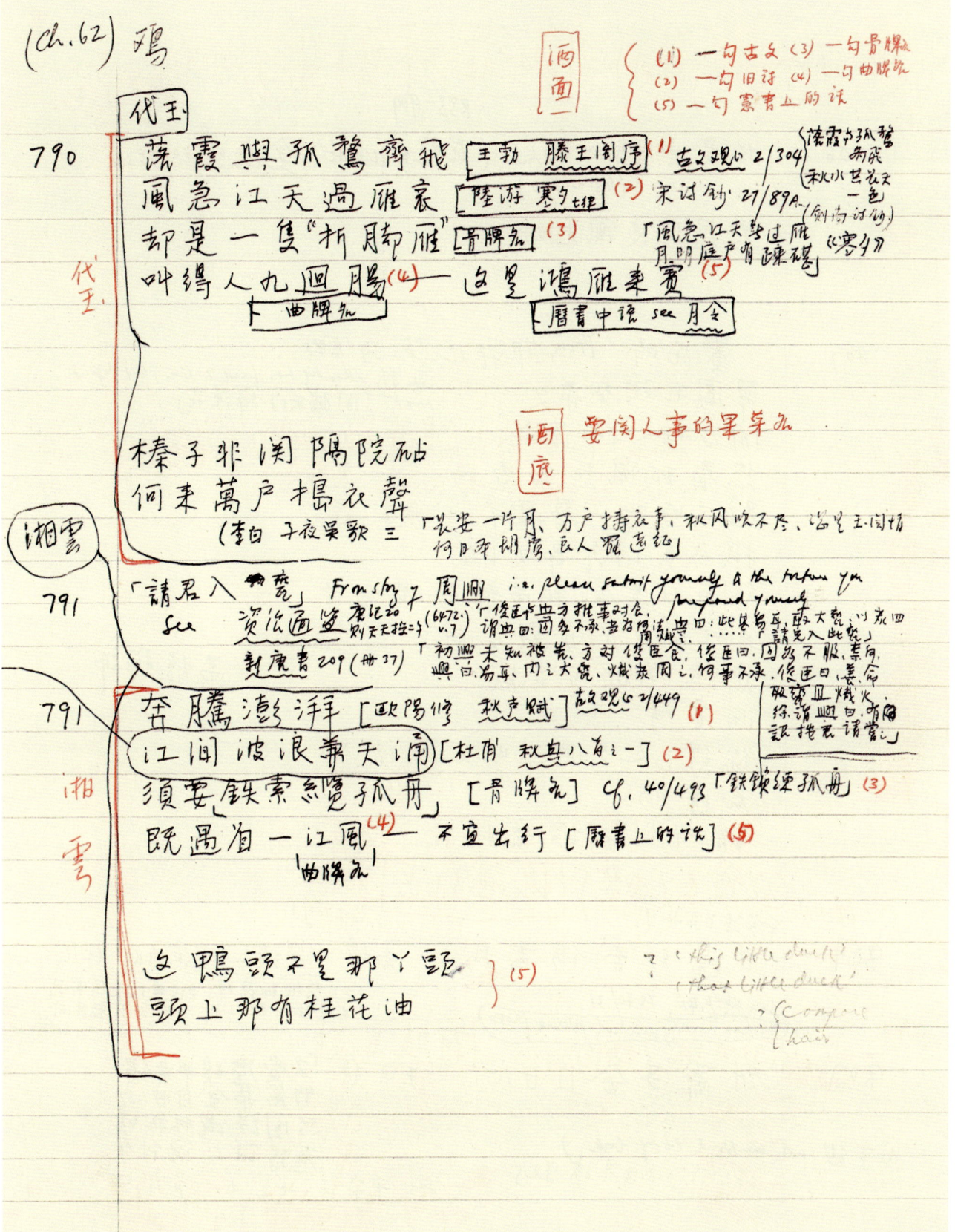

(Ch.63) ① 寶釵（牡丹） 艷冠群芳
833-909

806　任是無情也動人 （羅隱#「牡丹花」全唐詩 10/7532
　　　　　　　　　(before 790)

　　　壽道閑慶風光好

807　賣花時　From 邯鄲記 第三齣「度世」
　　　翠鳳毛翎紮帚叉　　高本 also only has first 2 lines, but different
　　　閑踏天人掃落花　　text: 「閑踏天門掃落花」
　　　　　　　　　　　（高本 only gives these first two lines）
　　　您看那人風起玉塵沙　　庚辰「一」
　　　猛可的那一層雲下　　庚辰「霞」
　　　抵多少門外即天涯
　　　您[再休要劍]斬黃龍一線兒差　庚辰「看那一風」
　　　再[休]向東老貰窮賣酒家　庚辰[林]
　　　您與俺眼向雲霞　　　　　　黃龍禪師

〈洞賓呵
　你得了人方便早些兒回話
〈荷仙呵〉
　錯叫人[留]恨碧桃花　庚辰「唱」

② 探春（杏花） 瑤池仙品
Apricot 千家詩七言絕句9.　　　　　(and 子桐)
807　日邊紅杏倚雲栽　高標下筆綠上永棠高待郎（七絕）
　　　　　　　　　　　「玉上認桃莉露神，晚霞紅杏倚雲栽,
　　　See chap.40, TS 40/31　　　　　　　芙蓉生在秋江上,不向東風怨未開」
　　　The sun rising, a red petalled flower
　　　　　　　　　　　　　　　　　　霜曉寒姿
③ 李紈（梅花）
807 plum 竹籬茅舍自甘心　王淇梅：「不受塵埃半點侵
　　　　　　　　　　　　　　　　竹籬茅舍自甘心
　　　　　　　　　　　　　　　　只因誤識林和靖
　　　　　　　　　　　　　　　　惹得詩人說到今」
（王淇 not mentioned in 唐 Cnk.）
　　千家詩的「字叢橫樓（宋人）　　See 千家詩七言絕句（p.32）

792   鄭谷 題邸間壁
(acc. 千家詩; but neither 全唐詩 nor 萬首唐人絕句
have this among the poems of 鄭谷)
   酒醒香夢怯春寒
   翠掩重門燕子閒
   敲斷玉釵紅燭冷
   計程應說到藍山

岑參 送張子尉南海
(appears not to be in 全唐詩 but appears in 唐詩別裁卷十)
                    (see also 唐詩合解箋註讀本卷八)
   不擇南州尉
   高堂有老親   尉 "comptroller" "one of the several superintendents
   樓臺重蜃氣   of employees + taxes in the subprefectural govt. ……"
   邑里雜鮫人   (Perspectives p. 418)
   海暗三山雨   Re 南海 commandery = Canton, see Pulleyblank 163/12
   花明五嶺春
   此鄉多寶玉
   慎勿厭清貧

李商隱 殘花
   殘花啼露莫留春
   尖髮誰非怨別人
   若但掩關勞獨夢
   寶釵何日不生塵

793　　1. 泉香而酒冽　　　　　　歐陽修「醉翁亭記」
　　　2. 玉盌盛來琥珀光　　　　李白「客中行」
　　　3. 直飲到梅梢月上　　　　骨牌名
　　　4. 醉扶歸　　　　　　　　曲牌
　　　5. 得為宜會親友　　　　　曆書句

1. (see 古文觀止 448)「臨溪而漁，溪深而魚肥。釀泉為酒、
　　泉香而酒冽⋯」
　　See James Liu p. 146: 'the wine is brewed with spring water, and
　　since the spring is sweet the wine is superb.'

2. 蘭陵美酒鬱金香　　　See Obata 75.
　 玉椀盛來琥珀光
　 但使主人能醉客
　 不知何處是他鄉

1. The spring-water being sweet, the wine is good （古文）
2. Pour me this Liquid amber in a jade cup （舊詩）
3. ~~Just~~ We'll drink till The moon shines on the Plum tree Bough （骨牌名）
4. Then Reeling Home （曲牌名）
5. It ~~would be~~ "A good time" ~~quite nice~~ to meet a ~~close~~ friend. （曆書上的話）

'garden' rather than 'gardener'
'market garden' (老圃)
'herb garden' (藥圃)

789　　紅香圃

　　　老(圃)　Analects 13.4 (論語・子路):「樊遲請學稼,子曰:吾不如老農,請學為圃,曰:吾不如老圃…」

790　　藥(圃)　王維　宴趙叟家 i.e.《濟州過趙叟家宴》箋注卷十一/p.212
「離心人境接、閉門成隱居、道言莊叟事、儒行魯人餘、深巷斜暉靜、閑門高柳疏、荷鋤修藥圃、散帙曝農書、上客搖芳翰、中廚饋野蔬、夫君弟高飲、景晏出林閭」

　　　(雞)人　王維《和賈至舍人早朝大明宮之作》
「絳幘雞人報曉籌,尚衣方進翠雲裘…」

　　　(雞)窗　羅隱《題袁溪張逸人所居》:「蒲楨獵獵燕差差、數里溪光日落時、芳樹之君機上錦、遠山孫壽鏡中眉、雞窗夜靜閑書卷、魚檻春深展釣絲、若使浮名拘絆得、世間何處有男兒」(CTS 10/7587)

　　　(雞)塒　詩經・王風・君子于役 (M.66):「君子于役、不知其期、曷至哉、雞棲于塒、日之夕矣、羊牛下來、君子于役、如之何勿思…」
　　　塒 shí: 鑿牆為雞棲處曰塒

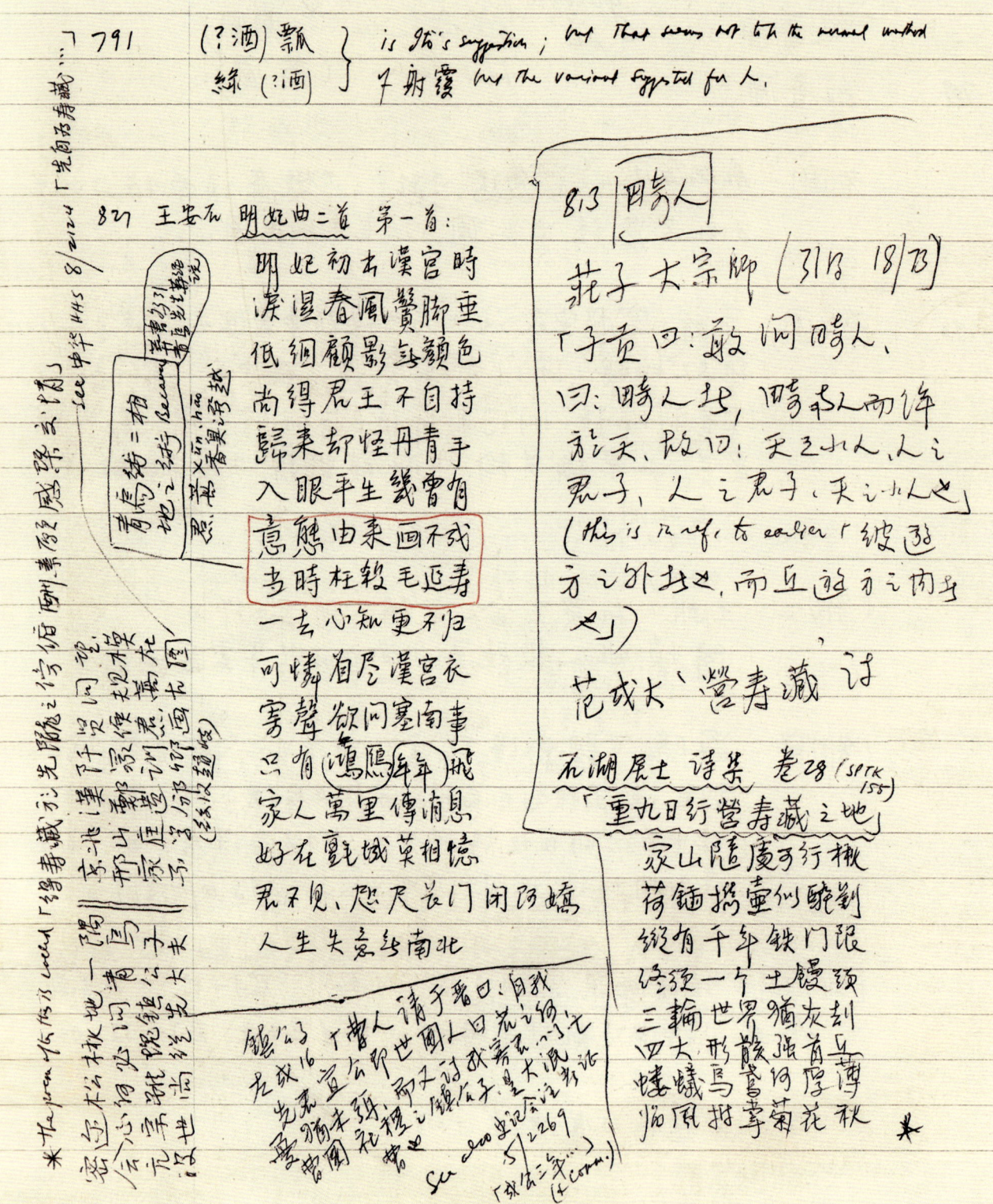

(ch. 63)   NOTES

807　邯鄲記 第三齣 '度世' (cf. '掃花')　(湯顯祖集 第2冊 p.2287)

　　何仙姑持箒上：

『賞花時』

　　翠鳳毛翎札箒叉　　　　　　箒 zhǒu　札 zhá = 紮 zhā

　　閒踏天門掃落花

　　你看風起玉塵砂

　　猛可的那一層雲下

　　抵多少門外即天涯

〔見介〕洞賓先生何往？〔呂〕恭喜你領了東華帝旨,證了仙班.
果老曾在仙翁誠恐你高班已上,掃花無人,着我再往塵寰.
度取一位,散支分散人也！〔何〕洞賓先生大巧行了.只此去未知
何處度人？蟠桃宴可趕的上也？

『么』

　　你休再劍斬黃龍一線差

　　再休向果老人貧窮賣酒家

　　你與俺高眼向雲霞

　　洞賓呵

　　你得了人早些兒回話

　　遲呵

　　錯教人留恨碧桃花　〔下〕

*人民ed. based on 世界文庫 影排 明葉敬池刻本 makes it 21. but 李田意's photos of 內閣文庫 cy makes it 22. This is because 人民 ed. excised 金海陵 (23) and put 張淑兒 after 呂洞賓: two [strikethrough] 中華刻本

For 「劍斬黃龍」, see 醒世恆言 No.21 "呂洞賓飛劍斬黃龍
Ref. to this story in 鐘呂二仙傳 by 黃魯曾 (in 叢書集成).
Cf. also 呂純陽戲化度黃龍 in 孤本元明雜劇 vol.4 ('度黃龍')
In the 恆言 story the attempt is a fiasco, but 傳 (指序) + 度黃龍 version
treat 劍 as symbolic (斬慾貪嗔三毒). 度 desiring successive conversion 7 the Buddhist 5 R Taoist 呂.

as follows: (1) (足本) 20 張廷秀, 21 張淑兒, 22 呂純陽, 23 金海陵
(2) (刪去) 20-21 張廷秀, 22 呂純陽, 23 張淑兒
Hence 人民 (3) 20 張廷秀, 21 呂純陽, 22 張淑兒 23 (刪)

(Ch. 70)   Graham trans. ('Clustered chrysanthemums have opened twice in tears of other days')

902   叢菊兩開他日淚
From 秋興八首 No.1:「玉露凋傷楓樹林、巫山巫峽氣蕭森、
江間波浪兼天湧、塞上風雲接地陰、叢菊兩開他日淚、
孤舟一繫故園心、寒衣處處催刀尺、白帝城高急暮砧」
See 仇 3/17/63, Index 467, Hung 233, Graham 52

902   紅綻雨肥梅 From 陪鄭廣文遊何將軍山林十首 No.5:
「騰水流江破、殘山礧石開、綠垂風折筍、紅綻雨肥梅、
銀甲彈箏用、金魚換酒來、興移無灑掃、隨意坐莓苔」
See 仇 1/2/84, Index 283, and cf. Hung 66-7. (H.h. Nos 1,4,9 and 10)

902   水荇牽風翠帶長 —(See 40/493)
From 曲江對雨:「城上春雲覆苑墻、江亭晚色靜年芳、
林花著雨臙脂落、水荇牽風翠帶長、龍武新軍深駐輦、
芙蓉別殿漫焚香、何時詔此金錢會、暫醉佳人錦瑟旁」
See 仇 @ 1/6/102, Index 308

歐陽文忠集 卷八   《再和明妃曲》
漢宮有佳人   耳目所及尚如此
天子初未識   萬里安能制夷狄
一朝隨漢使   漢計誠已拙
遠嫁單于國   女色難自誇   紅顏勝人多薄命
絕色天下無   明妃去時淚   莫怨春風當自嗟
一失難再得   灑向枝上花
雖能殺畫工   狂風日暮起   ↙ 落花辭
於事竟何益   飄泊落誰家   灘上空枝見風迎痕

(chap. 63)　　　Crabapple flower ④ 湘雲（海棠）　香夢沈酣

808　只恐夜深花睡去　（千家詩）
　　蘇軾 七絕 海棠：「東風嫋嫋泛崇光，香霧空濛月轉廊，只恐夜深花睡去，故燒高燭照紅粧」
　　For ninth version KHCPTS 蘇東坡集 1/4/11：「東風嫋嫋泛崇光，香霧霏霏月轉廊……」

rose (rosa rubus)　　開到荼蘼花事了　⑤ 麝月（荼蘼花）　韶華勝極
　　(宋) 王淇 春暮遊小園, according to 谷, but can't find this — nothing about 「王淇」
　　In fact it comes in 千家詩，「一絲梅粉龍殘粧，塗抹新紅上海棠，開到荼蘼花事了，絲絲天棘出莓牆」

⑥ 香菱 purple skullcap (並蒂花)　連理枝頭花正開　? = 並頭草 scutellaria scordifolia : purple skullcap
　　千家詩 朱淑貞《落花》　「連理枝頭花正開，妒花風雨便相催，願教青帝常為主，莫遣紛紛點翠苔」　聯春繞瑞

Lotus? (Hibiscus)　莫怨東風當自嗟　⑦ 黛玉（芙蓉）　風露清愁
　809　↑ 谷 says 歐陽修 七律《再和明妃曲》(Last line), but can't find this in 歐陽文忠詩鈔 (nor in 千家詩). 佩文韻府 quote 2 lines：「紅顏勝人多薄命，莫怨春風當自嗟」

peach　桃紅又見一年春　⑧ 襲人（桃花）　武陵別景
　　千家詩 謝枋得 (宋)《慶全庵桃花》七絕：「尋得桃源好避秦，桃紅又見一年春，花飛莫遣隨流水，怕有漁郎來問津」

(Ch. 64)　　　黛玉《五美》五首絕句

826　西施
　　一代傾城逐浪花
　　吳宮空自憶兒家
　　效顰莫笑東村女
　　頭白溪邊尚浣紗

827　意態由來畫不成　After 791 for whole poem
　　當時枉殺毛延壽
　　《明妃曲二首》王安石
　　臨川詩鈔

　　耳目所見尚如此　After 902 for whole poem
　　萬里安能制夷狄
　　歐陽修

(ch. 64)

虞姬　　　　　　　　　　　　　　　黥布属项籍，籍封之为九江王，汉遣随
826　　　　　　　　　　　　　　　何说布归汉，佐高祖定天下，封淮南王，继以韩信
　　腸斷烏啼夜嘯風　　　　　　　　彭越见诛，惧祸及己，发兵反，高祖讨破之，
　　虞兮幽恨對雲瞳　　　　　　　　布走越，为番阳人所杀。
　　黥彭甘受他年醢　　(醢: hǎi)　　彭越初事项羽，后率兵归汉，又征讨共
　　飲劍何如楚帳中　　　　　　　　封梁王，高祖既诛韩信越惧祸
　　　　　　　　　　　　黥布　　　及己，後祺固至洛阳序为废人庐舍
　　　　　　　　　　　　彭越　　　西，产活启之说，更三族，暴其骨。

明妃
絕艷惊人入漢宮
紅顏命薄古今同
君王縱使輕顏色　　　　　　予奪: 赐予与褫夺　yǔ duó
予奪權何畀畫工　　　　　　畀bi: 赐與.

綠珠　　　　　　　　　　　See (宋) 樂史's 綠珠傳 (唐宋傳奇集 247)
瓦礫明珠一例拋　　　　　　for an expanded
何曾瓦尉重嬌嬈　　　　　　version of 綠珠's story.
都緣頑福前生造　(石崇)　　頑福: 下品に縁なくとも、当世の功
更有同歸慰寂寥　　　　　　徳で然く不動の富貴を享ける
　　　　　　　　　　　　　ものをいう.

　　　　　　　　　　　　　　　　Qiá-rán
紅拂　　(=張一妹, from the Sty of Curlybeard 《虬髯客传》)
MSS 拮 running　　　　　　　　　For 紅拂記 (乡[明]張鳳翼), see
the correct text：　衣剑雄談戀自珠　　六十種曲 vol. 3. Curiously enough, there
拮 is correctly　美人巨眼識窮途　　seems to be no mention of this play in 典故
中國撑拭　　尸居餘氣楊公幕　(楊素)
乾轨印米　　豈得羈縻女丈夫

唐宋傳奇集 p.166 (杜光庭 虬髯客傳) 紅拂 herself says: 「彼尸居
餘氣，不足畏也…」

(Back to 827)

(ch. 66) (854 MS als has: 將軍不下馬　各自奔前程) Looks rather like an incorporated comment. Author omitted.

857　揉碎桃花紅滿地
　　　玉山傾倒再難扶

(ch. 70)

901　　　桃花行
　　桃花簾外東風軟。
　　桃花簾內晨妝懶。
　　簾外桃花簾內人
　　人與桃花隔不遠。
　　東風有意揭簾櫳
　　花欲窺人簾不卷。
　　桃花簾外開仍舊。
　　簾中人比桃花瘦。
　　花解憐人花亦愁(。)
　(─隔簾消息風吹透。
　　風透簾櫳花滿庭。
　　庭前春色倍傷情。
　　閒苔院落門空掩
　(─斜日欄杆人自憑。
　　憑欄人向東風泣。
　　茜裙偷傍桃花立。
　　桃花桃葉亂紛紛
　　花綻新紅葉凝碧。
　(樹)(樹)烟封一萬株
　　戚本作「霧裹」

Cf. poem + story 于 崔護 the 本事詩
(P.12): 「去年今日此門中
　　　　人面桃花相映紅
　　　　人面不知何處去
　　　　桃花依舊笑春風」

揭 jiē: 高舉

消息 flaps up + down, presumably (in blows in and out)

can't have mean on the ground in view of 「花綻新紅」 & the next stanza. No, it must mean full rows. — diff stanza? A conclusion?

茜裙 qiàn (赤色)

綻 zhàn

株 zhū

(Ch. 70)

901　烘樓照壁紅模糊
　　天機燒破鴛鴦錦　　　The loom of heaven (?dawn)
　　春酣欲醒移珊枕
　　侍女金盆進水來
(?)胭脂冷　　蘸 zhàn: 以物沾水
　　胭脂鮮艷何相類
　　花之顏色人之(淚)
　　若將人(淚)比桃花
　　(淚)自長流花自媚
　　(淚)眼觀花(淚)易乾
　　(淚)乾春盡花憔悴
　　憔悴花遮憔悴人
　　花飛人倦易黃昏
　　一聲杜宇春歸盡
　　寂寞簾櫳空月痕

(902 before 803)

柳絮詞　　　(Shi Xiang-yun)

(Ch. 70)
904　如夢令　(史湘雲)　(詞律 三十三字 2/3B)
　　豈是繡絨才吐　　　× × × ○ ○ ×
　　卷起半簾香霧　　　× × × ○ ○ ×
　　纖手自拈來　　　　× × × ○ ○
　　空使鵑啼燕妒　　　× × × ○ ○ ×
　　且住　且住　　　　× ×　× ×
　　莫使春光別去　　　× × × ○ ○ ×

addressed to the clouds 柳絮, presumably. (don't take the spring away with you as they do)　they would have killed it for their nests.

(ch. 70) 柳絮词 (ctd.) (Bao-yu, Tan-chun, Dai-yu)

905　南柯子 (探春)(宝玉续)—— (al. 南歌子) 加又一体 五十二字此 词律 1/3a

空挂纤纤缕。
徒垂络络丝。
也难绾系也难羁。
一任东西南北各分离。

落去君休惜
飞来我自知。
莺愁蝶倦晚芳时。
纵是明春再见隔年期。
(bis)

　　唐多令 (黛玉)—— 唐多令 六十字 词律 9/7

粉堕百花洲。(duò)
香残燕子楼。
一团团/逐对成毬。
漂泊亦如人命薄
空缱绻 qiǎn-quǎn
说风流。　缠绵不离之意

草木也知愁。
韶华竟白头。
叹今生/谁舍谁收。
嫁与东风春不管
凭尔去
忍淹留。
(bis)

柳絮詞 (ctd) (Bao-qin, Bao-chai)

(ch. 70)

西江月 (宝琴)　　　词律 6 五十字
906　漢苑零星有限　　　6/2b　××○○××
　　隋堤點綴无窮。 diǎn-zhuì "点缀"　　○○××○○
　　三春事業付東風。　　　　　○○××× ○○
　　明月梨花一夢。　　　　　　××○○×
　　幾處落紅庭院　　　　　　　三
　　誰家香雪簾櫳。　　　　　　(bis)
　　江南江北一般同。
　　偏是離人懷重。

臨江仙 (宝釵)　　　词律 又一体 60字
　　白玉堂前春解舞　　　8/3a (Model by 秦觀)
　　東風卷得均勻。 juǎn
　　蜂團蝶陣亂紛紛。　　　　××○○××
　　幾曾隨逝水　　　　　　　○○××○○
　　豈必委芳塵。　　　　　　○○××○○
　　萬縷千絲終不改　　　　　×○○××
　　任他隨聚隨分。 fèn　　　×××○○
　　韶華休笑本無根。　　　　bis
　　好風憑借力
　　送我上青雲。

「蜂團蝶陣」 i.e. 'swarming like bees....'

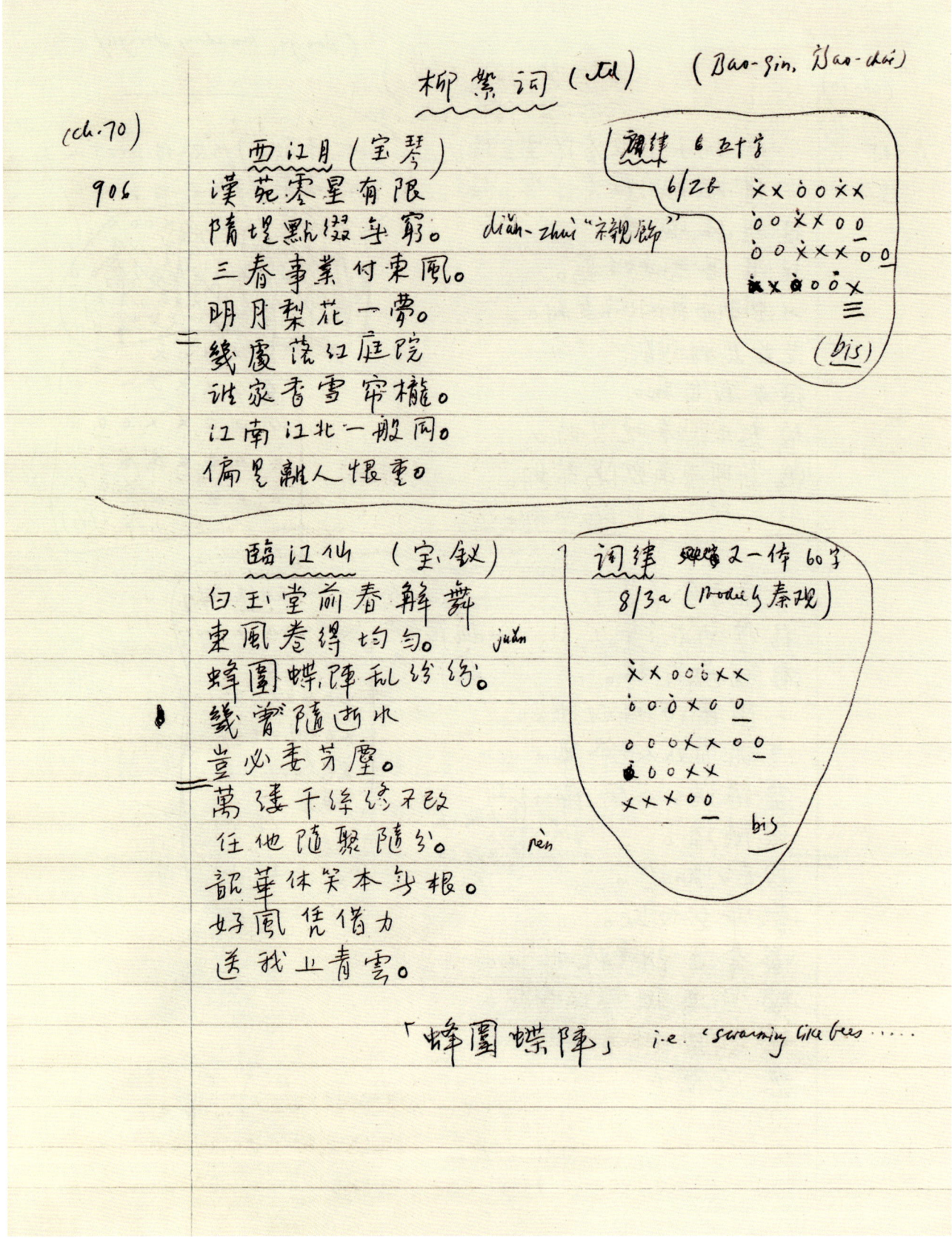

(ch.76) 中秋夜大觀園即景聯句三十五韻

983 代玉		三五中秋夕	
湘雲	①	清游擬上元	CELEBRATE ~~STIMULATE~~ 上元：正月十五日 擬 hau like 相似
	②	撒天箕斗燦	箕斗
984 代玉		匝地管弦繁	REVERBERATE zhā PULSATE
	③	幾處狂飛盞	
湘雲		誰家不啟軒	CELEBRATE STIMULATE SCINTILLATE
代玉	④	輕寒風剪剪	喧 (xuān) = push. 剪剪 (jiǎn) 風寒哨貌。韓偓 夜深：「側側輕寒剪剪風、小梅飄雪杏花紅」
湘雲		良夜景喧喧	喧 (xuān) was intended, but changed to 剪剪, which the PinYin changes 王安石 夜直：「金爐香燼漏聲殘、剪剪輕風陣陣寒」 班固 敘傳：「焱焱上天、擾擾萬姓」
代玉	⑤	爭餅嘲黃髮	餅此月餅 高元裕傳 新序 PNP 33/177/88 seq.
湘雲		分瓜笑綠嫒	綠嫒 like 綠女 ('young young girls'). cf. 燕京歲時記 「…旗人婦女、綠衣紅裳，聯袂遊諸…」 EIGHT
代玉	⑥	香新榮玉桂	the day lily (the 金針 are the dried unopened buds to eat)
湘雲		色健茂金萱	萱 xuān is called 「金針兒」and does a foot have a reddish yellow colour.
代玉	⑦	蠟燭輝瓊宴	SIMULATE (gold towels) 歐陽修 醉翁亭記
985 湘雲		觥籌亂綺園	觥 gōng (酒器). cf. 「觥籌交錯」 (籌者所以行酒令也) INEBRIATE
代玉	⑧	分曹尊一令	
湘雲		射覆聽三宣	? three times promulgate PROMULGATE
代玉	⑨	骰彩紅成點	
湘雲		傳花鼓濫喧	"傳花" game. 'passing the flower'. ROTATE
代玉	⑩	晴光搖院宇	
湘雲		素彩接乾坤	ILLUMINATE
代玉	⑪	賞罰無賓主	
湘雲		~~吟~~ 吟詩序仲昆	DELIBERATE
	⑫	~~構~~ 構思時倚檻	構思／構思 熟：「沈約製郊居賦、構思積時」 裏：「左思欲作三都賦、構思十年」
代玉		擬句或依門	GATE

(ch.76) 中秋夜大觀園即景

986

玉	13	酒盡情猶在		
湘雲		更殘樂已諼	xuān 忘 sta h. 'じみぬ' yaminu TERMINATE
代	14	漸聞語笑寂	
玉	15	空剩雲霜痕 DESOLATE	合歡 albizzia julibrissin. But tr. 'albizzia' here. This will be identified as 'mimosa' in the conversation that follows.
湘雲	15	階露團朝菌	hūn = 合歡 PERNOCTATE
代		庭煙斂夕楹	
湘雲	16	秋湍瀉石髓	湍 tuan (急流) 石髓 KWTT says = 石鍾乳 (Math. stalactites)
代 CONGRATULATE		風葉聚雲根	「唐宋詩人多稱山石為雲根」KWTT
玉	17	寶婺情孤潔	婺女 (wù) 星名 (寶婺 = 婺女) ? Aquarius or (女宿, 也須星)
湘雲 LAVEOLATE ILLUMINATE		銀蟾氣吐吞	yin-chán Rmoon. 吐吞 instead of 吞吐 (tūn-tǔ: 呼息者入) for rhyme's sake.
代	18	藥經靈兎搗	帝孫: Nrnnng 「天孫」Heavenly weaver 天河上 = 織女星 漢書·天文志: 「織女, 天帝孫也」	博物志: 「天河與海通, 舊傳海上, 年年八月浮槎去來不失期, 有人齎糧乘槎而往, 十餘日中一處逢見宮中有織婦, 一丈夫牽牛漸次飲之, 其人還至蜀問嚴君平曰, 某年某月有客星犯牽牛宿, 計年月, 正此人到天河時也」(宁 李義山箋注 3/188)
MANIPULATE ETIOLATE		人向廣寒奔	
玉	19	犯斗邀牛女	
湘雲 HUMAN FREIGHT		乘槎訪帝孫	
	20	盈虛輪莫定	

987

代	21	晦朔魄空存 INANIMATE	
玉		壺漏聲將涸	涸
湘雲	22	窗燈焰已昏	昏 ANNIHILATE LATE (nightfall late)
		寒塘渡鶴影	
代		冷月葬詩魂 ANNIHILATE	

989

妙	23	香篆銷金鼎	xiāo
玉		冰脂膩玉盆	COAGULATE
	24	簫憎嫠婦泣	嫠婦 lí-fù = 寡婦
		衾倩侍兒溫	衾 qīn「請人代為」MITIGATE ABATE
	25	空帳懸文鳳	程本「衾」从脂本改

380

(ch. 76)　　中秋夜大觀園即景

989

1. 閒屏設彩鴛　　ORNATE　　王本作「敞」，脂本作「搶」
26. 露濃苔更滑
    霜重竹難捫　　SERRATE
27. 猶步縈紆沼　　縈紆 yíng·yū
    還登寂歷原　　寂歷 jí·lì 又張謂詩：「空山寂歷道心生」PERAMBULATE
28. 石奇神鬼縛　　縛：fú（讀音）
    木怪虎狼蹲　　蹲：cún（讀音）PULLULATE
29. 贔屓朝光透　　贔屓 bì·xì「作力之貌」「壯士作力貌」又．碑下石龜．
    罘罳曉露屯　　罘罳 fú·sī：屏風，鏤木為之可透明．又．獵罝．
30. 振林千樹鳥　　ACCUMULATE
    啼谷一聲猿　　ULULATE　　脂「玉」→「雨」
31. 歧熟焉忘徑　　(qí)「旁出之路」
    泉知不問源　　INVESTIGATE
32. 鐘鳴櫳翠寺
    雞唱稻香村　　ANTICIPATE (the dawn, the sun)
33. 有興悲何繼　　極（程）　繼：脂本
    無愁意豈煩　　IRRITATE
34. 芳情只自遣
    雅趣向誰言　　COMMUNICATE
35. 徹旦休云倦
    烹茶更細論　　DEBATE

(ch.78)　　　　　姽嫿將軍詩

1017　（賈蘭）　　　　　　　　　　　　　青州 Shantung
　　　姽嫿將軍林四娘　　　　　　　　　and part of Liaoning
　　　玉為肌骨鐵為腸　　　　　　　（古州之一．今山東東部
　　　捐軀自報恆王后　　　　　　　舊青萊寧登州以東之地）
　　　此日青州土尚香
　　　　　　　　　　　　　　　　　姽嫿：
　　　（賈環）　　　　　　　　　　　靜好貌
　　　紅粉不知愁　　　　　　　　　Comes in 宋玉「神女賦」
　　　將軍氣未休　　　　　　　　　「既姽嫿于幽靜兮，
　　　掩啼離繡幕　　　　　　　　　又婆娑乎人間」
　　　抱恨去青州
　　　自謂酬王德
　　　誰能復寇仇
　　　好題忠義墓
　　　千古獨風流

─────────────────────

1018　（寶玉）　　　Necessary to follow the aaxa rhyme scheme in
　　　　　　　　　　order to make sense of the comments.
　　　　　　　　　　　46 lines.
　　　恆王好武兼好色　　賈政搖頭道：「粗鄙」一幕賓道：「要這樣
　　　　　　　　　　　　方古．究竟不粗...」
眾人聽了，便
拍手笑道：「一　遂教美女習騎射
發畫去了，　　　鼙歌艷舞不成歡　（presently 'First (aft.) line') (presumably 'll.1-4.')
再畫見寶　　　列陣挽戈好自矜　眾人都道：「只這第三句便古樸老健，極妙，這句
公之花容．　　　　　　　　　　　平敘出才是好體」
見其嬌閒裊，
不然終　　　　眼前不見塵沙起　「好個《不見塵沙起》！又承了一句《俏影紅燈裏》
停貼至此．」　將軍俏影紅燈裏　　用字用句皆入神化了」
　　　　　　　叱咤時聞口舌香　　叱咤 chi-zha 怒聲．
　　　　　　　霜矛雪劍嬌難舉
　　　　　　　丁香結子芙蓉縧　眾人都道：「轉《縧》〈蕭〉韻
　　　　　　　　　　　　　　　更妙，這才流利飄蕩」
　　　　　　　　＊

(ch. 78)　＊宝玉道：「好姐姐，底下一句我想不出，想出再念。」
　　　　　贾政道：「……好！今又要一句连得萆然，岂不心有馀而力不足些！」

1019
不系明珠系宝刀　（宝玉问：「这一句可使得？」　众人拍掌叫绝。
战罢夜阑心力惟　　宝玉道：「若使得，我便要一气下去；若使不得，索性
脂痕粉渍污鲛鞘　　涂了，我再想别的意思出来再另措词」
明年流寇走山东　　　　　　　　　贾政 says「又一段」, i.e. it's assumed
强呑虎豹势如蜂　众人道：　　　 that this is a 4-line stanza.
王率天兵思剿减　「好个"走"字　But in fact it doesn't continue in
一战再战不成功　便见的高径　　 4-line stanza.
腥风吹折陇中麦　　了。且通句　　　　　jiǎo
日照旌旗虎帐空   对的也工稳」

青山寂寂水澌澌　　　　　　　lǒng=垄 (田中高处)
正是恒王战死时
雨淋白骨血染草　众人都道：「妙极，妙极！布置较多，词藻甚
月冷黄昏鬼守尸　不尽美，且看如何至丫鬟，必另有妙转奇句」

1020
纷纷将士只保身
青州眼见皆灰尘　众人都道：「铺叙已委婉」
不期忠义明闺阁　贾政道：「太多了，底下只怕累赘呢」
愤起恒王得意人

恒王得意数谁行
姽婳将军林四娘
号令秦姬驱赵女
秾桃艳李临疆场　　疆场：本指战场（KYTT）
绣鞍有泪春愁重
铁甲无声夜气凉
胜负自难先预定
誓盟生死报前王

(ch. 78)

1020
　　賊勢猖獗不可敵
　　柳折花殘血凝碧　　抄 conform「步了場」
　　馬踐胭脂骨髓香　　order wd. g 抄 con.
　　魂依城郭家鄉(隔)　　　　　戚本「近」　com. probably made
　　星馳時報入京師　　　　　星馳：「諧戴星乘夜馳行」　in 抄本, but have
　　誰家兒女不傷悲　　　　　　　　　　　　　　　to fall.
　　天子驚慌愁失守
　　此時文武皆垂首
　　何事文武立朝(綱)
　　不及閨中林四(娘)　　　　程乙
　　我為四娘長嘆息　　　　　always 隔
　　歌成餘意尚徬(徨)

1020
　　古人云：
　　潢汙行潦、荇藻蘋蘩之賤、可以羞王公、
　　薦鬼神。

(ch. 78)

1021 Ⓐ 芙蓉女兒誄　(ch. 78 癡公子杜撰芙蓉誄)
庚辰（鏡）
維太平不易之元、 cf. ch. 13/148「四大部洲至中之地，奉天永建太平之國……國……」
蓉桂競芳之月　　　蓉＝芙蓉 'Lotus' (Ito 'hachisu')
　　　　　　　　　The time is mid-autumn.
無可奈何之日
怡紅院濁玉
謹以群花之蕊　　jr̃
冰鮫之縠　「用晴雯素日所喜之冰鮫縠一幅楷字寫成」
沁芳之泉 (Qin-Fang: Drenched Blossoms)　「又備四樣晴雯所喜之物」
楓露之茗 ◦ cf. 8/102「早起沏了碗楓露茶」T198 'Fung Loo'
四者雖微
聊以達誠申信
乃致祭于白帝宮中撫司秋艷芙蓉女兒之前曰：

Ⓑ 竊思女兒自臨人去、迄今凡十有六載
其先之鄉籍姓氏、湮淪而莫能考者久矣。
而玉得于衾枕櫛沐之間、栖息宴遊之夕、
親昵狎褻、相與共處者、僅五年八月有奇。
qīn-nì xiá-xiè

Ⓒ 憶女曩生之者、其為質則金玉不足喻其貴、
　　　　　　　其為體則冰雪不足喻其潔　庚辰作性
náng　　　　　其為神則星日不足喻其精　(modern 明
　　　　　　　其為貌則花月不足喻其色　咸不如神)

Ⓓ 姊娣悉慕媖嫻　zǐ-dì yīng-xián
　姬媵鹹慧慧德　yù-xián
　　　咸

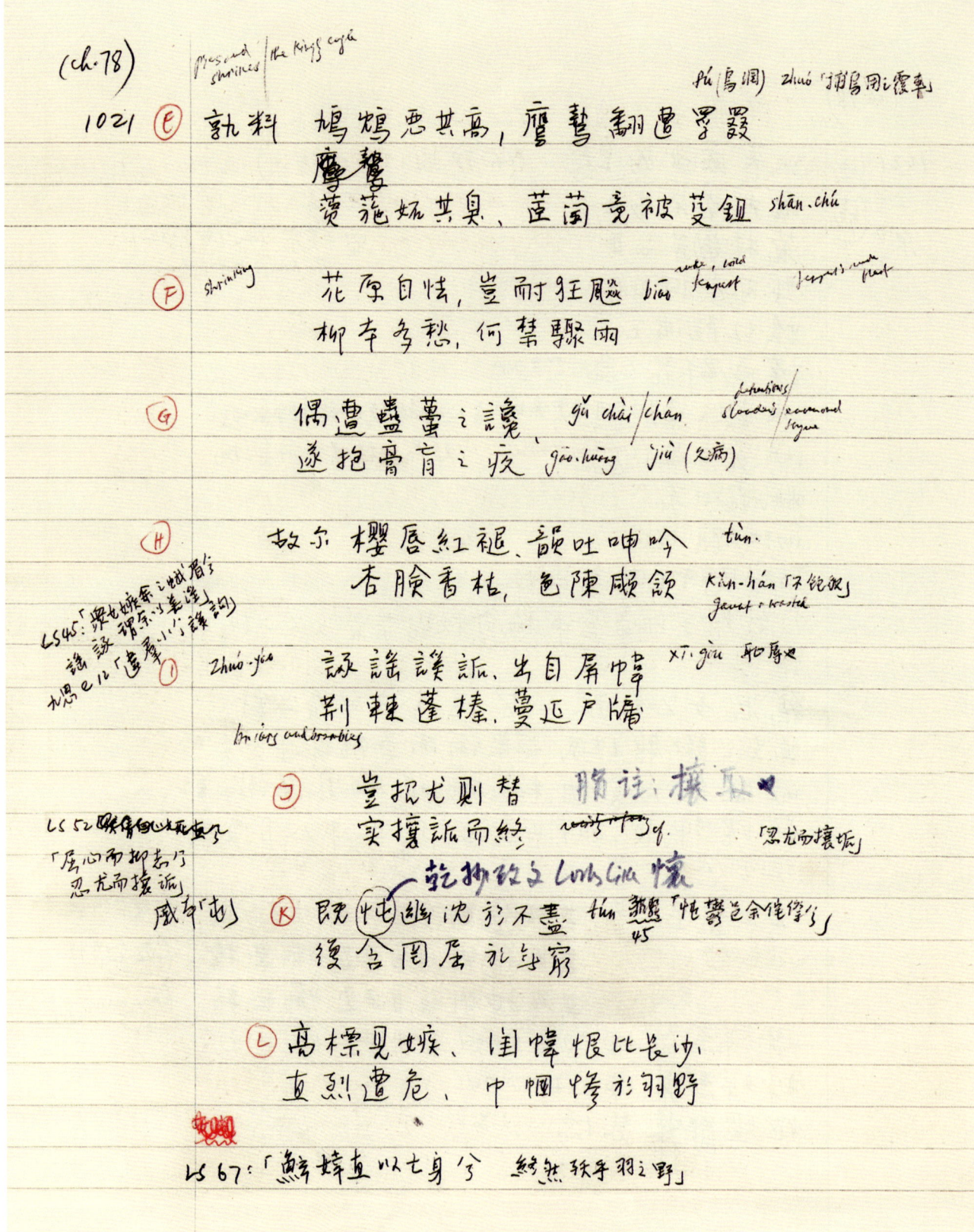

(ch. 78)

1021

Ⓜ 自蓄辛酸、誰憐夭折
　　仙雲既散、芳蹤難尋

Ⓝ 洲迷聚窟、何來卻死之香　　聚窟：海內十洲記：
　　海失靈槎、不獲回生之藥　　「聚窟洲在西海中申未之地，
　　　　　　　　　　　　　　　地方三千里，北接崑崙，上多
　　　　　　　　　　　　　　　真仙靈官，宮第比門，不可勝
　　　　　　　　　　　　　　　數」

Ⓞ 眉黛煙青、昨猶我畫
　　指環玉冷、今倩誰溫　　　　qiàn

Ⓟ 鼎爐之剩藥猶存
　　襟淚之餘痕尚漬　　　　　　漬

Ⓠ 鏡分鸞別、愁開麝月之奩　　　劉敬叔異苑：「罽賓王
　　梳化龍飛、哀折檀雲之齒　　 一鸞三年不鳴，夫人曰、聞鳥
　　cf. 23/267「窗明麝月開宮鏡、　 見影則鳴，懸鏡照之，鸞覩
　　　　　　　　　室靄檀雲品御香」 影悲鳴，中宵一奮而絕」

Ⓡ 委金鈿於草莽
　　拾翠𪄆於塵埃　　　　　　　(掂, peruse)

Ⓢ 樓空鳷鵲、徒懸七夕之針
　　帶斷鴛鴦、誰續五絲之縷

Ⓣ 況乃金天屬節、白帝司時
　　孤衾有夢、空室無人

Ⓤ 桐階月暗、芳魂與倩影同銷　　倩影: moon,
　　蓉帳香殘、嬌喘共細言皆絕　　Sinn「空九い な月か忙」
　　　　　　　　　　　　　　　　 adds HLM 37
from 探春's "海棠" poem. (姑 there has sings 〈月かげ〉)　「芳心一點嬌無力
　　　　　　　　　　　　　　　　 倩影三更月有痕」

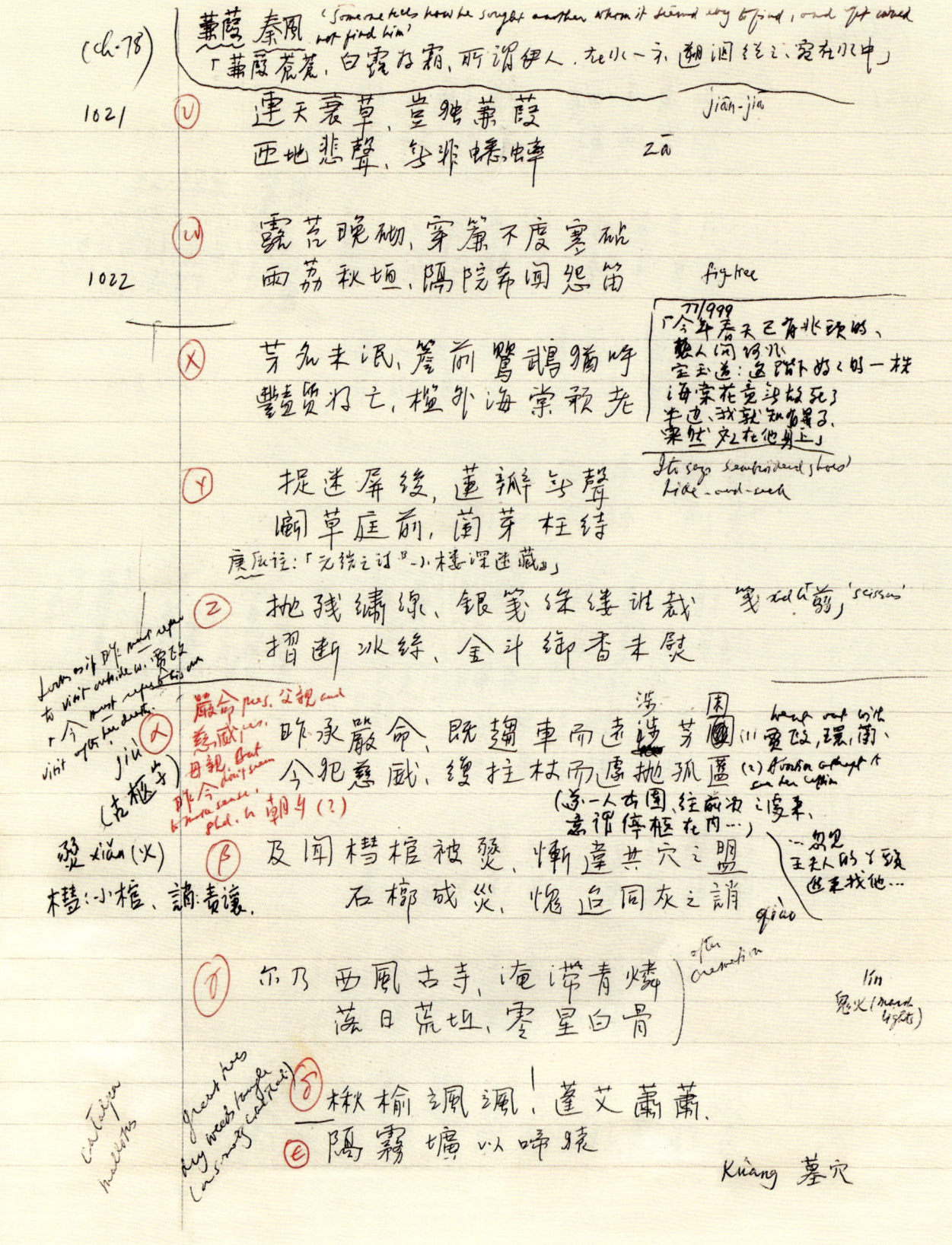

(ch. 78)
1022

※ 汝南涙血 Ref. probably to 碧玉, YFSJ〈碧玉歌〉attrib. to "宋汝南王". Actually no such person: but 南平王鑠, commander at the time of the production of 碧玉 songs of 汝南, may well have been so called. (See 宋書 27/32/1B and 南史 4/14/11A, which says he is a poet)
梓澤 obviously a ref. to 石崇's favorite 綠珠 (see 晉書 8/33/13A: [介士孙], 崇謂綠珠曰 我今好子目累, 綠珠泣曰 当效死於官前, 因自投於楼下而死). Don't know where CXQ gets 远烟膜而注思, his sty about 碧玉 (?) but either most sures he way is making this a ref to
(金竟帝) The most in each case to really write a girl who died before her master. And in any case 碧玉 and 綠珠 come quite close together in YFSJ

⑤ 自为红绡帐里，公子情深 See note to 46〈懊儂歌〉 加石崇/綠珠
  始信黃土壠中，女兒命薄

Cheng (稻田之界蹊)

①「黃紗窗下，公子多情」 ②「黃紗窗下，小姐多情, 黃土壠中, 卿何薄命」 ③「黃紗窗下，我本多情
                                                                              黃土壠中, 卿何薄命

⑦ ※ 汝南涙血, 斑斑洒向西風
    梓澤餘衷, 默默訴憑冷月   zǐ-zé 衷
                                            梓澤: 石崇別館

⑧ 嗚呼! 因鬼蜮之為災, 豈神靈而亦妬

⑨ 箝詖奴之口, 討豈能寬   ⑨仙箝詖柬 箝口: 脅制之使不
  剖悍婦之心, 忿猶未释   詖奴: 奴之不正者 敢言.
                                       悍婦(hàn) 凶暴之婦人

⑩ 在君之塵緣雖淺
   然玉之鄙意豈终

⑪ 固蓄惓惓之思   quán = 拳拳: 懇摯
   不禁諄諄之問   (拳拳之思)
                              zhūn: 忠謹貌.

⑫ 始知上帝垂旌, 花宮待詔
   生侪蘭蕙, 死辖芙蓉   chái   xiá (管辖)

⑬ 聽小婢之言, 似涉無稽
   以濁玉之思, 則深为有據

   何也

(Ch. 78) 葉法善 HTS 204 (36/129/4A) CTS 191 (34/141/12B) Neither has this story.
Compelled 李邕's spirit (Son 子李邕) to come and write an epitaph for his grandfather — in his sleep.

李商隱 李長吉小傳：「...長吉將死時，忽晝見一緋衣人，駕赤虯，持一板書若太古篆或霹靂石文者，云當召長吉。長吉了不能讀，欻下榻叩頭，言阿嬤老且病，賀不願去。緋衣人笑曰，帝成白玉樓，立召君為記，天上差樂不苦也...」

1022   昔葉法善攝魂以撰碑
　　　李長吉被詔而為記
　　　事雖殊，其理則一也

9tā's suggestion that 「澄乎」(all texts) shd. be 「鎣乎」seems right.
KYTT：「誘秀韓娥子、喻竽才而展絡充數」... 肉儀説上：「齊宣王使人吹竽，必三百人，南郭處士請為王吹竽，宣王説之。廩食以數百人，宣王死，湣王立，好一一聽之，處士逃。」

① 故相物以配才，苟非異人，惡乃鎣乎

　　　權衡：權力：「觸探進指揮之威力」

⑪ 始信上帝委託權衡
　　可謂至治至協　庶不負其所畫東賦也

⑥ 固希其不昧之靈，或陟降於茲，
　　特不掃鄙倖之詞，庸洿慧聽，乃歌而招之曰：

qióng-lóng
高者向上奪
而自向下垂瓏　虬qiú

天何如是之蒼蒼兮　秉玉軋以遊乎穹窿耶
地何如是之茫茫兮　駕瑤象以降乎坱壤耶

繳sān: 望繳蓋之陸離兮　抑箕尾之尨耶   i.e. the splendour of the
全傘   　　 canopy outshines the light
箕尾 Sagittarius   列羽葆而為前導兮　綴危虛於旁耶   of the stars.
9 stars in Scorpio
危虛   　 (風伯) Wind God
not Aquarius   LS 100:「前望舒使先驅兮 絳飛廉使奔屬」
or Pegasus   　　　　　　　　　　　　　　　　　　乾枯非酷
3 of Aqu & 4 of Equuleus 驅蜚廉以為比從兮　⑪望舒月以角隆耶   This can't be right
Perhaps it shd.   聽車軌而伊軋兮 ②御鷥鷺以結耶   because it doesn't
be 「望舒卿以生騅」 ③「嘗興騂以下紀」 V.軋伊   rhyme.
                              X seem to indicate 「騁：「駕玉軋以車鷥兮
                              王逸 sez, 鷥, a kind of swan」 鹽塘風余上征」
闖馥郁而蓊然兮　紉蘅杜以為纕耶   蘋蘅：莎、南蘅
火衣裎褐之燦燦兮　鑲明月以為琦耶   芳：多才植物
　　　　　　　　　　　　　　　　　　　　　　　　　但上LS風雨既椒糈
時zhi (茶天地之雨)
葭yán   al. 葌葽, polygonatum officinale (jade bamboo)
(蓮蓋兒 pres. a
Lotus-shaped canopy
is intended)   藉葳蕤而成壇畤兮　掔蓮皌以爨蘭膏耶
                    文飛鉋以為罇罍兮　瀝西霆酥以浮桂酒香耶
蔬shuo
飛bó　　　　　　　 罍瓦盛酒器   瀝lu   ling-lu 姜酒ech
鉋pào   No 酉脣 seems to be word for 糈 (both 米皆)

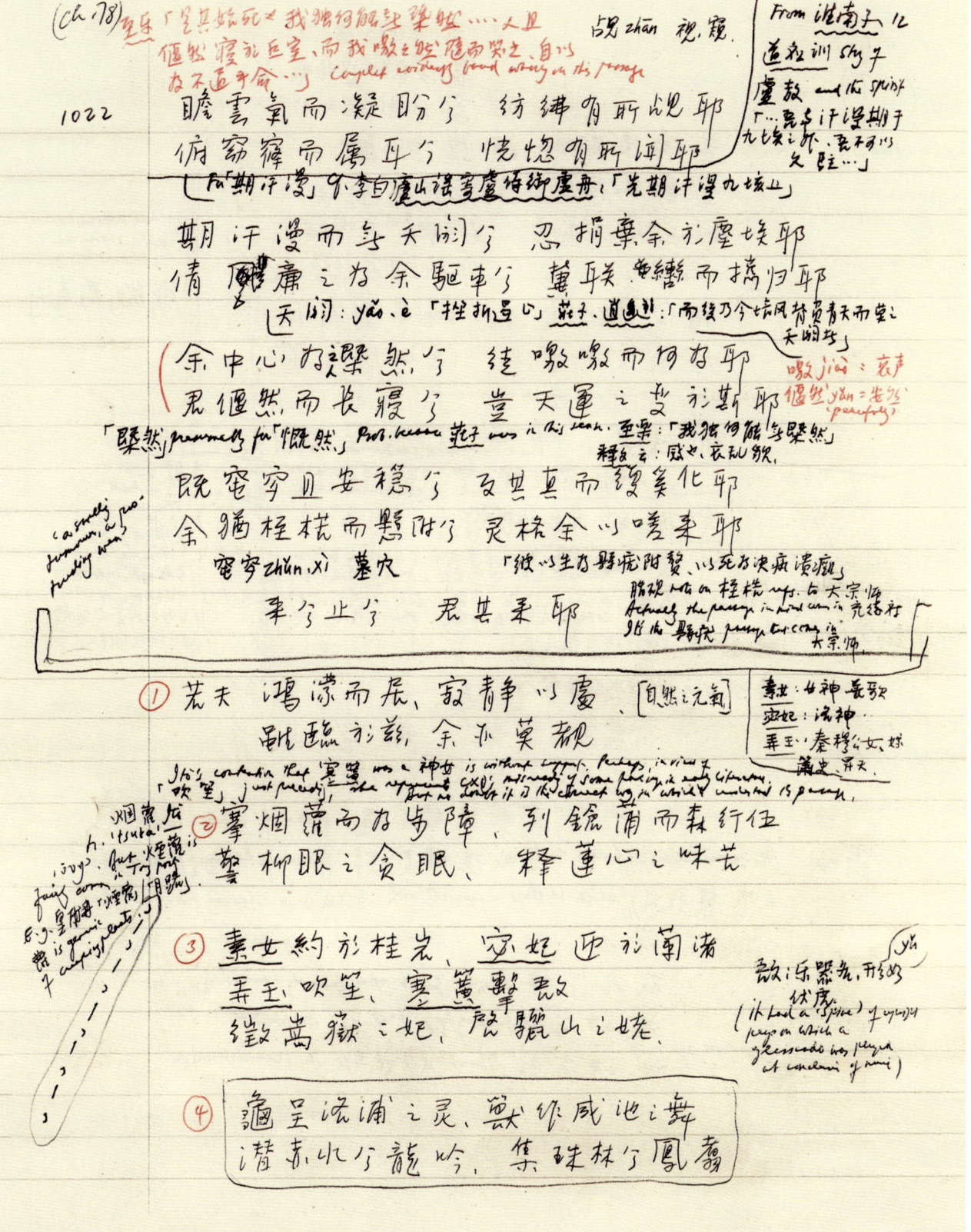

(ch. 78)

簋：古祭祀盛稻粱器
笲：竹圆形盛米之竹器

1023 《⑤ 姜棳姜藗、匪簋匪笲
發韌于霞域，迄推于宮闈
既顯微而若通、復高氤而條阻》

⑥ 離合兮烟雲，空濛兮霧雨
塵霾斂兮星高，溪山麗兮月午

yīn-yūn「烟雲瀠漾状」

murky vapours / a murky vapour coming from...
「顯微易聲碟」話。

⑦ 何心意之忡忡，若寤寐之栩栩
(chōng：心憂貌)   栩栩 xǔ: usually glossed in 喜貌, but it can't mean that here. CXQ must be talking about... the expression is the 莊子 passage: 不知 周之為胡蝶，栩栩然胡蝶也... (whether you're dreaming or not)

寂歷 jí-lì Poem 張說：「空山寂歷道心生」

余乃欷歔悵望，泣涕縹緲
⑧ 人謠兮寂歷，天籟兮篔簹

篔簹 yuán-dāng 竹名 (薄肌而長節，竹之最大者) comes fr. 左思 吳都賦。Also in 游記 fr. 柳宗元。

嗟嘆 shā-die「水鳥聚食声」

⑨ 鳥驚散而飛，魚唼喋以響

⑩ 誌哀兮是禱，成禮兮期祥
嗚呼哀哉，尚饗

霞城：this connects w. ch. 50「霞城隱曙赤標」(one of 湘雲's contributions to the 排聯詩), which he there associates with 赤城山 in Chekiang (N. of 天台縣).

「成禮兮期祥」conventional ending for a dirge; a bit like 'The peace of God be upon you all, amen'.
嗚呼哀哉 Perhaps best left in transliteration.

(ch. 79)

1028　池塘一夜秋風冷
　　　吹散菱荷紅玉影　←
　　　蓼花菱葉不勝悲
　　　重露繁霜壓纖梗　←
　　　不聞永晝敲棋聲
　　　燕泥點點污棋枰
　　　古人惜別憐朋友
　　　況我今當手足情

蓼荇蒿之菱
蓼花 Knotgrass
菱葉 caltrop leaves

枰 ping 棊局
〈棋枰＝棋盤〉

* 4/7/83　「…進入房內, 只見迎春探春二人正在窗下
圍棋…」　And of course 迎春's maid
is 司棋 (and In 22/259 the answer to 迎春's
riddle is a 算盤)

「…再看那岸上的蓼花葦葉之類覺
搖々落々, 似有追悼故人之意,
迥非素常逞妍鬥色可比…」

Wuhu aizai ※ Receive this offering.

①-④ Must sing to 芙蓉神 (not the poet)

⑤ 謹 旌 must also (sung) to 芙蓉神; so must 題絨.
yet to conti. is thinking that the poet himself goes out to
meet 〈the soul of 晴雯〉 (道中さしきよしと心躍らせつつ, 晴雯の
魂を迎えんとて, 天気の霞城より⊙出, 西牡のかた玄圃まで
おもむいたが逢うことがかなわずして引き返す)

On the other hand 歌 14「倩風廉之為余驅車兮…」does suggest
that the poet himself goes after her.

× Prob. best to take「寧妃」to「凰翥」of 芙蓉神 and
「發軔…」of the poet.

740

The spring-time flowers, white and red,
Before the thieving wind have fled;
And in among the green boughs now
The young fruit hangs oly the bough.

1. 牡丹 Peony　宝钗：艳冠群芳　Empress of the Garden
   《任是无情也动人》

2. 杏花 Apricot　探春：瑶池仙品　Spirit of the Mystic
   《日边红杏倚云栽》

3. 梅花 Plum (Winter)　李纨：霜晓寒姿　Beauty of the Snow
   《竹篱茅舍自甘心》

4. 海棠 Crabflower　湘云：香梦沈酣　Sweet Drunken Dreamer
   《只恐夜深花睡去》

5. 荼蘼 Rose　麝月：韶华胜极　Swan's Crowning
   《开到荼蘼花事了》

6. 并蒂花 Purple Skullcap 香菱：联春绕瑞　Three Springs' Harbinger
   《连理枝头花正开》

7. 芙蓉 Lotus　黛玉：风露清愁　Autumn Mourner
   《莫怨东风当自嗟》

8. 桃花 Peach Blossom　袭人：武陵别景　Beyond the Hidden Paradise / Fisher's Paradise Lost
   《桃红又见一年春》

790　(1) "Scudding clouds race the startled mallard across the water"
(2) "A wild goose passes lamenting across the wind-swept sky."
(3) It must be "The wild goose with the broken leg".
(4) So sad a sound makes "The Heart Tormented".
(5) "The cry of the wild goose is heard in the Land"

(6) This cob I take up from the table
　　Came from a tree, not from a stable.

791　What's wrong with your own formula? As Lai Jun-chen said to
Zhou Xing when he showed him the fiery furnace: "P[...] step inside,"
　　　　　　　　　　　　　　　　　　　　　　Just

(1) "A swift-rushing swirl and shock"
(2) "The sky heaves and rocks in the river's swelling waters."
(3) Better now "The love boat tied with an iron chain".
(4) Since there is "A Storm on the River",
(5) "This day stir not abroad"

(6) This little duck can't with that little duck compare:
　　This one's quite bald; that one has a fine head of hair.

806　You that lack passion yet can others move

　　The sumptuous birthday feast begins...

807-8
(1) 艷冠群芳　Empress of the Garden
(2) 瑤池仙品　Spirit of the Afterglow
(3) 霜曉寒姿　Beauty of the Snow
(4) 香夢沈酣　Sweet Drunken Dreamer
(5) 韻華勝極　Summer's Crowning Glory
(6) 聯春綬瑞　Three Springs' Harbinger
(7) 風露清愁　Mourner of the Autumn Dew
(8) 武陵別景　Fisherman's Lost Paradice

黃頭草　Scutellaria scordifolia
　　　　　baikalensis is called 'purple skullcap'

807

With my little phoenix-feather broom I stood at heaven's door
To sweep away the fallen flowers that lie on heaven's floor;
And when, by yonder cloud-bank,
The wind begins to rise,
It stirs the peach dust up,
Round and round it flies.
O! sweeping heaven's floor
Is like any earthly chore!

(2) Apricot-trees make the sun's red-petalled floor

(3) Content by cottage fence to bloom unseen

808 (4) Fear the flowers at dead of night should sleep

(5) After the roses there is no more blooming

(6) Even as the twy-stemmed blossoms break in bloom

809 (7) Your own self, not the East Wind, is your undoing

(8) Peach-trees in pink, and another spring is here.

826

Xi Shi

That Kingdom-quelling beauty dissolved like the flower of foam.
In the foreign palace, Xi Shi, did you yearn for your old home?
Who laughs at your ugly neighbour with her frown-and-simper now,
Still steeping her yarn at the brook-side, and the hair snow white on her brow?

Yu Ji

The very crows are grieving as they caw in the cold night air.
She faces her beaten Tyrant King with a haggard look of despair:
'Let the others wait for the hangman, to be hacked and quartered and rent;
'Better the taste of one's own steel in the decent dark of a tent.'

Lady Bright

To a loveliness that dazzled, the palace of Han showed the door;
For 'the fair are mostly ill-fated', as has been said often before.
Yet it seems strange that an emperor — even one with such tepid views —
Should abandon his eyes' own judgement and let a painter choose!

Green Pearl

Pebble or pearl — to Shi Chong it was only a rich man's whim:
Do you really believe your undoubted charms meant so very much to him?
It was fate, from some past life preordained, that made him take his rash stand,
And the craving to have a companion in death's dark, silent land.

826 Red Duster
She marked the firm, courteous protest, the well-phrased, confident plan,
And, under the unsuccessful clerk, saw the essential Man.
The great Yang Su in her eyes was finished from that hour:
He could not hold a girl like her for all his pomp and power.

827 What brush could ever capture a beauty's breathing grace?
The painter did not merit death who botched that lovely face.

A prince so ill able to control what went on under his nose
Might hope in vain to impose his reign on remote barbarian foes.

857 Red scatter of broken blossoms, and the jade column fallen,
Never to rise again...

901   THE FLOWER OF THE PEACH
Peach pink the tender flowers outside the window blow;
Peach pink on sleepy face the morning colours glow.
Tree-flowers outside the room and lady-flower inside;
Only a few short steps the flowery forms divide.
Slyly the conspiring wind tugs at the blind below:
Tree-flowers would peep inside if they could do so.
        x   x   x

901　　Outside the window tree-flowers are blooming still;
　　　　Inside the window Lady-flower looks ill.
　　　　If the flowers could understand, surely they would grieve?
　　　　The anxious wind flaps the blind against the window-sill.
　　　　　　　　x　　　　　x　　　　　x
　　　　The anxious wind flaps the blind; spring crowns the courtyard trees;
　　　　Spring sights fill the Lady's eyes, but bring her heart no ease.
　　　　In her closed, untrodden court the moss grows green on the stones:
　　　　She leans there at the sunset hour, in the soft evening breeze.
　　　　　　　　x　　　　　x　　　　　x
　　　　In the soft breeze the Lady's face is wet with many a tear.
　　　　Her silken peach-skirt billows out, the peach-trees to be near.
　　　　The peach-flowers and the peach-leaves nod in a rich array;
　　　　The leaves, against the peach-pink, dark emerald appear.
　　　　A thousand trees, ten thousand trees, crowding close together,
　　　　Walls and buildings everywhere in a red mist smother.
　　　　　　　　x　　　　　x　　　　　x
　　　　Heaven's new bed-spread is burning on the dawn loom of the skies:
　　　　It's time now for sleeping Lady-flower from dreams of spring to rise.
　　　　Her maid comes in with a golden bowl as she leaves her coral bed,
　　　　And the peach-pink stain from her sleepy face the chilly water dyes.
　　　　　　　　x　　　　　x　　　　　x
　　　　If with the water's rosy hue comparison be made,
　　　　Carmine tears and dewy flowers seem of the self-same shade.
　　　　Yet lady's tears and flowers in this unalike I find,

901   That the flowers are still and smiling, but the tears flow unallayed.
      As she gazes on the smiling flowers, her tears at last grow dry;
      But as they dry, the springtime ends and the flowers fade.
              x   x   x

      The flowers fade, and an equal blight the lady's fair cheek palls.
      The petals drift; she is weary; and soon the darkness falls.
      A nightingale is singing a dirge for the death of spring,
      And moonlight steals through the casement and dapples the silent walls.

902   Chrysanthemums have opened twice in tears of other days.

      Rain-fattened plum-buds, crimson-slashed

      The wind's green duckweed-trails on the water bright.

904   WILLOW FLOSS POEMS
      Shi Xiang-yun   (Tune: Ru-meng-ling)
            'Not chewed-off ends of the sky's embroidery?'
            'What are they?' — 'Raise the blind a bit and see.'
            A white hand snatches some and draws it in,
            Pursued by the swallows' chiding din.
               Oh stay, oh stay!
            The lovely spring drifts after you away.

905

Tan-chun, Bao-yu (Tune: Nan-ge-zi)

Once in the air you start,
The creatures of the wind, the breezes' sport,
Not to be bound or held back by any art,
To north and south and east and west
You drift apart.

Your drifting fate not fear:
I understood the message that you bear.
Though orioles mourn and the flowers' end seems near,
Spring will return, but I must wait
Another year.

Dai-yu (Tune: 'Tang-duo-ling')

The pollen is spent in the Island of Flowers;
From the House of the Swallow the perfume has fled.
    The fluff-balls dance,
      Pursue, embrace,
Their floating lives, as our lives, quickly sped,
    That, craving Beauty,
    Find it dead.

The creatures of nature, they too know our sorrow,
Their beauty, like ours, must soon end in decay.
    Our fate, like theirs,

905
     Uncertain hangs,
 Wed to the wind, our bridegroom of a day,
     Who cares not if we
     Go or stay.

906 Bao-qin (Tune: ~~Here~~ 'Xi-jiang-yue')

In the Han palace gardens, a scatter thin and slight,
But along the Sui embankment, in legions falling:
Spring's three-month handiwork before the wind in flight,
A day-dream of pear-blossom on a moonlit night.

In many a courtyard petals fall through the air,
And the floss collects like fragrant snow on the casements:
In North and South the same sight is seen now everywhere,
But for the sad exile ~~not~~ hard to bear.

 Bao-chai (Tune: ~~Here~~ 'Lin-jiang-xian')

 In mazy dances over the marble forecourt,
 Wind-whorled, into trim fluff-balls forming,
 Like fluttering moths or silent white bees swarming:
 Not for us a tomb in the running waters,
 Or the earth's embalming.

 The filaments whence we are formed remain unchanging,
 No matter what separates or unifies.

906.   Do not, earth-child, our rootlessness despise:
       When the strong wind comes he will whirl us upwards
       Into the skies.

               MID-AUTUMN NIGHT IN PROSPECT GARDEN: A
               POEM IN THIRTY-FIVE COUPLETS

983 (1) [DY] Fifteenth night of the Eighth, Mid-Autumn moon —

         [XY] Whose joys the First Full Moon's do emulate:
    (2)   Under your crystal, constellated heaven —

984   [DY] The sounds of music everywhere pulsate.
                    In many a house
    (3)   ~~Now everywhere~~ the reckless wine-cups fly —

         [XY] When friends are met your feast to celebrate.
    (4)   The air is crisp, the wind more bracing blows —

         [DY] In the clear sky the cold stars scintillate.
    (5)   Grey hairs are mocked when they for cakes dispute —

                   Green
         [XY] ~~And~~ girls divide the melons, eight and eight.
    (6)   New scents the jade-like cassia have enriched —

         [DY] Lilies do golden needles simulate.
    (7)   Candle-light gleams on the faces of the feasters —

985 [XY] Whom frequent sconcings soon inebriate.
(8)   Competing, they observe the game's strict order —

[DY] And rules for 'I spy' gravely promulgate.
(9)   Some shake the pretty dice and make them roll —

[XY] Or, to the drum's quick beat, the flower rotate.
(10)   The clear rays glint on roofs and courts below —

[DY] And all in silvery light illuminate.
(11)   Prizes and forfeits impartially they ponder —

[XY] Competing verses they adjudicate,
(12)   Poets lean on railings, seeking inspiration —

[DY] Or hunt for rhymes, propped up against a gate.
(13)   ~~Noisy~~ Excitement lingers, though the party's over —

986 [XY] The sounds of music softly terminate.
(14)   Slowly the talk and laughter fade to silence —

[DY] Leaving a moonscape hushed and desolate.
(15)   On dewy steps the tiny toadstools sprout —

[XY] Tight-curled albizzia bushes prostrate.

986	(16)	A rain-swelled swirl rips through the brook-bed rocks —
	[DY]	And wind-combed leaves on ledges congregate.
	(17)	The Spinning Maid in lonely splendour shines —
	[XY]	Damp airs the silver toad of the moon inflate.
	(18)	See where the hare immortal medicine pounds —
	[DY]	Thither Chang E was forced to emigrate.
	(19)	A man moves upwards through the constellations —
	[XY]	A raft floats skywards with a human freight.
	(20)	Waxing or waning, the moon's face, ever changing —
	[DY]	Its substance, changeless and inanimate.
	(21)	Soon the clepsydra's night-long drip will cease —
	[XY]	Black shades the lamp's last gleam annihilate.
	(22)	A stork disturbs the cold brightness of the water —
	[DY]	Where, moon-embalmed, a dead muse lies in state.
989	[MY]	
	(23)	In golden censers figured incense burns;
		Unguents in their jade pots coagulate.

989 (24) A flute provokes the grieving widow's weeping;
She craves some warmth her bed's chill to abate.

(25) Its cheerless hangings stir in the wind of autumn,
Its love-ducks mock a mistress without mate.

(26) Thick dews make treacherous the slippery moss,
And spears of frost the tall bamboos serrate.

(27) Better the winding lakeside path to follow,
Or lonely hill-tops to perambulate.

(28) Bound demons seem to writhe in the tortured rock-shapes;
In the trees' black shadows wild things pullulate.

(29) Light's harbingers begin with the dark to struggle,
And morning's first dews to accumulate.

(30) Birds in a thousand treetops wake the woodland;
In the echoing valley sad apes ululate.

(31) My footsteps tread the path's familiar turnings,
Nor need the stream's source to investigate.

(32) From Green Bower convent sounds the matin bell;

989   And Sweet Rice cocks the dawn anticipate.

(33)   Why should this rapt enjoyment end in sorrow,
        Or timid cares our conscience initiate?

(34)   Poets ought in themselves to find their pleasure,
        Not in the message they communicate.

(35)   As daylight breaks, let none of us plead tiredness,
        But over tea continue our debate.

1017   <u>Jia Lan</u>
        Fourth Sister Lin was the Winsome Captain's name:
        She was beautiful and gentle, yet her valour none could tame.
        In Qing-zhou where, her Prince to avenge, she threw her life away,
        The very ground on which she fell is fragrant to this day.

        <u>Jia Huan</u>
        The lovely lady would not sit and grieve;
        with sterner thoughts her warlike breast was filled.
        She dried her woman's tears and fearless rode
        Through Qing-zhou's gates (to be killed to kill)   (and
        'However great the odds,' she said, 'I can
        'My debt repay, if not avenge his ill.'
        The inscription graved upon her tomb shall be:
        'Here lies the world's fidelity.'

The Winsome Captain

1018
Prince Heng was fond of a pretty face, ~~and~~ of martial arts also,
So he trained the ladies of his court to ride and draw the bow,
In ravishing songs and beguiling dances the Prince took no delight,
But to watch the pike-drill he was fain of ~~his~~ fair maids all in a row.

    x   x   x

As he watched them drill, he scarcely saw the clouds of dust arise;
'Twas the lovely Captain's lamplit face that swam before his eyes.
When the rosy lips framed their harsh commands, he could smell the mouth's sweet breath;
~~But~~ the weapons oft shook in the fair white hands, too weak for such exercise.

    x   x   x

Rhymes: 'eyes', 'eyed' 1019

The lotus belt round the Captain's waist in a clove ~~shaped knot~~ was tied:
~~But it~~ was not ~~the~~ strung pearls that hung from it, but the good sword at her side.
When late at night the jousting ended, her courage was quite spent,
And her handkerchief with the carmine sweat of her steaming face was dyed.

    x   x   x

Next year the whole North-~~east~~ land with rebels was a-run,
Like ravening beasts, or swarming bees after the queen has flown.
The Prince led forth the Emperor's men the rebel hordes to quell,
~~But~~ though he fought them once and ~~fought them~~ twice, ~~but~~ his army was overthrown.
A steach of blood upon the wind blighted the standing corn,
~~And~~ on empty tents and on empty camp the setting sun went down.

    x   x   x

'Twas the rainy time, and sounding rills down the lone green hillsides sped
When Prince Heng, his fighting ended, on the battlefield lay dead.

Now rain has washed the white bones clean, but not the blood-soaked grass,
And as the moon rises, shivering ghosts stand at each corpse's head.
        x   x   x

1020 The Officers refused to fight, for fear they might be killed,
      And with no defenders Qing-chou's fate seemed already to be sealed.
      But though the men were all afraid, the girls were loyal and true:
      Among them Prince's favourite with especial zeal was filled
        x   x   x

And who the Prince's favourite was to you shall be revealed:
Fourth Sister Lin she was by name, the Winsome Captain called,
She rallied her companions fair and issued a command,
And like a troop of lovely flowers they rode into the field.
        x   x   x

Their heavy saddle-cloths are wet with tears of the spring sky's woe,
The iron of their armour chills, as through the cold night they go.
Though the outcome may be uncertain, they have taken a solemn vow,
Whatever befall, before they die, for the Prince to strike a blow.
        x   x   x

But what hope against a savage foe had the gallant band?
Like gentle flowers they perished, crushed by a brutal hand.
The horses' hooves are fragrant yet that trod them in the mud;
Near the city walls their poor ghosts flit, where they made their final stand.
        x   x   x

A courier riding through the night to the Emperor's city came,
And all who heard his heavy news with sadness did exclaim.

1020 The Son of Heaven looked aghast when he learned of Qing-zhou's fall,
And his captains and his counsellors all hung their heads for shame.
　　　　　×　　　　　×　　　　　×
The captains and the counsellors and men of high degree
Were put to shame by Fourth Sister Lin's fidelity.
For Fourth Sister Lin my heart with grief does swell,
And though my song is ended, my thoughts still on her dwell.

1028 (ch. 79)

The pool's pink-petalled lotus crowns have gone,
By nightlong blast of autumn breeze blown.
Like grief-stricken mourners, knotgrass and coltsfoot-heads
Under the weight of frost and dew bow down.
Her board that once with Go-stones clicked all day
With sluttish swallows' mud is now blotched brown.
Old poets for parked friends made such a din:
What grief must mine be for my own close kin?

The pool's pink-petalled lotus crowns have gone,
     one night's ripping
By nightlong ~~broad blast~~ of autumn blown;
Like stricken mourners, knotgrass and coltsfoot-heads
Under the weight of frost and dew bow down;
The   in
    board ~~~~~~~~~~~~~~~~~~~~~~~~~ where Go-stones clicked
                                        the long day through
With sluttish swallows' mud is now blotched brown.
Old poets for parked friends made such a din,
What grief must mine be for my own close kin?

ELEGY FOR A LOTUS SPIRIT

1021

The year being in the era of Immutable Peace; the month, that in which the sweet odours of lotus and cassia compete; the day, a heavy and doleful day — I, most wretched and disconsolate JADE of the House of Green Delights, having with due reverence prepared and got together buds of flowers, silk of mermaids, water of the Drenched Blossoms stream and Fung Loo tea (all things of small account in themselves, yet sufficient to attest the devotion of a true believer) — do here offer them up in sacrifice to her that has now, in the Palace of the White God, become the SPIRIT OF THE LOTUS, having power and dominion over the flowers of autumn.

It is, now, sixteen years since the BLEST SPIRIT descended into this world of men. As to her native place and the lineage in which she was born, they were long since forgotten and past recall; but for five years and eight months of that time she was, in my rising up and lying down, in my washings and combings, in my rest and in my play, my constant close companion and helpmate.

It is to be recorded of her that in estimation she was more precious than gold or jade, in nature more pure than ice or snow, in wit more brilliant than the sun or stars, in complexion more beautiful than the moon or the flowers. Who of the maidens did not admire her accomplishments? Who among the matrons did not marvel at her sagacity?

But if baleful screech-owls that hate the heights can cause the kingly eagle to be taken in a net, and rank and stinking weeds, envious of another's fragrance, can cause the sweet herb of grace to be uprooted,

1021 it is not to be thought that a shrinking flower could withstand the whirlwind's blast, or a tender willow-tree to pray against the buffetings of the tempest. When the envenomed tongue of slander was wagged against her, she pined inwardly with a wasting sickness; the red of her cherry lips faded and only sad and plaintive sounds issued out of them; the bloom of her apricot cheeks withered and none but lean and haggard looks were to be seen upon them.

Slanders and slights crept from behind every curtain; thorns and thistles choked up the doors and windows of her chamber. Yet truly, although she ended her days in infamy, she had done no infamous thing. She entered a silent sufferer into the eternal, a wronged innocent into the everlasting, a more notable martyr (though but a mere girl) to the envy of excellence than he who was drowned at Long Sands, a more pitiable sufferer from the peril of plain dealing than he that was slain upon Feather Moor.

Yet since she stored up her bitterness in silence, none recognized the treasure that was lost in her, cut off so young. The fair Cloud dispersed, leaving no means to trace the beauteous outline of its former shape. For it were a hard thing to hunt out the Isle of the Blest from among the multitudinous islands of the ocean and bring back the immortal herb that should restore her: the rest is lost that went to look for it.

It was but yesterday that I painted those delicate smoke-black eyebrows; and who is there today to warm the cold jade rings for her fingers? The medicine she drank yet stands upon the stove; the

1021 tears are still wet on the garment she once wore. The phoenix has flown, and MUSK's vanity-box has burst apart for sorrow; the dragon has departed, and RIPPLE's comb has broken its teeth for grief. The magpie has forsaken my chamber; it is in vain for the maidens to hang up their needles on Seventh Night and pray for nimble fingers. My buckle with the love-ducks is broken; the sapphire is no more who could repair the silk-work of its girdle.

And this being the season of autumn when the power of metal predominates and the White God is master of the earth, the signs themselves are melancholy. I wake from dreams of her on a lonely couch and in an empty room.
A> The moon varies barely behind the trees of the garden, the moonlight and the scent from I dreamed of any extinguished.
A> The perfume fades in the hangings of my bedchamber; the laboured breath and the whispered words that I strove to catch fall silent. Dew pearls the moss on the pavement and the blind of loneliness's beat is borne in unceasingly through my window. Rain wets the fig-tree by the wall; a flute's complaint carries unceasing from a neighbouring courtyard.

1022 Her sweet name is not extinguished, for the parrot in his cage under the eaves ceases not to repeat it; and the crabtree in my courtyard, whose half-withered boughs foretokening of her doom, stands yet for her memorial. But no more shall the sound of her little lotus-feet betray her at hide-and-seek behind the screen; no more will her fingers cull budding orchids for the game of match-my-flower in the garden. The embroidery silks are thrown aside in a tangle: never again will she snip at them with her silver scissors. The sheeny satin lies creased and crumpled: her hot-iron shall never smooth out its perfumed folds.

In her last hour, when I might else have gone to her, I was called in haste from the Garden by my Father's summons; when, grieving, I sought to take leave of her abandoned body, I could not see it, for it had been removed by my Mother's command; and when I was told that her coffin had been covered, I repented me of my jesting vows that we should share the same grave-hole together, for that were now impossible, and that our ashes should commingle, for ash is what now she is become.

In the burning-ground by the old temple green ghost-fires flicker when the west wind blows. On its derelict mounds scattered bones gleam whitely in the setting sun. The wind sighs in the tall trees and rustles in the dried-up grasses below. Gibbons call sadly from tombs that are hidden in mist and ghosts flit weeping down the alley-ways between the tombs. At such times must the young master in his crimson-curtained bed seem most cruelly afflicted and the maid beneath the yellow earth most cruelly ill-fated.

The tears of Ru-nan fall in bloody drops upon the wind and the complaint of Goddess Volky is made to the moon in silence. Vengeance is for demons and baleful bogles; the gentle spirits of maids are not moved to be jealous, though Nathless wronged. the backbiters shall not escape; their mouths shall be squeezed in vices. The hearts of those cruel harridans shall be ripped for Her anger is kindled against them.

1022   Though the bond between us was a slight one, yet was it not lightly to be broken; and because she was ever close to me in my thoughts, I could not forbear to make earnest inquiry concerning her. Thus I [heard] that God had sent down the baton of his authority, summoning her to his Palace of Flowers, to the end that she who in life was like a flower (in death should) have dominion over the Lotus-flower. At first, when I heard the words of the little maid touching this appointment, I thought them fantastical; but now that I have pondered them in my heart, I know them to be worthy of the most perfect credence.

   How so?
   Did not Ye Fa-shan compel Li Yong's sleeping spirit to compose an epitaph? And was not the soul of Li He summoned that he might write a memorial in heaven? The circumstances may be different, but the principle is the same. God chooses his ministers according to their capabilities, else how could they discharge the duties that are required of them? And who more fit and meet than her to be given this charge that He has laid upon her? Truly, here at last she has a work that is worthy of her.

   And because I would hereby ⟨BLEST SPIRIT⟩ descend here in this place, I have composed these verses with which to invoke her, fearing that the common speech of mortals might be offensive to her immortal ears:

   The Invocation
   All's clearest azure above—a,   where her team of white wyverns
       → through the welkin wends,
   And the world in a haze below—a,   as her chryselephantine car
       to the earth descends.

1022   Her awning's relucent splendour-a   outshines Antares and his starry band,
Her guidons and gonfalons go before-a,   and the stars of Aquarius guard her on either hand.
Cloud-cleaver follows as escort-a,   Moondriver gallops to clear the way ahead.
I can hear the creak and trundle of chariot-wheels-a,   of her phoenix-figured car's majestic tread,
I can smell the enveloping scent-a   of her cincture from fragrant stalks of asarum twined,
See the dazzle of her dress-a   gleaming with worm-jade ruches fretted and lined,
I'll strew the altar with lily-of-the-valley leaves-a   and have water-lilies for lamps fed with orchid oil,
And in chalices cunningly fashioned from calabash-a pour rarest metheglin flavoured with pennyroyal.
As I fasten my gaze on the clouds-a,   methinks I see a faint glimmer of her face;
As I strain my ear on the silence-a,   I seem to hear a faint echo of her voice.
But she, on a tryst with eternity, brooking no coarctation-a, has abandoned me, cruel, below in the dust to lie,
Calling on Wind-Lord in vain to drive me up after-a   and side by side ride with her across the sky.
My heart is all wracked with keen-a,   yet it boots not to weep and wail:

1022 You are gone now to your long sleep—a   against Nature's order no
                                              power on earth can prevail;
      In the grave-vault secure you rest—a,   the bourne after which there
                                              is no more transformation
      But to me still in bonds in this hateful men below—a, o Spirit,
                                              succouring come for my consolation!
      O Spirit, come and abide for my consolation!

      But what though she is present in this place? She is girt about with
silence, and veiled in a mist of invisibility; I cannot see her.
      I see only the green wreathed creepers that make her side-screens
      And the ranks of tall bullrushes, her guardsmen's spears.
      Yet sleepy willow-buds waken as she approaches,
      And the bitter lotus-seeds sweeten as she nears.
      The White Virgin waits for her on the Cliffs of Cassia;
      From Orchid Island the Water Spirits come to greet her;
      Jade-player plays for her on a little organ,
      And Cold-Keys sweeps the iron spine with his metal beater;
      The God of the Mill Peak's consort comes at her bidding;
                    Crone of Li Mountain
      The ~~Mountain wife of~~ is summoned forth to meet her;
      The two River turtle brings her his magic offering;
      Wild beasts to the heavenly music gambol and prance;
      In the deeps of the Red River dragons turn their turns,
      And in pearly grasses the Birds of Paradise dance

1023 Seeing my reverence and my devoutness of heart (notwithstanding that

1023 I have no vessels of gold neither of bronze in which to make my offering; she drove forth her chariot from the City of the Sunrise; but even now her banners are returning to the Garden of Night. For a little moment it seemed that the invisible would become visible; but murky vapours rose up (between us and suddenly) we are cut off.

  Clouds and mists drifted and drew together,
  Rain and fog veiled the heaven's light,
  Then, rolling back, revealed the high stars
  And earth all radiant in the noon of night.

And now ~~But~~ My mind is in a turmoil, uncertain whether I awake or dream. I gaze at the sky with sighs of disappointment; I wait in uncertainty with weeping eyes. My speech grows silent; only the music of the wind in the grove of bamboos is heard, and the wing-beats of birds as they fly off startled, and the plopping sounds of fish nibbling at the surface of the water.

  Blest Spirit, may my lament go up to thee; may my rite be acceptable to thee.

  <u>Wuhu aijai</u>! Receive this offering!

FOR 1028 see before 1020 (Elegy)

后记

范圣宇（澳大利亚国立大学亚太学院文化历史语言系）

英国汉学家霍克思先生（1923—2009）的《红楼梦》前八十回译文（企鹅出版公司，1973—1980），早已被学界公认为汉译英的经典，至今无人超越。他的《〈红楼梦〉英译笔记》（下称"《英译笔记》"），无疑是研究霍氏译文的必读书。只是这本书十分不容易读，因为它本来就不是写给其他人看的。这是霍克思当年在翻译《红楼梦》时所做的笔记与部分草稿。笔记一共四册，写明日期的有三册，从1970年11月到1979年6月，还有第四册无日期，主要是《红楼梦》中诗词的注释、解释与翻译草稿。香港的岭南大学文学与翻译研究中心曾于2000年5月影印出版《英译笔记》，印数可能不多，早已不易得见。现在商务印书馆重新影印并在内地出版，这对学界研究霍克思与他的《红楼梦》译文，都是可喜可贺、功德无量的一件好事。

我们今天来研究霍氏的译文，《英译笔记》是极其重要的第一手材料，因为它是译者思考与阅读过程的忠实记录，也是现存为数不多的霍氏亲笔文件之一。《英译笔记》是霍氏留下的吉光片羽，弥足珍贵，记录了不少译者在翻译过程中的犹豫反复、字斟句酌，值得我们仔细研读、深入分析，它对我们理解霍克思的译文，具有不可替代的作用，因为这可以说是翻译过程的"黑匣子"，值得研究者进一步破译其中包含的信息，并以此为进阶，更深入地研究霍氏的译文。或者我们也可以说，《英译笔记》是打开霍氏译文这个百宝箱的一把钥匙，当然，这把钥匙并不是现成的，它需要经历一个聚沙成塔、集腋成裘的过程并反复打磨。[1]《英译笔记》从头到尾都一直在提醒我们，像霍克思这样的汉学家、翻译家，是如何读书、如何思考、如何翻译的。我们如果能够从中学习到一些做学问、搞翻译的方法，并对研究《红楼梦》或者其他中国文学作品英译而能有所启发，那无疑是霍氏喜闻乐见的结果，也是我们阅读《英译笔记》的意义所在。

霍氏通晓希腊文、拉丁文、法文、德文、日文等多种文字，这在笔记中随处可见。由于霍氏的笔记原本只是为他自己的翻译做准备，所以这些语言都是自然而然地出现在他笔下的，当然也因此增加了阅读的难度，不过也许这就是通晓多种语言的人的特点吧。霍氏归隐威尔士乡间之后还在努力学习当地的威尔士语，真正做到了"活到老学到老"。霍氏日文水平也相当精湛，他在翻译过程中不时参考伊藤漱平在平凡社出版的《红楼梦》日语译文，而且在《英译笔记》中不断记录下了他对伊藤氏译文的评价，或正面或反面的意见，都可见他日文的功底深厚。霍氏的博学多闻，从他参考过的各语种书目（第5、23、25页等处）当中就可见一斑。如果要求读者都能阅读这些文字，那也未免强人所难，毕竟通晓这些文字对大多数人来说只

是某种愿景或期望。但我们还是可以从已知的文字当中追随霍氏的脚步，进一步深入研究从而读懂并更好地理解他的翻译。

除了不同语种的参考书，霍氏更让人惊叹的是他对众多中文原典的参照。他为了翻译所参考、阅读的深度与广度，都值得我们学习并向他致敬。例如为了理解"星宿不利，祭星"到底是什么意思，他参考了《大正藏》的七种佛典：《宿命智陀罗尼经》《宿命陀罗尼》《文殊师利菩萨及诸仙所说吉凶时日善恶宿曜经》《宿曜仪轨》《七曜攘灾诀》《七星如意轮秘密要经》《七曜星辰别行法》。此外，他也借阅过《道藏·太玄部》中的《黄帝内经素问补注释文》《素问入式运气论奥》，六译馆丛书中的《平脉考》《脉经》等。语言方面，《佩文韵府》《国语辞典》《北京话语汇》《小说词语汇释》，是他常用的参考书。而史部要籍，他参考过并且留下记录的有《汉书》《后汉书》《新唐书》《唐书·乐志》《宋书》《南史》《明史》等。还有其他常用书如《诸子集成》《六十种曲》《曲海》《中国戏曲史》《古今小说》《唐宋传奇集》，不常用书如《月令广义》《钦定宫中现行则例》《大清通礼》《大清会典》《清朝续文献通考》，专书如《中国医学大辞典》《中国药学大辞典》《中国植物图鉴》《清代货币金融史稿》。对于端午习俗，他参考过《东京梦华录》《西湖老人繁盛录》《梦粱录》《武林旧事》《燕京岁时记》，而对于抹骨牌游戏中骨牌副的不同组合，他参考了《牙牌参禅图谱》《牌谱》《新定牙牌数》等。刘勰在《文心雕龙·神思》中曾说："张衡研京以十年，左思练都以一纪。虽有巨文，亦思之缓也。"[2] 我们从《英译笔记》就能很清楚地知道，霍氏翻译《红楼梦》前八十回，也整整用了十年。这里简单列举的书目，就足以说明他为什么需要这么长的时间，霍氏的翻译过程可与曹公"批阅十载、增删五次"的创作过程相提并论，正所谓"字字看来皆是血，十年辛苦不寻常"。

霍氏力求在下笔之前透彻地理解原文的每一处细节、每一个字。读者诸君不要忘记，中文对母语是英文的霍克思来说挑战也是不小的，例如他曾经列出对他来说很难翻译的词（"bad" words for translators）："痴、抽身、风流、知己、生分、薄命、造次"（第110页）；甚至有些相对来说比较简单的词，对他也造成困扰，比如"明日""一日"（第135、165、170页等处）。但他的优点或者说长处在他敢于接受这种挑战，而且愿意全身心地投入到这项浩大工程中去，甚至为了专心致志翻译《红楼梦》而辞去了牛津大学汉学教授的工作。这在当时已经是惊天骇俗的举动，即便是在今时今日，无疑也不是一般人等闲能做到的。试问还有其他哪一位世界名

校的教授为了翻译自己喜欢的文学作品而辞去工作吗？霍克思之所以这么做，固然是由于深爱这部中国古典小说，还有一个重要原因是他无羁独行，也很不喜欢自己的工作进程不断地被行政、会议等身外琐事打断。这样一个极具独创性的译者，是不愿意遵循任何特定的规则的。他从牛津大学辞职这一举动，现在回头看当然是正确的决定，但在当时不能不说他胆识过人，因为谁也无法保证他辞职以后一定可以顺利完成这项极具挑战性的任务。据闵福德先生说，霍氏辞职之后曾经尝试过申请当运奶工、邮递员，却均被告知资格过高而无法录用。幸运的是，他的妻子波金丝（Jean Hawkes, 1927–2017）十分理解并全力支持他的决定。如果没有家庭这个坚强后盾，恐怕霍氏连维持生计都难，译文可能更要大打折扣，遑论完成了。幸而不久牛津大学万灵学院就聘请他为研究员，有了稳定的收入，这才缓解了他的燃眉之急。

研究和翻译中国古典文学作品，首先要注意的是底本问题。就《红楼梦》来说，底本的选择与校勘，这是成功解释与翻译的第一步。霍克思就是这样做的，他着手翻译不久，就敏锐地注意到了底本的版本问题，有时他也会记录版本选择的原因，或改写的原因（第17、18、145页等处）。《英译笔记》记录了不同版本详细对比、校勘的结果，如王熙凤对时间安排的指示（第11页），以及宁国府总管究竟是来升还是赖升的异文（第113页），甚至第三回与第十五回两次宝玉不同装束的描绘对比（第14页），第五十六回甄府礼单的异文（第202、203页），都说明霍氏对原文的阅读一丝不苟、极其认真。版本校勘其实也是正确理解与研究霍氏译文的第一步。笔者从2009到2012年在闵先生的指导与帮助下花了整整三年的时间整理校勘《红楼梦》汉英对照双语版，目的不光是"为读者提供一个可靠的汉英对照本，同时如实地反映出霍克思先生在翻译过程中到底做了哪些增删改动"[3]，也是为了更准确更全面地理解并读懂霍氏的译文。

霍克思幽默的性格，在《英译笔记》中也偶尔流露。比如他因为小说中许多时间、年纪、细节等前后不吻合，而把曹雪芹戏称为"Our Careless Author"（第54页）或者"Our Forgetful Author"（第127页），曹公若地下有知，当也浮一大白。与曹公相仿，霍氏也多才多艺，除了掌握多种语言之外，他会画水彩，弹钢琴，吹竖笛，还整得一手好园子，能种花种蔬菜（曹公在北京西郊"不如著书黄叶村"的时候，恐怕也没有少当灌园叟吧？），据闵先生说，他每次搬家，都能把家里的园子搞得生意盎然、五彩缤纷。在园子里劳作也是他休息脑子的一种好方法。有时候找不到某个合适的韵脚，与其枯坐书斋苦思冥想而无所得，不如去园子里舒展身心，

虽然身体可能劳累，但往往就能灵光一闪，找到答案。霍克思躬耕南亩、灌溉田园，从牛津大学辞职以后归隐威尔士山村，都像极了不为五斗米折腰的晋代大诗人陶渊明，也正暗合陶氏所云："衣沾不足惜，但使愿无违。"闵先生家中墙上曾挂了一幅霍克思与杨宪益这两位《红楼梦》译者手持酒杯、无言微笑的照片，底下的标注也是陶诗："天运苟如此，且进杯中物。"闵先生曾说这是他最喜欢的霍氏与杨氏的合照，确实可能没有另外一张照片更能抓住这两位大翻译家淡然微醺、陶然忘机的神情了。这两位牛津大学校友都是著作等身、博学多闻的一代学者，都在中国文学英译这一领域内做出了卓越的贡献，而其人品也都如寒江钓雪、光风霁月，对身外之名毫不介怀。这张照片恰如其分地点明了他俩惺惺相惜、遥相呼应的性情与友谊。

《英译笔记》也记录了霍克思与同时代其他学者的交往，"独学而无友，孤陋而寡闻"这种情况对霍氏而言并不存在。与此恰恰相反，另一位《红楼梦》的译者班索尔（Bramwell S. Bonsall, 1890–1960），却是独自完成他的译文的，而且除了家人以外几乎没有任何人知道这件事。班氏译文质量显然远不如霍氏，固然可以说是学养不及，但他没有一个可以随时帮助他的朋友圈，也是重要原因之一。霍氏与几位图书馆员如托尼·海德（Tony Hyder）、玛丽·特里盖尔（Mary Tregear）等都成了好友。来自天津的刘容恩、刘程荫夫妇，是霍氏经常讨教的对象，据说程荫女史当年离开中国的时候带的就是一套《红楼梦》，这套书早已纸质发黄，闵先生特意把它买下留作纪念，现在还在他家书房的书架上。《英译笔记》中记录了霍氏与科技史专家李约瑟、鲁桂珍的通信（第174页），法国汉学家程纪贤（程抱一）当年的通讯地址（第181页），与红学家赵冈的往来（第231页），还有考古学家郑德坤建议霍氏参考的书目（第20页），向香港翻译家刘殿爵的咨询（第72、221页），等等。霍氏在企鹅版各卷的序言中曾提到过这些朋友、同事及同好的鼎力相助。文学翻译家如果不尽可能地寻求母语读者及专家的帮助，利用各种渠道解决所遇到的语言、文化、背景知识问题，很难想象他可以高质量地完成任务。

《英译笔记》还记录了不少霍氏译文的初稿，也值得研究者注意。"怡红院"他曾经考虑译作 Rozy Joy Lodge，后来才定为 Green Delights，"秋爽斋"曾经考虑过 Snug-in-autumn Studio 或 Autumn Chill，最后定为 Autumn Studio。"潇湘妃"他考虑过 Hsiang Lady, River Sprite, River Queen（第36页）。"风露清愁"从 Autumn Mourner 改为 Mourner of the Autumn Mere；"武陵别景"，典出陶渊明《桃花源记》，霍氏尝试了多种译法，从 Fisherman's Lost World, 到 Lost World of Fisherman，再

到Beyond the Hidden Paradise，最后定为Fisherman's Lost Paradise（第394页）。此外如人名译法，"鸳鸯"原译作Ducksie，"傻大姐"原译作Daftie，"小红"的名字则从Reddie, Rosie到Rosey, Rosy，最后才确定为Crimson，这些都可以形象地说明严复所说的"一名之立，旬月踟蹰"究竟是什么意思。

笔者与霍氏的交往，是从2005年开始的。笔者2003年在北京师范大学中文系完成的博士论文讨论的正是霍氏的前八十回译文与杨宪益译文的比较，在写论文期间就与闵先生互通过邮件，他总是耐心细致地回答我的各种问题，并提出各种建议和反馈意见。博士论文完成以后以《〈红楼梦〉管窥——英译、语言与文化》为题于2004年由中国社会科学出版社出版，我在书出版之后寄了两本给闵先生，托他转交一本给霍先生。2005年暑假我去台湾辅仁大学访学，回程经过香港，闵先生交给我一封霍氏亲笔信，信中告诉我他已经读完了《〈红楼梦〉管窥》，从此我与霍先生也开始陆续通信。2009年年初闵先生联系我说霍先生与他都希望我来校勘《红楼梦》汉英对照版，在我当然是求之不得，所以很兴奋地答应了。也正是因为这个机缘，我辗转来到了澳大利亚国立大学。笔者与霍氏的通信因他2009年7月突然去世戛然而止，但我深信他所秉承的学术却不会因此而中断，薪尽火传，总会遇到有心人能从中获益并将之发扬光大。笔者虽与霍克思先生缘悭一面，甚至从未通过电话，但从他的经典译文，他留下的发表与未发表的文字，他的家人、朋友或澳大利亚国立大学当年见过他的同事的口中，还是可以遥想霍氏当年的风采。笔者在撰写英文专著《译者的风月宝鉴：曹公的红楼梦与霍氏的石头记》[4]的过程中曾大量参考过《英译笔记》，以及霍氏的打印稿、手写稿，还有霍闵两位先生之间的通信，笔者尝试对这些珍贵的第一手资料的解读，也许可以为感兴趣的读者提供些切实的帮助。拙著之所以取这个题目，首先是愉快地接受了闵先生的建议，同时也暗喻司空图《二十四诗品》中的一句："空潭泻春，古镜照神"[5]，希望能聊备学者参镜，并期盼能与诸位同好"奇文共欣赏，疑义相与析"。

笔者认为，以霍克思的《英译笔记》为线索，追踪蹑迹地紧跟这位汉学家、翻译家的脚步，对我们提高阅读理解文学与翻译的能力和修养是大有好处的。莱布尼茨1714年给布尔格的信中曾说："可是研究旁人的创造发明的方式如果能使我们见出那些创造发明的来源，使那些创造发明仿佛成为我们自己的，这毕竟是件好事。所以我想望作家们肯告诉我们他们的创造发明的历史，告诉我们他们如何一步一步地达到了那些创造发明。如果他们没有当心这样源源本本地说出来，我们就必

须把那些步骤探求出来，这样才能使人从他们的作品中得到更多的益处。"⁶ 有趣的是，清代学者黄汝成在《日知录集释》序中也说过："呜呼，学识远不逮先生毛发，而欲以微埃涓流上益海岱之崇深，抑愚且妄矣！然先生之体用具在，学者循其唐涂，以窥贤圣制作之精，则区区私淑之心，识小之悁，或不重为世所诟病者矣。"⁷ 在笔者看来，这与莱布尼茨所说遥相呼应。文学翻译家也必须是作家，霍克思译的《红楼梦》毫无疑问地证明，他是一位出色的英语作家，他重新用英文创造发明了这部著名的中国古典小说，成功地让贾宝玉林黛玉说上了英语，而他的《英译笔记》就源源本本地告诉读者，霍氏是如何一步一步地达到了他的创造发明的。这样一部奇特的书，值得我们仔细研究、详加探寻。如果我们确实能够"循其唐涂，以窥贤圣制作之精"，那《英译笔记》无疑就是这条道路上一枚不可或缺的指南针。

2022 年元月

1 周仲华（Christina Chau）2019 年在闵福德先生指导下于澳大利亚国立大学完成的博士论文 "Translators in the making, the work of David Hawkes in the making of the Hawkes-Minford translation of *The Story of the Stone*, with special reference to Hawkes' *Translator's Notebooks*"，是迄今为止对霍克思《英译笔记》最详细的解读。
2 刘勰，《文心雕龙注释》，周振甫注，人民文学出版社，1998 年，第 296 页。
3 范圣宇，《红楼梦》（汉英对照版）前言，上海外语教育出版社，2012 年，第 7 页。
4 FAN Shengyu, *The Translator's Mirror for the Romantic: Cao Xueqin's Dream and David Hawkes' Stone* [M]. London: Routledge, 2022.
5 司空图，《诗品集解》，郭绍虞集解，人民文学出版社，2006 年，第 14 页。
6 维科，《新科学》，朱光潜译，人民文学出版社，1997 年，第 610 页。
7 顾炎武，《日知录集释》，黄汝成集释，上海古籍出版社，2013 年，第 2 页。